Microsoft Office 365 Administration Cookbook

Enhance your Office 365 productivity with recipes to manage and optimize its apps and services

Nate Chamberlain

BIRMINGHAM—MUMBAI

Microsoft Office 365 Administration Cookbook

Commissioning Editor: Wilson D'souza
Senior Editor: Shazeen Iqbal
Content Development Editor: Ronn Kurien
Technical Editor: Sarvesh Jaywant
Copy Editor: Safis Editing
Project Coordinator: Neil D'mello
Proofreader: Safis Editing
Indexer: Tejal Daruwale Soni
Production Designer: Shankar Kalbhor

First published: September 2020

Production reference: 1080920

Published by Packt Publishing Ltd.
Livery Place
35 Livery Street
Birmingham
B3 2PB, UK.

ISBN 978-1-83855-123-0

www.packt.com

`Packt.com`

Subscribe to our online digital library for full access to over 7,000 books and videos, as well as industry leading tools to help you plan your personal development and advance your career. For more information, please visit our website.

Why subscribe?

- Spend less time learning and more time coding with practical eBooks and Videos from over 4,000 industry professionals

- Improve your learning with Skill Plans built especially for you

- Get a free eBook or video every month

- Fully searchable for easy access to vital information

- Copy and paste, print, and bookmark content

Did you know that Packt offers eBook versions of every book published, with PDF and ePub files available? You can upgrade to the eBook version at `packt.com` and as a print book customer, you are entitled to a discount on the eBook copy. Get in touch with us at `customercare@packtpub.com` for more details.

At `www.packt.com`, you can also read a collection of free technical articles, sign up for a range of free newsletters, and receive exclusive discounts and offers on Packt books and eBooks.

Contributors

About the author

Nate Chamberlain, a Microsoft 365 Enterprise Administrator Expert and Microsoft MVP in Office apps and services since 2019, has over 5 years of experience in helping organizations deploy and maximize their usage of Office 365 apps and services. His work has included administrative and analyst roles in the higher education, healthcare, corporate, and finance sectors.

Nate is the author of several other books, including an MS-101 exam guide, an MS-500 exam guide, and a handful of smaller publications on SharePoint, OneNote, and leading advocate groups. Nate speaks at user groups and conferences both in person and virtually throughout the year, and he can be found blogging regularly at `NateChamberlain.com` and tweeting as `@chambernate` on Twitter.

About the reviewers

Greg Swart has been working with Microsoft Modern Workplace tools for 8 years and is passionate about business process transformation. He has worked in higher education, engineering, and construction as an expert and is leveraging Office 365 to increase efficiency and implement changes from the ground up. He now works as a senior consultant focusing on the middle market and helping smaller organizations achieve the same benefits as large enterprises.

> *I'd like to thank my wife, Mikayla, and our three children, Sierra, Riley, and Hayley, for their daily support and patience. I'd also like to thank Nate for his boundless energy, positive attitude, and dedication to building a community by sharing what we learn.*

Mike Swantek is a senior consultant and seasoned business professional partnered with a nationwide consulting firm. Mike uses his corporate experience, strategy, and vision to add significant value in companies utilizing Microsoft products and solutions. Mike has demonstrated achievements in SharePoint, SharePoint Online, business intelligence, process improvement, enterprise content management, information security, and project management in his 25+ year career in business and IT. Mike enjoys speaking at various SharePoint Saturday events throughout the year and is also a musician.

Suzanne Hunt has been in the IT industry for 15 years, with a career ranging across frontend and backend support, administration, system configuration, and development roles. Working in both technical and development roles has given her a broad base of skills. She has an applied interest in all things web-based, in particular SharePoint and the Microsoft 365 stack, having both administration and development experience across the product range. She is enthusiastic about helping community groups, having been part of the team that set up the Enderly Computer Clubhouse as well as being the chairperson of the governing board. More recently, she has taken up a position on the Web Access Waikato Trust and has been volunteering with Hospice Waikato for over 10 years.

Packt is searching for authors like you

If you're interested in becoming an author for Packt, please visit `authors.packtpub.com` and apply today. We have worked with thousands of developers and tech professionals, just like you, to help them share their insight with the global tech community. You can make a general application, apply for a specific hot topic that we are recruiting an author for, or submit your own idea.

Table of Contents

Preface

1

Office 365 Setup and Basic Administration

2

Office 365 Identity and Roles

3

Administering Office 365 with PowerShell

4

Managing Exchange Online

5

Setting Up and Configuring Microsoft Search

6
Administering OneDrive

7

Configuring the Power Platform

8
Administering SharePoint Online

9
Managing Microsoft Teams

10

Configuring and Managing Users in Azure Active Directory (Azure AD)

11

Understanding the Microsoft 365 Security & Compliance Center

12

Deploying Data Loss Prevention and eDiscovery

13

Monitoring Office 365 Apps and Services

14

Appendix – Office 365 Subscriptions and Licenses

Other Books You May Enjoy

Index

Preface

Thank you for buying this *Microsoft Office 365 Administration Cookbook*. Throughout the chapters that follow, you'll find over 100 recipes that walk you through administrative functions in the various apps and services that are to be found in Office 365. While that may seem like a lot, we're just scratching the surface. And in many cases, we've made a decision in recipes to focus on a specific way of configuring a policy or setting that could be configured a dozen other ways. The flexibility and potential for variation in how you administer your unique Office 365 environment in your organization is seemingly endless. This cookbook should simply spark ideas and get you on the right track to where you want to take your own apps and services. Always consult your organization's compliance and governance guidelines before making any significant changes, especially regarding security and compliance, and be sure to include others in decision-making where appropriate.

Who this book is for

The target audience for this book is new Office 365 administrators or those with beginner-level experience. Recipes will vary from beginner to advanced in complexity, but overall, they should be accessible to new administrators. Experienced administrators may also find value with the inclusion of newer apps and services, including those to do with the Power Platform and Microsoft Search.

What this book covers

Chapter 1, Office 365 Setup and Basic Administration, covers connecting a domain to your tenant, enabling PowerShell abilities, and migrating data to your new tenant, as well as basic navigation and routine tasks for administrators.

Chapter 2, Office 365 Identity and Roles, explores recipes that involve provisioning and managing users and groups in Office 365.

Chapter 3, Administering Office 365 with PowerShell, focuses exclusively on tasks that can be performed in Office 365 as an administrator using PowerShell.

Chapter 4, Managing Exchange Online, takes a look at configuring the user experience and security of your mail environment. Recipes range from Exchange basics to more advanced topics involving security.

Chapter 5, Setting Up and Configuring Microsoft Search, dives into one of the latest additions to Microsoft 365 and covers basic setup and configuration tasks, such as adding bookmarks and Q&A results, as well as utilizing data to improve and enhance the user experience.

Chapter 6, Administering OneDrive, looks at managing default and security settings and migrating data from local network locations to OneDrive.

Chapter 7, Configuring the Power Platform, explores important settings and administrative recipes for each of the Power Platform applications.

Chapter 8, Administering SharePoint Online, includes recipes on provisioning new site collections, managing sharing and site sprawl, and improving the user experience.

Chapter 9, Managing Microsoft Teams, covers Microsoft Teams, covering creating new teams and configuring policies and settings for live events, meetings, teams, external access, guests, and messaging.

Chapter 10, Configuring and Managing Users in Azure Active Directory (Azure AD), explores customizing the Azure AD portal, administering with PowerShell, enabling self-service password reset, access reviews, and more.

Chapter 11, Understanding the Microsoft 365 Security & Compliance Center, covers the essentials of the Office 365 Security & Compliance Center, such as monitoring audit log activities, working with Secure Score, and configuring advanced threat protection features.

Chapter 12, Deploying Data Loss Prevention and eDiscovery, covers data loss prevention policies, sensitive information types and labeling, eDiscovery cases, and more.

Chapter 13, Monitoring Office 365 Apps and Services, demonstrates how to procure reports on important and helpful topics that will enable you, as an administrator, to respond to risks and plan for growth in Office 365.

Chapter 14, Appendix – Office 365 Subscriptions and Licenses, contains links to helpful and current resources on subscriptions and licenses.

To get the most out of this book

Because everything covered in this book involves Office 365, a cloud-based and subscription-based service, you'll need a constant internet connection and an Office 365 subscription. In most cases, an E3 or E5 subscription will be sufficient, and recipes that require add-ons will specify that.

If you have a subscription through your organization, you may be able to perform some of these recipes if you've been granted the proper administrative role for the recipe(s) you wish to perform. If you're unable to obtain proper permissions and just want to practice the recipes, you can get a personal trial of Microsoft 365 at `https://www.microsoft.com/en-us/microsoft-365/try`. You can also get a Microsoft 365 tenant pre-populated with users and content specifically intended for development and testing at `https://developer.microsoft.com/en-us/microsoft-365/dev-program`.

If you are using the digital version of this book, we advise you to type the code yourself. Doing so will help you avoid any potential errors related to the copying and pasting of code.

Download the color images

We also provide a PDF file that has color images of the screenshots/diagrams used in this book. You can download it here: `http://www.packtpub.com/sites/default/files/downloads/9781838551230_ColorImages.pdf`.

Conventions used

There are a number of text conventions used throughout this book.

`Code in text`: Indicates code words in text, database table names, folder names, filenames, file extensions, pathnames, dummy URLs, user input, and Twitter handles. Here is an example: "Mount the downloaded `WebStorm-10*.dmg` disk image file as another disk in your system."

Any command-line input or output is written as follows:

```
Install-Module AzureADPreview
```

Bold: Indicates a new term, an important word, or words that you see onscreen. For example, words in menus or dialog boxes appear in the text like this. Here is an example: "Select **Show all** from the left navigation menu."

> **Tips or important notes**
> Appear like this.

Sections

In this book, you will find several headings that appear frequently (*Getting ready, How to do it..., How it works..., There's more...,* and *See also*).

To give clear instructions on how to complete a recipe, use these sections as follows:

Getting ready

This section tells you what to expect in the recipe and describes how to set up any software or any preliminary settings required for the recipe.

How to do it...

This section contains the steps required to follow the recipe.

How it works...

This section usually consists of a detailed explanation of what happened in the previous section.

There's more...

This section consists of additional information about the recipe in order to make you more knowledgeable about the recipe.

See also

This section provides helpful links to other useful information for the recipe.

Get in touch

Feedback from our readers is always welcome.

General feedback: If you have questions about any aspect of this book, mention the book title in the subject of your message and email us at customercare@packtpub.com.

Errata: Although we have taken every care to ensure the accuracy of our content, mistakes do happen. If you have found a mistake in this book, we would be grateful if you would report this to us. Please visit www.packtpub.com/support/errata, selecting your book, clicking on the Errata Submission Form link, and entering the details.

Piracy: If you come across any illegal copies of our works in any form on the Internet, we would be grateful if you would provide us with the location address or website name. Please contact us at copyright@packt.com with a link to the material.

If you are interested in becoming an author: If there is a topic that you have expertise in and you are interested in either writing or contributing to a book, please visit authors.packtpub.com.

Reviews

Please leave a review. Once you have read and used this book, why not leave a review on the site that you purchased it from? Potential readers can then see and use your unbiased opinion to make purchase decisions, we at Packt can understand what you think about our products, and our authors can see your feedback on their book. Thank you!

For more information about Packt, please visit packt.com.

1
Office 365 Setup and Basic Administration

Welcome to the Microsoft Office 365 Administration Cookbook. This book will share step-by-step instructions for completing basic to advanced administration tasks throughout the Office 365 ecosystem and is geared toward newer Office 365 administrators.

Many of the basic administration and tenant setup tasks are simple, but they require making decisions that are difficult to reverse or adjust later. In this first chapter, we'll cover important topics such as connecting a domain to your tenant, enabling PowerShell abilities, and migrating data to your new tenant. We'll also go over basic navigation and ongoing tasks administrators should commit to a routine.

We will cover the following recipes in this chapter:

- Accessing the admin centers
- Setting up the PowerShell environment
- Viewing and filtering the roadmap
- Discovering upcoming changes
- Opening a service request
- Monitoring service request status

- Adding a domain

- Changing the domain for users

- Assigning a license to a user

- Assigning a license to a group

- Customizing navigation of the admin center

- Personalizing your admin center home page

Technical requirements

This chapter requires users to have administrative privileges in Office 365. Those with a global administrator role will be able to perform every task in each recipe. Specific app and functional administrators will be able to do many of the recipes. Throughout the book, we'll cover recipes requiring certain admin roles. All of these can be assigned by a current global administrator via the Microsoft 365 admin center's **Users** blade if they're not already.

For the second recipe, *Setting up the PowerShell environment*, you will need to download the Microsoft Services Online Sign-in Assistant, but this is covered in the recipe. For all other recipes, no downloads/installations are required.

Accessing the admin centers

Admin centers provide an interface through which you'll configure global settings, restrictions, and allowances for each app and service in Office 365. In this recipe, you'll learn how to find the admin centers for all apps and services used for configuration, management, and reporting of Office 365 apps and services.

Getting ready

You must be a user assigned as a global administrator or have a specific app administrator role to be able to access the corresponding app's admin center.

How to do it...

1. Go to the Microsoft 365 admin center at `http://admin.microsoft.com`.

2. Select **Show all** from the left navigation menu:

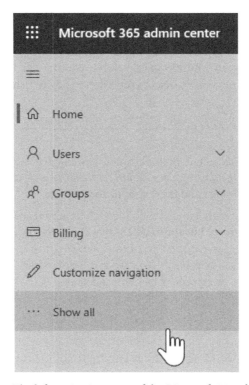

Figure 1.1 – The left navigation pane of the Microsoft 365 admin center

3. Select the admin center you wish to access from those that appear by default, or select **All admin centers** to view a complete list. The **All admin centers** view is seen here:

Nate LLC

All admin centers

	Name	Description
△	Azure ATP	Identify, detect, and investigate advanced threats, compromised identities, and malicious insider actions directed at your organization.
◆	Azure Active Directory	Go deep with identity management. Enable multi-factor authentication, self-service password reset, and edit company branding.
○	Compliance	Manage your compliance needs using integrated solutions for data governance, encryption, access control, eDiscovery, and more.
▣	Endpoint Manager	A single management experience for the End User Computing team in IT to ensure employees' Microsoft 365 devices and apps are secured, managed, and current.
▣	Exchange	Manage advanced email settings, such as quarantine, encryption, and mail flow rules.
▣	Power Automate	The Azure free-to-use workflow automation service to automate repetitive and time-consuming tasks by setting up a connection to access web services, files,
◯	Microsoft Search	Manage Microsoft Search settings including services and content that are available for people in your organization. Make finding internal tools, documents,
▶	Stream	Choose how Microsoft Stream works for your organization.
◈	OneDrive	Control access and sharing settings, default storage, and allowed file types.

Figure 1.2 – All admin centers available to a user displayed in the Microsoft 365 admin center

How it works...

By default, admin centers are "hidden" behind a **Show all** menu node in the Microsoft 365 Admin Center. Depending on your assigned role(s), you may be unable to access certain admin centers. In this recipe, you've discovered where they're listed and which of them are available to you.

> **Tip**
>
> Check out the last two recipes in this chapter, *Customizing navigation of the admin center* and *Personalizing your admin center home page* to make your admin experience simpler and more specific to your role.
>
> Also, as you become more familiar with the various admin centers, you'll notice other **Uniform Resource Locators** (**URLs**) that will save you a couple of clicks, such as `security.microsoft.com`, `compliance.microsoft.com`, `TenantName-admin.sharepoint.com`, `admin.powerplatform.microsoft.com`, and so on.

See also

- Learn more about specific admin roles and their abilities at `https://docs.microsoft.com/en-us/microsoft-365/admin/add-users/about-admin-roles`.

Setting up the PowerShell environment

PowerShell is an ever-growing scripting language that allows network and system admins to interact with Microsoft products in an elevated manner. Admins can use PowerShell to create new users, make changes to users, interact with MS-SQL tables, move and manipulate files, and much more. PowerShell cmdlets are single-purpose functions with specific rules and syntax, but there are hundreds of these cmdlets, giving admins a flexible and extensible toolset with which to customize, administer, and run their tenant.

As there are so many possible uses of PowerShell, *Chapter 3*, *Administering Office 365 with PowerShell*, is dedicated to the topic. However, every admin must start somewhere, and that is why the basic steps to setting up your PowerShell environment are presented here in the following recipe—steps for connecting your desktop or laptop to your Office 365 tenant.

Getting ready

To start, an admin must have PowerShell installed, either the command-line, black screen version or an **Integrated Scripting Environment** (**ISE**). You must have valid credentials and have an appropriate admin role (such as **Global Admin**).

As PowerShell for Office 365 has advanced, additional tools have become available to minimize previously known obstacles when making a connection to your tenant. For this, you must download the Microsoft Online Services Sign-In Assistant (the link for this appears in the *See also* section of this recipe). Download the files and install it on your PC.

The first time you connect to your Office 365 tenant, you'll want to set the **Execution Policy** to RemoteSigned. This is done by opening a PowerShell window with elevated rights (**Run as administrator**) and executing the following code:

```
Set-ExecutionPolicy RemoteSigned
```

Once prompted, press *Y* and hit *Enter*.

Additionally, you will need to execute and install the following PowerShell modules:

```
Install-Module MSOnline
```

You may be prompted that the NuGet provider is required in order to continue. Press *Y* and press *Enter* to continue. As it downloads, you may see an additional warning regarding an untrusted repository. The repository is Microsoft and is trusted, so press *Y* and press *Enter* to continue:

```
PS C:\WINDOWS\system32> Install-Module MSOnline

NuGet provider is required to continue
PowerShellGet requires NuGet provider version '2.8.5.201' or newer to interact with NuGet-based repositories. The NuGet
 provider must be available in 'C:\Program Files\PackageManagement\ProviderAssemblies' or
 'C:\Users\14196\AppData\Local\PackageManagement\ProviderAssemblies'. You can also install the NuGet provider by running
 'Install-PackageProvider -Name NuGet -MinimumVersion 2.8.5.201 -Force'. Do you want PowerShellGet to install and
import the NuGet provider now?
[Y] Yes  [N] No  [S] Suspend  [?] Help (default is "Y"): Y

Untrusted repository
You are installing the modules from an untrusted repository. If you trust this repository, change its
InstallationPolicy value by running the Set-PSRepository cmdlet. Are you sure you want to install the modules from
'PSGallery'?
[Y] Yes  [A] Yes to All  [N] No  [L] No to All  [S] Suspend  [?] Help (default is "N"): Y
PS C:\WINDOWS\system32> Connect-MsolService -Credential $credential
PS C:\WINDOWS\system32>
```

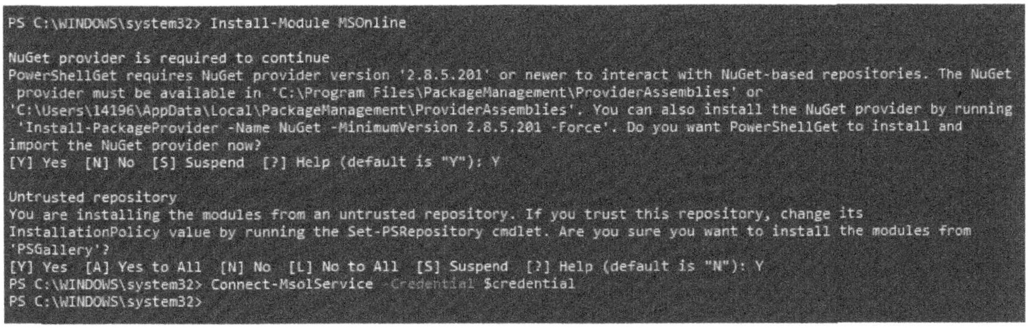

Figure 1.3 – Screenshot of PowerShell commands when installing the MSOnline module

How to do it...

1. Open Windows PowerShell or the PowerShell ISE as an administrator by searching for PowerShell in your applications, right-click, and select **Run as administrator**:

Figure 1.4 – Right-clicking PowerShell from Start menu provides Run as administrator option

2. Assuming a standard login (see *There's more…* section for information about **multi-factor authentication** (**MFA**)), you'll create a Windows PowerShell credentials object by executing the following command:

```
$credential = Get-Credential
```

Once executed, the PowerShell window will prompt you for your credentials. Click **OK** to proceed:

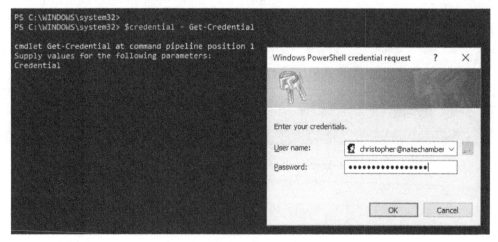

Figure 1.5 – PowerShell prompts for credentials when using Get-Credential

3. With the credentials saved to the `$credential` variable, you can connect to Office 365 by executing the following command:

```
Connect-MsolService -Credential $credential
```

This is shown in the following screenshot:

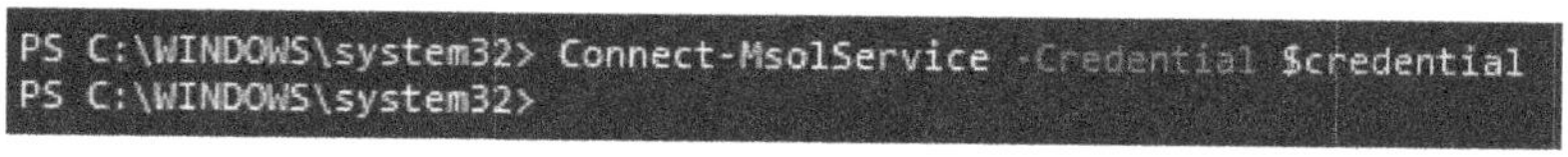

```
PS C:\WINDOWS\system32> Connect-MsolService -Credential $credential
PS C:\WINDOWS\system32>
```

Figure 1.6 – PowerShell screen showing use of stored credential variable to connect to MsolService

4. As the preceding screenshot shows, it is not clear if the system is connected. At this point, you can test to see if you are connected by executing the following command:

```
Get-MsolDomain
```

The `Get-MsolDomain` cmdlet shows you all domains associated with the connected tenant and proves you are ready to start using PowerShell as an admin tool on your tenant:

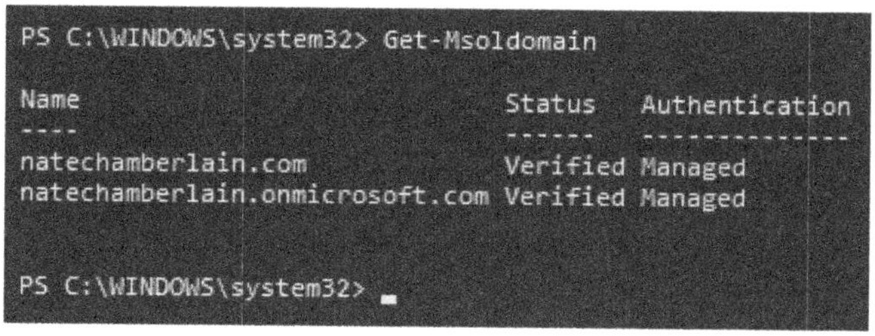

```
PS C:\WINDOWS\system32> Get-Msoldomain

Name                                Status    Authentication
----                                ------    --------------
natechamberlain.com                 Verified  Managed
natechamberlain.onmicrosoft.com     Verified  Managed


PS C:\WINDOWS\system32>
```

Figure 1.7 – PowerShell screen showing domains found using Get-MsolDomain

How it works...

You've just configured the essentials needed to complete most PowerShell cmdlets you'll need as an Office 365 admin.

PowerShell has been around for many years but historically has not required setup. On-prem network admins are expected to log in to a server and start executing commands. Interacting from your PC with an online tenant is technically a remote session (something PowerShell experts will recognize). Connecting in this way requires passing credentials to gain access to the tenant.

This recipe focused on getting you ready to use PowerShell in your tenant. *Chapter 3, Administering Office 365 with PowerShell* will cover many of the options available to an admin.

There's more...

If using MFA (not standard login), you'd authenticate by skipping *Step 2* and removing the credential parameter from *Step 3*. *Step 3* would instead resemble the following:

```
Connect-MsolService
```

This brings up the modern Office 365/Azure login screen that supports MFA.

See also

- Microsoft Online Services Sign-In Assistant for IT Professionals RTW download page: `https://www.microsoft.com/en-us/download/details.aspx?id=41950`

Viewing and filtering the roadmap

Microsoft 365 Roadmap lets you know what's in development and being released in Office 365 for all subscription types. You can filter the roadmap to identify only the changes and releases relevant to your environment and purchased licenses, then use that news to coordinate change management and communicate with your organization's leaders and users. In this recipe, we will explore the roadmap and learn how to maximize its usage.

Getting ready

The roadmap is publicly available and only requires internet access.

How to do it...

1. Go to the Microsoft 365 Roadmap site at `http://roadmap.office.com`.

2. Under **Filters** > **Products**, select **Office 365**:

Figure 1.8 – The Microsoft 365 Roadmap filter pane's Products section

3. If you know your organization's chosen release phase, select it from under **Release Phase** to narrow down the results to only those relevant to your schedule:

Figure 1.9 – The Microsoft 365 Roadmap filter pane's Release Phase section

4. Lastly, choose your organization's subscription type (**Education**, **GCC**, **Standard**, and so on) from under **Cloud Instance** as they each have different schedules and available features.

Now, you can view and download (as a **comma-separated values** (CSV) file) the relevant releases and developments that affect your organization's tenant:

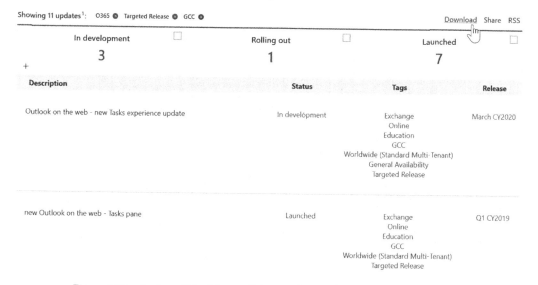

Figure 1.10 – A view of the Microsoft 365 roadmap when filtered to show O365 Targeted Release for GCC

How it works...

After accessing the roadmap online, you can filter, search, download, and share its contents that pertain to your environment and needs.

The roadmap is constantly updated and contains much more information than is relevant to any single organization. Using the filters in the filter pane to narrow down results first makes sure you're only consuming and sharing the updates that apply to your available apps and services included in your specific subscription and release phase. For example, GCC (Microsoft 365 Government) customers may never see certain features released to standard customers. This is because GCC tenants involve strict government data compliance, which may disallow utilization or potential risk of using certain features, connectors, and tools.

There's more...

You can use the Roadmap's **Really Simple Syndication (RSS)** feed to be alerted when new items are added, just as you might use to subscribe to a blog.

Also, utilize the search bar to find updates related to a specific app or service (such as SharePoint):

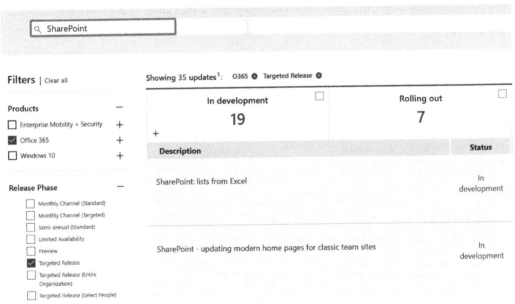

Figure 1.11 – The Microsoft 365 Roadmap's search function

See also

- Check out the *What's New with Microsoft 365* playlist on Microsoft Office 365's YouTube channel for quick, monthly videos reviewing the latest developments and news: `https://tinyurl.com/NewInM365`.

- You can also stay up to date with the Microsoft 365 blog: `https://www.microsoft.com/en-us/microsoft-365/blog`.

Discovering upcoming changes

The Microsoft 365 Message center, found within the Microsoft 365 admin center, is a place to keep track of all upcoming changes, new features, and planned maintenance relevant to your environment. Official announcements from Microsoft are released through the Message center, giving a high-level overview and links to additional information. In this recipe, you'll access upcoming changes via the Message center.

Getting ready

You must have been assigned to an appropriate admin role in Office 365 or assigned the Message center reader role.

How to do it...

1. Go to the Microsoft admin center for your tenant at `https://admin.microsoft.com/`.

2. Under **Health**, select **Message center**.

3. Now, you can see a list of active messages, messages filtered as being of high importance, or a filtered view of unread or archived messages:

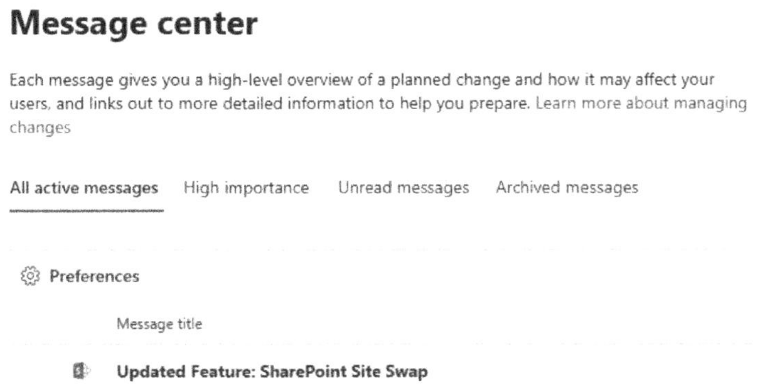

Message center

Each message gives you a high-level overview of a planned change and how it may affect your users, and links out to more detailed information to help you prepare. Learn more about managing changes

All active messages   High importance   Unread messages   Archived messages

⚙ Preferences

      Message title

      Updated Feature: SharePoint Site Swap

Figure 1.12 – The Office 365 Message center All active messages view

4. Click on any message title, and a right-side pane will open with the message details:

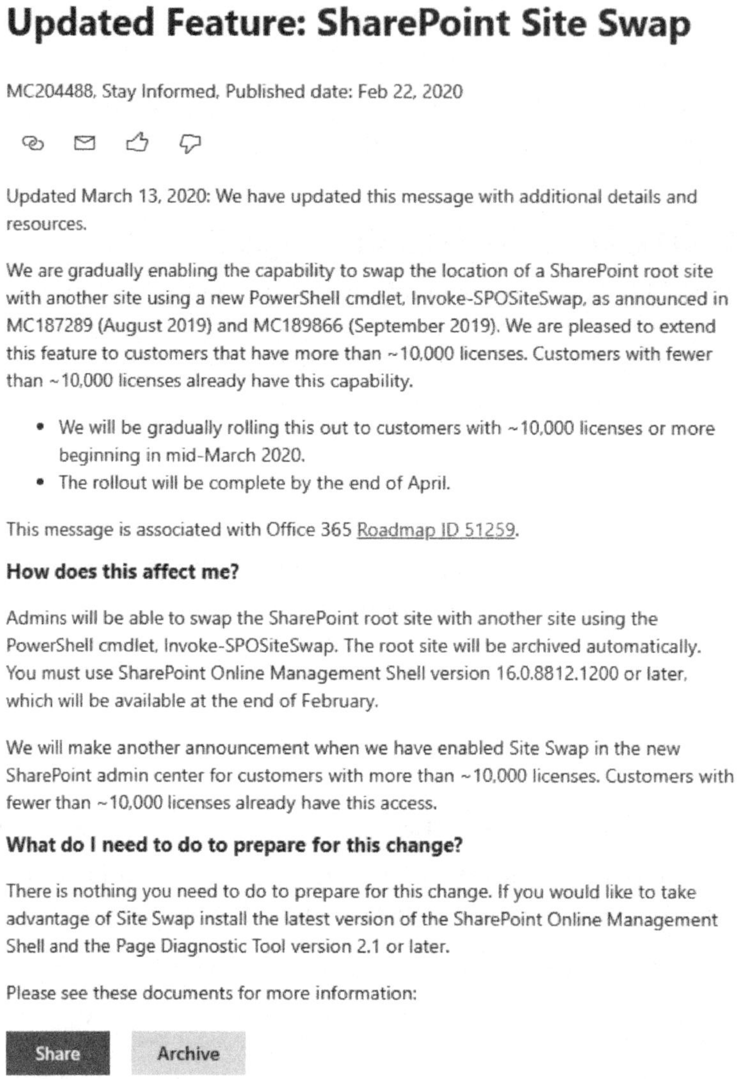

Updated Feature: SharePoint Site Swap

MC204488, Stay Informed, Published date: Feb 22, 2020

Updated March 13, 2020: We have updated this message with additional details and resources.

We are gradually enabling the capability to swap the location of a SharePoint root site with another site using a new PowerShell cmdlet, Invoke-SPOSiteSwap, as announced in MC187289 (August 2019) and MC189866 (September 2019). We are pleased to extend this feature to customers that have more than ~10,000 licenses. Customers with fewer than ~10,000 licenses already have this capability.

- We will be gradually rolling this out to customers with ~10,000 licenses or more beginning in mid-March 2020.
- The rollout will be complete by the end of April.

This message is associated with Office 365 Roadmap ID 51259.

How does this affect me?

Admins will be able to swap the SharePoint root site with another site using the PowerShell cmdlet, Invoke-SPOSiteSwap. The root site will be archived automatically. You must use SharePoint Online Management Shell version 16.0.8812.1200 or later, which will be available at the end of February.

We will make another announcement when we have enabled Site Swap in the new SharePoint admin center for customers with more than ~10,000 licenses. Customers with fewer than ~10,000 licenses already have this access.

What do I need to do to prepare for this change?

There is nothing you need to do to prepare for this change. If you would like to take advantage of Site Swap install the latest version of the SharePoint Online Management Shell and the Page Diagnostic Tool version 2.1 or later.

Please see these documents for more information:

Share   Archive

Figure 1.13 – An example message provided in the Office 365 Message center

How it works...

Accessing the Message center will give you the information you need to stay on top of changes and enhancements and provide you with other information that may impact your business and its processes. In this recipe, we discovered available messages in the Message center and opened a message as an example.

Once each message loads, you are given several options. You can share the message (click the blue **Share** button or the **Copy link** button). Click the **Mark unread** button to leave the message as active/unread, which keeps it bold on the main Message center page.

Additionally, you can like/dislike announcements, mark for archive, or click on various information links for additional details.

There's more...

Using the Message center reader role is a smart way of keeping superusers or technology champions in the know about what is coming and how to prepare for it.

And for mobile-centric admins, the Microsoft Admin app for your mobile device will give you access to the Message center, on the go: `https://go.microsoft.com/fwlink/p/?linkid=627216`.

See also

- For a list of admin roles that do not provide access to the Message center: `https://docs.microsoft.com/en-us/microsoft-365/admin/manage/message-center?view=o365-worldwide#admin-roles-that-dont-have-access-to-the-message-center`

Opening a service request

Service requests are how you ask Microsoft for assistance in resolving an issue in Office 365. By submitting a service request, you're asking to be contacted to elaborate on and discuss an issue further in pursuit of a resolution. In this recipe, we'll create a new service request.

Getting ready

You must be an Office 365 administrator to create service requests.

How to do it...

1. Go to the Microsoft 365 admin center at `http://admin.microsoft.com`.

2. Hover over the teal question mark icon in the lower right of the screen and select **Need help?** once it appears:

Figure 1.14 – The Need help? button appears in the lower right-hand corner
of the admin center

OR from the left navigation menu, select **Show all** > **Support** > **New service request**:

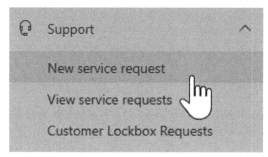

Figure 1.15 – The Microsoft 365 admin center's left-hand navigation menu's Support section

3. A panel opens on the right hand of the screen and, by default, you're able to chat with the automated **Support Assistant** to identify (and hopefully resolve) your issue. You can, instead, choose to toggle the automated assistant off and use **Search** instead:

Figure 1.16 – The Support Assistant is selected instead of Search when creating a new service request

4. For this recipe, we'll utilize the automated assistant. Type in your question or issue and click the **send** icon.

5. The automated assistant will respond, attempting to resolve your issue without the need to open a service request. Check the suggested resources or options to see if your issue can be resolved without a request or choose **None of the above** or **No** when prompted, to be given the option to contact support. Select **Contact support**:

Figure 1.17 – Contact support appears as an option when the assistant cannot help

6. Enter the details of your request, including any relevant screenshots or attachments, and choose **Contact me**:

Figure 1.18 – Service request fields and options

How it works...

In this recipe, we created a service request in which we indicated our preference to be contacted as soon as possible via phone to discuss changing our subscription.

Microsoft has a wealth of resources out there to help you through most problems. By requiring you to search for a potential existing solution before allowing the creation of a new service request, they're making sure they use their time most efficiently (contributing to their prompt response time estimates) while being respectful of yours in hoping you don't have to wait for a response to get back to work.

Depending on your selected preferred contact method, a Microsoft support representative will be in touch to gather information and work with you until the request can be closed.

There's more...

The **Search** function (rather than the automated assistant) is similar in requiring you to first search for a potential solution before **Contact support** becomes an option:

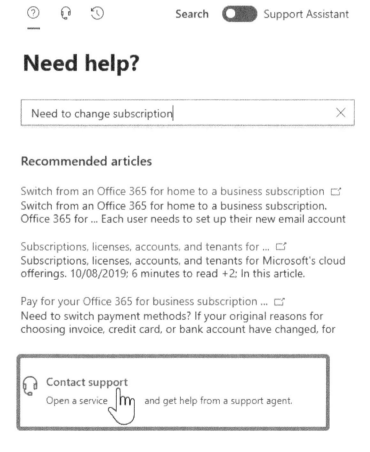

Figure 1.19 – When searching instead of using the assistant, Contact support appears at the bottom

See also

- Check out the next recipe, *Monitoring service request status*, to learn how to track your service request once submitted.

Monitoring service request status

Once your service request is submitted, you receive an email confirmation with its details. But as you get more requests in simultaneously, this can become difficult to manage. This recipe will share how you can monitor all service requests and their statuses in the Microsoft 365 admin center.

Getting ready

You must be an Office 365 administrator to monitor and manage service requests.

How to do it...

1. Go to the Microsoft 365 admin center at `http://admin.microsoft.com`.

2. Select **Show all** > **Support** > **View service requests**.

3. From here, you can export, search, or filter your service requests and see current statuses:

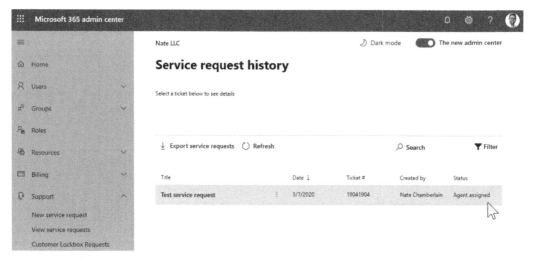

Figure 1.20 – View of service request history in the Microsoft 365 admin center

4.   Select a service request to see its case notes and history:

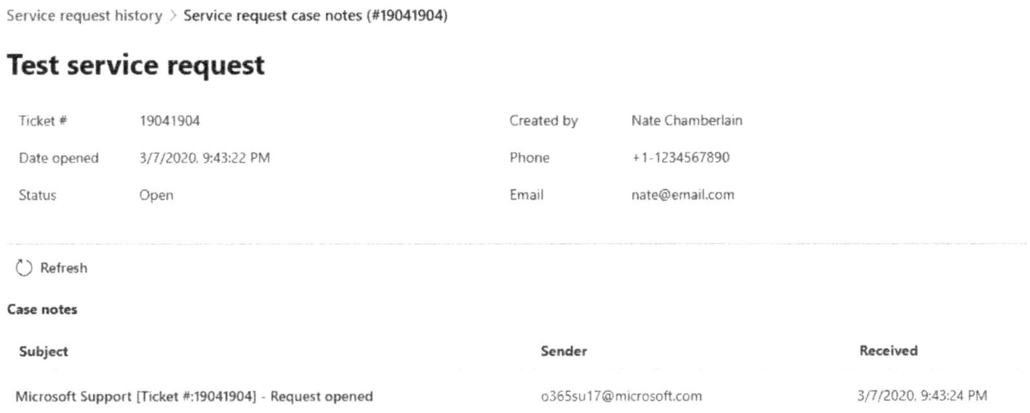

Service request history > **Service request case notes (#19041904)**

Test service request

Ticket #	19041904		Created by	Nate Chamberlain
Date opened	3/7/2020, 9:43:22 PM		Phone	+1-1234567890
Status	Open		Email	nate@email.com

○ Refresh

Case notes

Subject	Sender	Received
Microsoft Support [Ticket #:19041904] - Request opened	o365su17@microsoft.com	3/7/2020, 9:43:24 PM

Figure 1.21 – An active service request's details screen

How it works...

The service request history screen in the Microsoft 365 admin center displays all of your tickets in an exportable, searchable, and filterable screen, making it easy to find previous issues that may have arisen again or to aid in reporting issue resolution to your users and leadership. In this recipe, you accessed the **Service request history** screen to monitor the status of existing service requests and any case notes added to them.

There's more...

If you need to edit a request:

1. Find it by selecting **New service request** > **history icon** > **Test service request:**

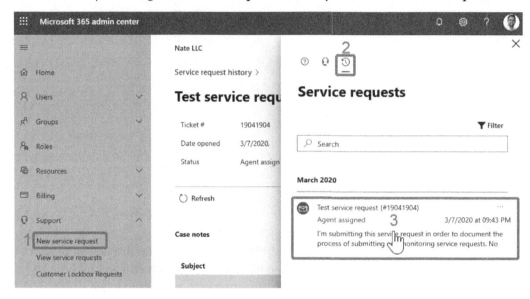

Figure 1.22 – Service request history is available from the New service request pane as well

2. Select **Edit** from the bottom of the service request:

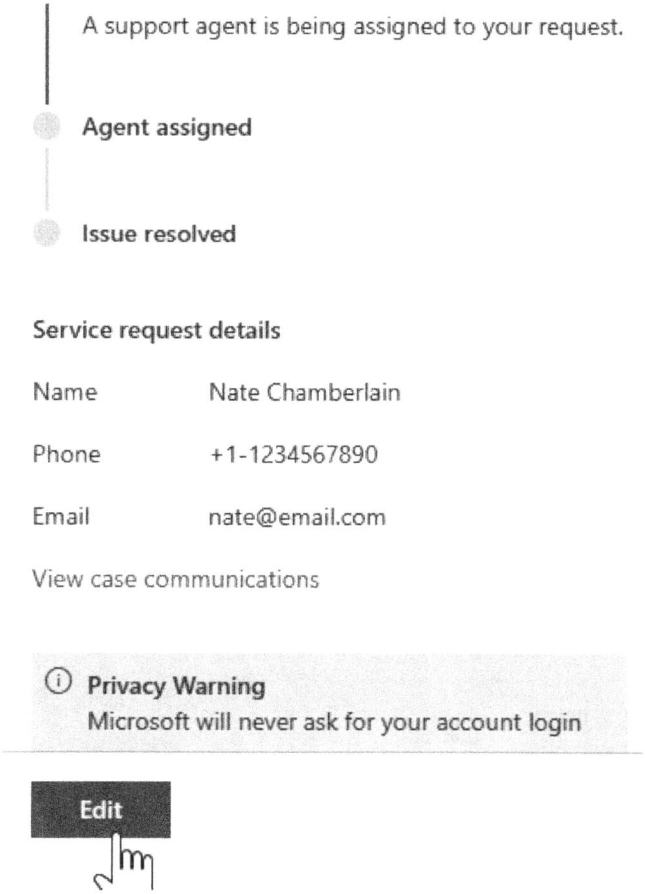

A support agent is being assigned to your request.

● **Agent assigned**

● **Issue resolved**

Service request details

Name   Nate Chamberlain

Phone   +1-1234567890

Email   nate@email.com

View case communications

ⓘ **Privacy Warning**
Microsoft will never ask for your account login

Figure 1.23 – The Edit button appears on existing service requests

3. Enter any additional notes or modify your contact info, then click **Save**:

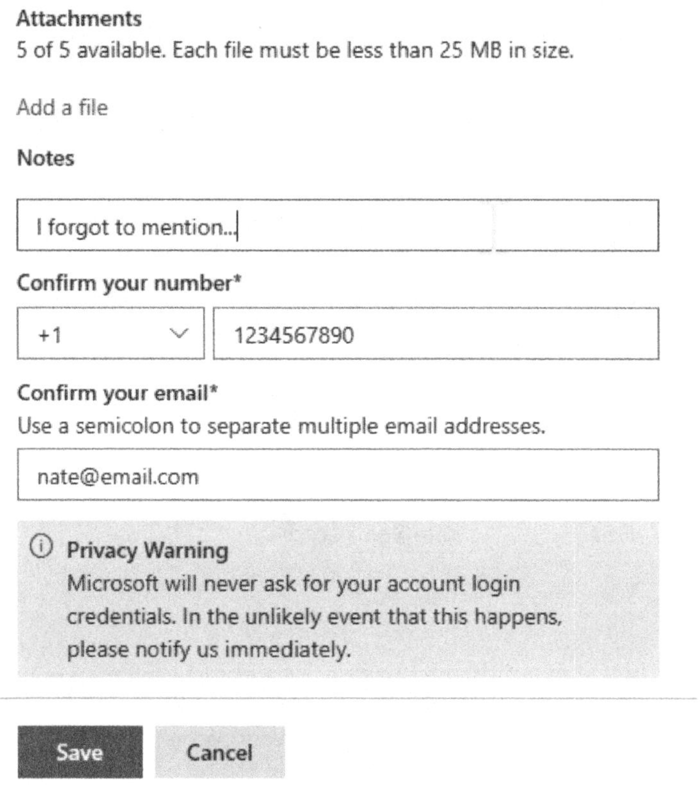

Attachments
5 of 5 available. Each file must be less than 25 MB in size.

Add a file

Notes

I forgot to mention...

Confirm your number*

+1   ∨   1234567890

Confirm your email*
Use a semicolon to separate multiple email addresses.

nate@email.com

ⓘ **Privacy Warning**
Microsoft will never ask for your account login
credentials. In the unlikely event that this happens,
please notify us immediately.

Save   Cancel

Figure 1.24 – Additional attachments and notes can be added when editing an existing service request

See also

- Learn more about admin roles and their abilities, such as the Office 365 administrator roles currently capable of managing service requests, at `https://docs.microsoft.com/en-us/microsoft-365/admin/add-users/about-admin-roles`.

Adding a domain

By default, new tenants' users are given addresses with their tenant name followed by `onmicrosoft.com`, such as `nate@contoso.onmicrosoft.com`. Adding your own domain, such as `contoso.com`, means you can change that user format to `nate@contoso.com` and have Outlook for Office 365 handle mail for that domain. In this recipe, we'll add the `natechamberlain.com` domain to our tenant.

Getting ready

You must be a **Global Administrator** to add a domain. You do not need to have already purchased a domain, as that can be done through this process.

How to do it...

1. Go to the Microsoft 365 admin center at `http://admin.microsoft.com`.

2. Select **Show all** > **Setup** > **Domains** to add or buy an existing or new domain.

3. For this recipe, we will choose **Add domain**, but note the option to also purchase your domain if you don't already have one or would just like an additional domain. Select **Add domain**.

4. Enter your **Domain name**, then select **Use this domain**.

5. In order to use email and instant messaging with your domain, you'll need to add **Domain Name System** (**DNS**) records for it at the registrar or hosting provider. Some registrars can connect directly to Office 365 to have this done automatically (WordPress, 1&1, and GoDaddy). Otherwise, you can manually add records by entering a provided list of DNS records via your host's administrative portal. Make your choice and select **Continue**:

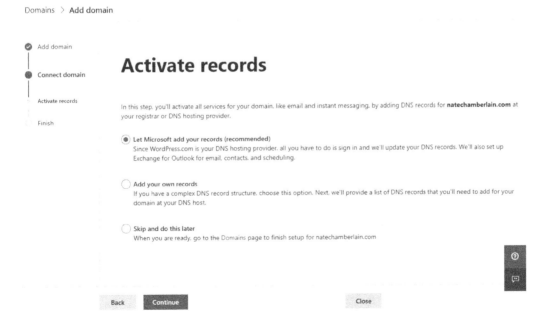

Figure 1.25 – The Activate records screen of adding a domain

6. Once the records have been added, your domain can now be used with Exchange, Teams, Skype, Intune, and so on. Follow the prompts to complete the wizard and click **Done** when finished:

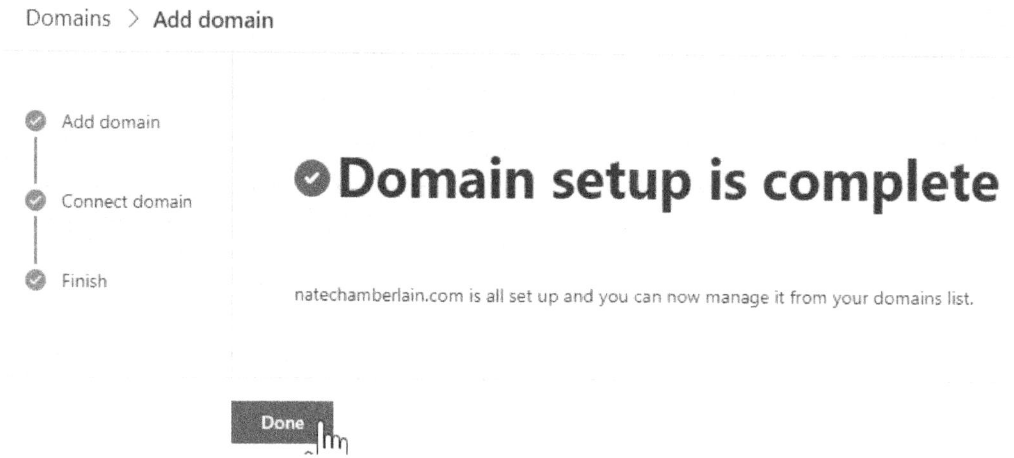

Domains > **Add domain**

Figure 1.26 – The domain setup confirmation screen when adding a domain

How it works...

You've added your own domain to Office 365. By configuring your domain within Office 365, you're telling your domain to direct all mail to Microsoft 365 so that users on your domain can access mail via Outlook/Exchange and log in to services such as Teams using your customized domain (nate@contoso.com) versus the default domain (nate@contoso.onmicrosoft.com). We'll cover changing the domain for users from the default (*onmicrosoft*) domain to your custom domain in the next recipe, *Changing the domain for users*.

> **Important note**
>
> If you have multiple domains, users could have secondary email addresses and administrators could apply policies and licenses per domain by utilizing dynamic security groups. Multiple domains are common in situations such as when companies acquire other companies that already have their own domains, which may or may not be converted to your primary domain. You could also have multiple subdomains, such as staff.contoso.com and faculty.contoso.com.

See also

- Read more about adding a domain to your Office 365 subscription at `https://docs.microsoft.com/en-us/microsoft-365/admin/setup/add-domain`.

Changing the domain for users

Once you've added a custom domain, or if you've acquired multiple domains and need to move existing users between domains, you can use the **Change domains** option. This changes users' email addresses and login credentials and can affect any scheduled meetings, so be sure to communicate this important fact prior to performing the steps in this recipe. In this recipe, you'll change selected users' domains.

Getting ready

You must be an Office 365 administrator to be able to change a user's domain.

How to do it...

1. Go to the Microsoft 365 admin center at `http://admin.microsoft.com`.

2. Select **Users** > **Active users**.

3. Select all users for whom you're making the domain change and select **Change domains**:

Figure 1.27 – Two users selected and the ellipsis menu showing the Change domains option

4.   Select the new domain from the drop-down list and read the disclaimer:

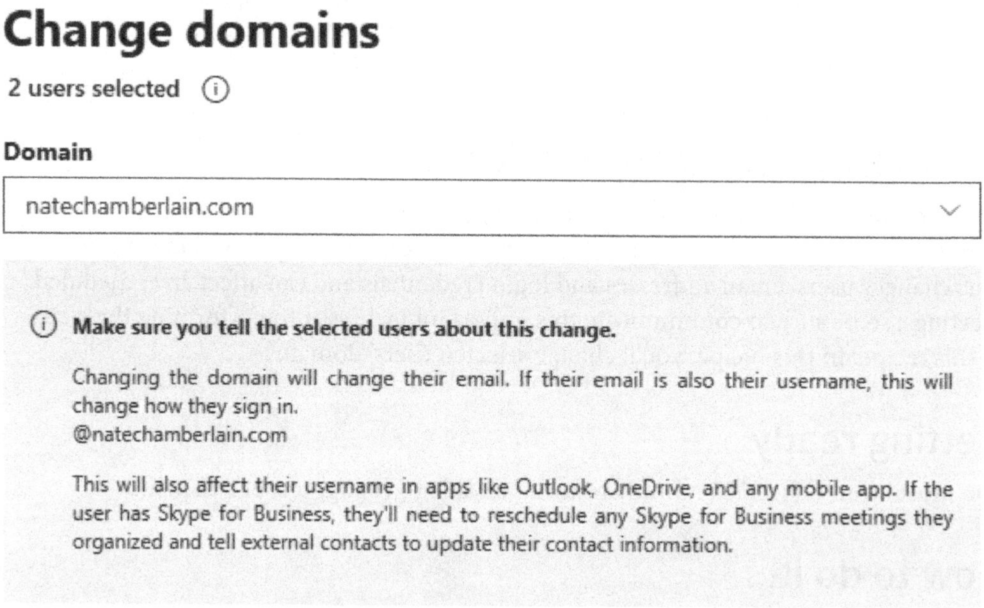

Change domains

2 users selected ⓘ

Domain

natechamberlain.com   ⌄

ⓘ **Make sure you tell the selected users about this change.**

Changing the domain will change their email. If their email is also their username, this will change how they sign in.
@natechamberlain.com

This will also affect their username in apps like Outlook, OneDrive, and any mobile app. If the user has Skype for Business, they'll need to reschedule any Skype for Business meetings they organized and tell external contacts to update their contact information.

Figure 1.28 – The warning provided when changing users' domains

5.   Click **Save changes**.

How it works...

In this recipe, we changed users' domains. Changing domains isn't common. Typically, you buy an Office 365 subscription, set up your custom domain as the default, then add your users, and they have the correct domain from the start.

However, you could change domains after your users have already been established. This could be done during acquisitions, company rebranding, or moving an employee to a new position that falls under a different domain owned by the company.

Once you select **Save changes**, the change is immediate, and the affected users will need to know the change has been made so that they log in with the correct credentials and share the correct email address with others.

> **Important note**
> The old domain (the `onmicrosoft` domain, in this example) can still be
> used as an email alias for the user, meaning mail sent to the old address will be
> forwarded to the new/primary address.

See also

- Check out *Change a user name and email address in Office 365*: `https://docs.`
  `microsoft.com/en-us/microsoft-365/admin/add-users/change-`
  `a-user-name-and-email-address`.

Assigning a license to a user

Users are restricted on what they can do within your environment based on the license(s)
that have been assigned. Even basic functions—such as navigation through the tenant, the
ability to email, and using various applications—all require some form of license.

This recipe demonstrates how to assign a product license to individual users or even all
members of a group via the Microsoft 365 admin center.

Getting ready

Only a user with an appropriate admin role (such as **Global Admin**, **License Admin**, and
so on) can assign a user license. Also, the tenant must have licenses of the appropriate type
free/available to be assigned. This requires the correct number of licenses to have been
purchased for your tenant.

How to do it...

1. Go to the Microsoft 365 admin center at `http://admin.microsoft.com`.

2. Select **Users** > **Active users**.

3. Select the user(s) for whom you're making the license change and select **Manage product licenses**:

Figure 1.29 – A user selected and the ellipsis menu showing the Manage product licenses option

4. Review the user's current licensing, which appears in a right-side window. This may require scrolling through all the available product licenses and clicking the *collapse/expand* arrows on the right side of the window:

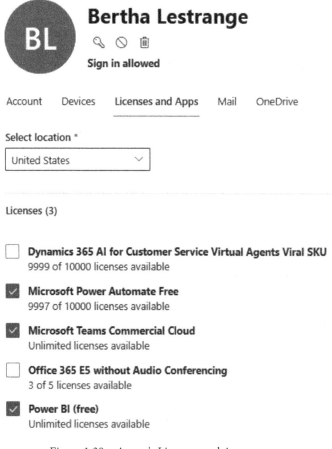

Figure 1.30 – A user's Licenses and Apps screen

5. The **Select location** dropdown should reflect the tenant default, but can be switched to access product licenses based on other locations/regions/countries:

Figure 1.31 – Location dropdown in a user's Licenses and Apps screen

6. Locate the product you wish to license to the user and check the box or toggle the button, then click the **Save changes** button to commit your selections:

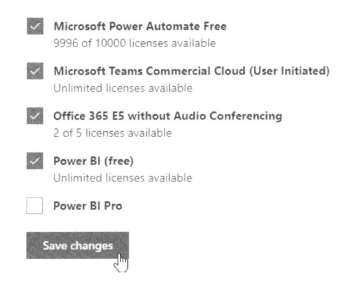

Figure 1.32 – Selected products to license for a user and the Save changes button

How it works...

You've assigned a product license to a user via the Microsoft 365 admin center's **Users** blade.

By accessing an active user's profile within Office 365, you can review, add, or remove licenses. Selecting some product licensing (such as **Enterprise licenses**) will automatically give a user access to a host of licenses/products. Lower-level licenses (such as Kiosk or unlicensed users) can be given ad hoc or à-la-carte access to various applications within the **Licenses and Apps** section.

There's more...

Managing users one at a time can become tedious. There are several ways to update product licensing in bulk. This can be accomplished by selecting multiple users at once in *Step 3* of this recipe, or by using a CSV upload process or through PowerShell commands. These processes are covered by recipes in the *Office 365 Identify and Roles* and *Administering Office 365 with PowerShell* chapters, found later in this book.

Assigning a license to a group

Assigning licenses to individual users can become a pain point for large organizations, or even smaller organizations that hire infrequently. The ability to quickly assign licenses based on groups of users is an efficient method of managing user licensing, especially if changes need to be made to all users within a group. In this recipe we'll do just that—assign a license to a group.

Getting ready

Only a user with an appropriate admin role (such as **Global Admin**, **License Admin**, and so on) can assign a user license. Also, the tenant must have licenses of the appropriate type free/available to be assigned. This requires the correct number of licenses to have been purchased for your tenant.

Finally, user locations play an active role in the assigning of licenses to a group process. Microsoft licenses are not available in all locations. A user's location property must be set before a license from a specific location can be assigned. When making a group license assignment, companies with multiple locations may need to be reviewed so that users are not given services in locations where that service is not allowed or available.

How to do it...

1. Go to the Azure **Active Directory** (**AD**) admin center at `https://aad.portal.azure.com`.

2. Click on **Azure Active Directory** and then **Licenses**.

3. Click on **All products** to see the available licenses in your tenant:

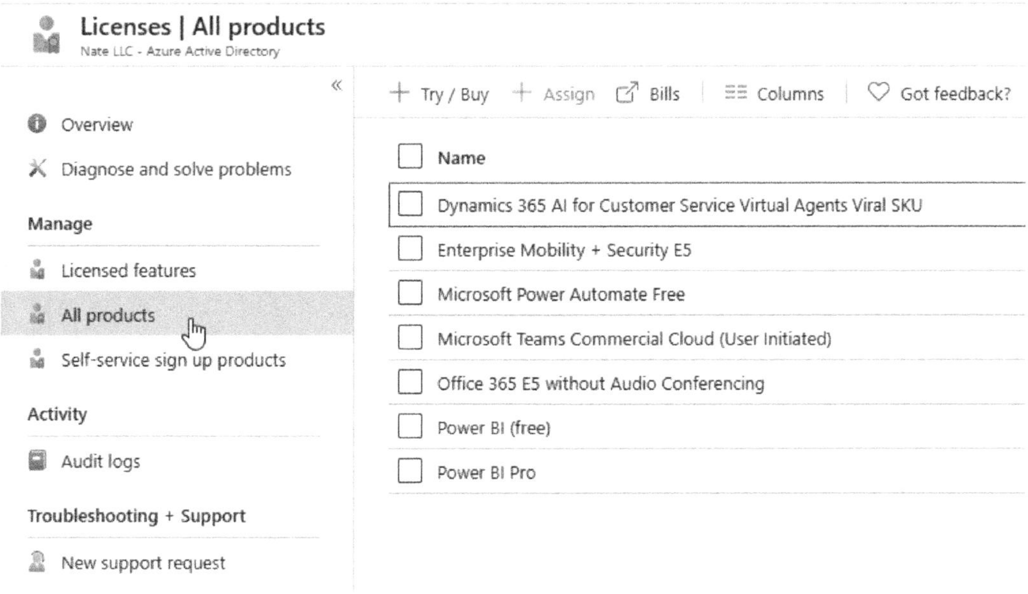

Figure 1.33 – Azure AD's All products screen

4. Check the box next to the license type you wish to assign, then click **Assign**:

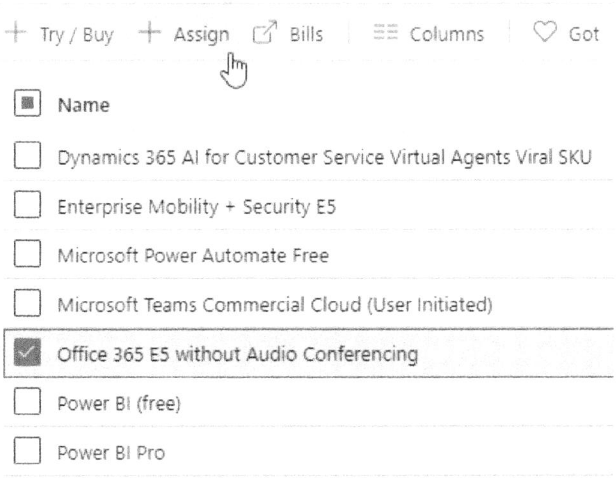

Figure 1.34 – Assign option in Azure AD when assigning an Office 365 license

5. On the **Assign license** page, select the group(s) you wish to assign the license to by clicking **Users and groups**, searching for the correct group and clicking on the group to add it as a selection, and, finally, clicking **Select**:

Figure 1.35 – Users and groups pane in Azure AD when assigning licenses

6. Next, review the assignment options by clicking the **Assignment options** section, toggling the various options based on your need, then clicking **OK**:

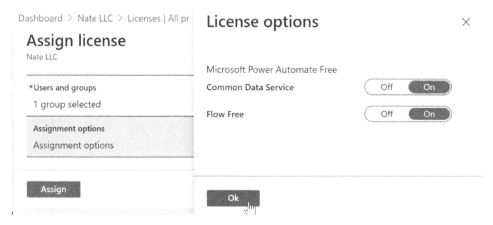

Figure 1.36 – License-specific options selected for a group in Azure AD

7. Complete the process by clicking **Assign**.

How it works...

In this recipe, you saved time by assigning a license to an entire group by utilizing Azure AD.

Azure AD processes all the members of the group, one at a time, but behind the scenes. This can take time, depending on the size of the group.

As the assignments are systematically added, a notification will display, stating the status and outcome of the process. If an error occurs—such as an assignment that could not be applied due to pre-existing licenses in the group—you may click the notification to review the details.

See also

- Verifying group license assignments were completed: `https://docs.microsoft.com/en-us/azure/active-directory/users-groups-roles/licensing-groups-assign#step-2-verify-that-the-initial-assignment-has-finished`

- Checking license issues and resolving: `https://docs.microsoft.com/en-us/azure/active-directory/users-groups-roles/licensing-groups-assign#step-3-check-for-license-problems-and-resolve-them`

- Known issues when using groups to manage licensing in Azure AD: `https://docs.microsoft.com/en-us/azure/active-directory/users-groups-roles/licensing-group-advanced`

Customizing navigation of the admin center

If you use certain admin centers frequently, you can adjust the navigation menu of the Microsoft 365 admin center so that those admin center links are always visible and not hidden beneath the **Show all** link. In this recipe, we'll make sure Azure AD, Exchange, and SharePoint admin centers are always visible on our menu.

Getting ready

A user must be an admin with the appropriate role (such as **Global Admin**). These steps are based on the "new" admin center (released for preview in 2018-2019).

How to do it...

1. Go to the Microsoft 365 admin center at `http://admin.microsoft.com`.

2. On the left-hand navigation panel, click **Customize navigation**. The **Customize your navigation pane** panel will open on the right side of the screen:

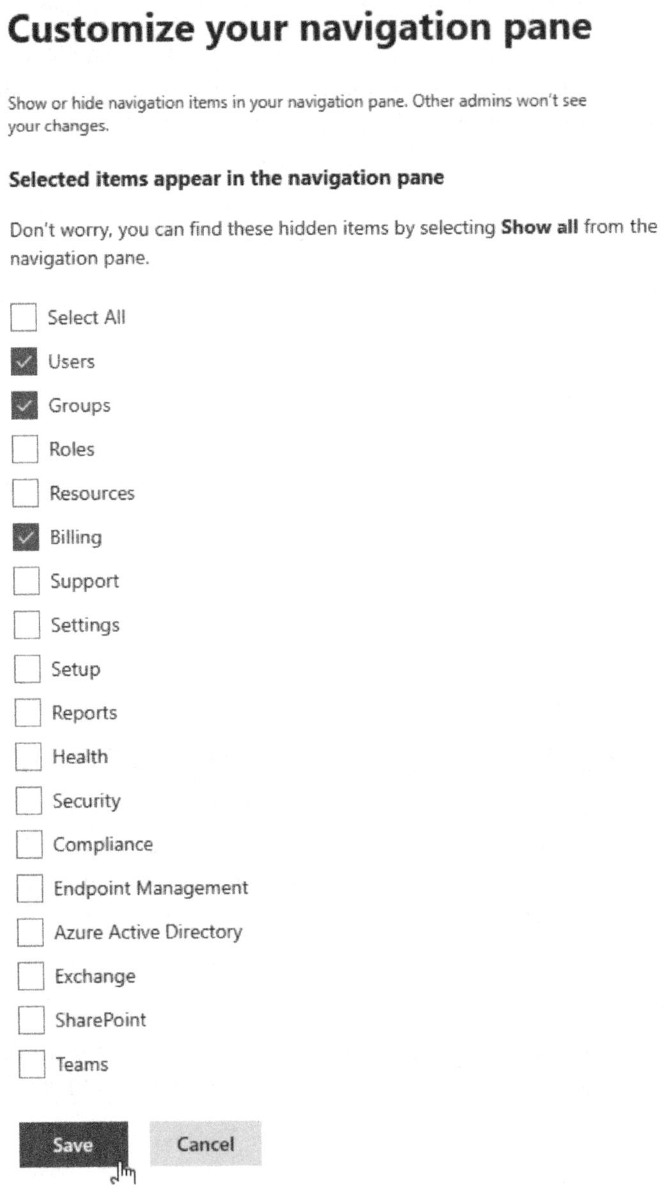

Customize your navigation pane

Show or hide navigation items in your navigation pane. Other admins won't see your changes.

Selected items appear in the navigation pane

Don't worry, you can find these hidden items by selecting **Show all** from the navigation pane.

- [ ] Select All
- [x] Users
- [x] Groups
- [ ] Roles
- [ ] Resources
- [x] Billing
- [ ] Support
- [ ] Settings
- [ ] Setup
- [ ] Reports
- [ ] Health
- [ ] Security
- [ ] Compliance
- [ ] Endpoint Management
- [ ] Azure Active Directory
- [ ] Exchange
- [ ] SharePoint
- [ ] Teams

Save   Cancel

Figure 1.37 – The configuration pane for choosing what appears in the left-hand navigation pane

3. Check the box next to the various links and admin centers you want to appear above the **Show all** section (such as **Azure Active Directory**, **Exchange**, and **SharePoint**), and click **Save.**

4. The links will group into basic admin navigation and admin centers, with the **Show all** link still available to expand the list to see all navigation choices:

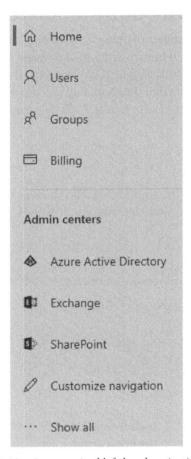

Figure 1.38 – A customized left-hand navigation pane

How it works...

In this recipe we added Azure AD, Exchange, and SharePoint admin centers as permanent links on our Microsoft 365 admin center left navigation pane by selecting **Customize navigation**.

As the Microsoft admin center ecosystem grows, the list of functions and admin centers continues to grow. Custom navigation allows your admins to target the items they need instant access to, based on how your tenant is used, but does not restrict a quick view of the other available links.

Personalizing your admin center home page

As with any application, the number of options, selections, and settings grows over time, having quick and ready access to information and common tasks. For example, the **User management** card allows an admin single-click access to add, delete, edit, or reset the password of a user. This kind of flexibility goes beyond simply changing colors and themes and helps improve the overall user experience. Let's personalize what appears on our home page.

Getting ready

A user must be an admin with the appropriate role (such as **Global Admin**). These steps are based on the "new" admin center (released for preview in 2018-2019).

How to do it...

1. Go to the Microsoft 365 admin center at `http://admin.microsoft.com`.

2. To the right of the main panel, click **Add card**:

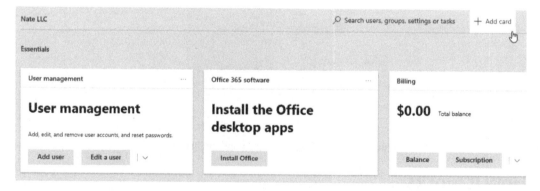

Figure 1.39 – The Microsoft 365 admin center landing page with the **Add card** button in the upper right

A variety of preconfigured cards are made available:

Add cards to your home page

Drag a card to the location you want, or select Add card (+).

Setup

Discover and set up your services, solutions, and add-ons.

Office 365 Advanced Threat Protection

Keep an eye on malicious content blocked by Advanced Threat Protection, and add protection when it's needed.

Azure Active Directory

Get access to common Azure AD tasks like self-serve password resets, customizing sign-in, and adding apps.

Data loss prevention

See how many files containing sensitive info are protected by data loss protection policies, and change those policies.

Figure 1.40 – Some of the available card options to choose for the Microsoft 365 admin center

3. Drag and drop the selected card or click the plus sign (+) (which appears when hovering over the card) to add it to your admin center.

How it works...

In this recipe, we added data cards of interest to our Microsoft 365 admin center's home page. This allowed us to have easy access to relevant, interesting data without having to dig for it elsewhere.

While the ability to customize your admin center is limited to the preconfigured options, the options span most of the major admin functions/centers, consolidating data and allowing you to build a powerful dashboard.

> **Tip**
>
> Admins can customize the theme for an entire tenant and toggle between **Light mode** and **Dark mode**.

2
Office 365 Identity and Roles

Users and groups are at the core of every administrative decision you will make. Before you can create policies or configure some admin center features, you will need to have groups thoughtfully provisioned to be used for appropriate licensing, security, and experience enhancement.

In this chapter, we'll cover Microsoft 365 identity management basics. This includes creation and management of both users and groups and introduces you to a couple of essential security topics such as enabling **multi-factor authentication** (MFA) through **Security Defaults** and assigning admin roles.

The recipes included in this chapter are as follows:

- Creating a new user
- Importing users in bulk
- Creating a new Office 365 group
- Enabling Security Defaults (MFA)
- Exporting users
- Managing guest users
- Creating a user template
- Restricting users from creating new O365 groups
- Assigning the User Administrator admin role in Azure **Active Directory** (**AD**)
- Managing admin roles in the Microsoft 365 Admin Center

Technical requirements

This chapter requires users to have administrative privileges in Office 365. Those with a global administrator role will be able to perform every task in each recipe. Specific app and functional administrators will be able to do many of the recipes. No installations/downloads are required for the recipes in this chapter.

Creating a new user

When someone joins your organization, you will need to create a new user profile so that person can be assigned credentials to your tenant. In this recipe, we'll walk through the steps of creating a single user via the Microsoft 365 Admin Center.

Getting ready

The user creating the account must be an admin with the appropriate role (such as **Global Admin**).

How to do it...

1. Go to the Microsoft 365 Admin Center at `http://admin.microsoft.com`.

2. Select **Users** > **Active users**.

3. Select **Add a user**.

4. A form will display, in which you enter the user's basic information. Fill in the first section, **Set up the basics**:

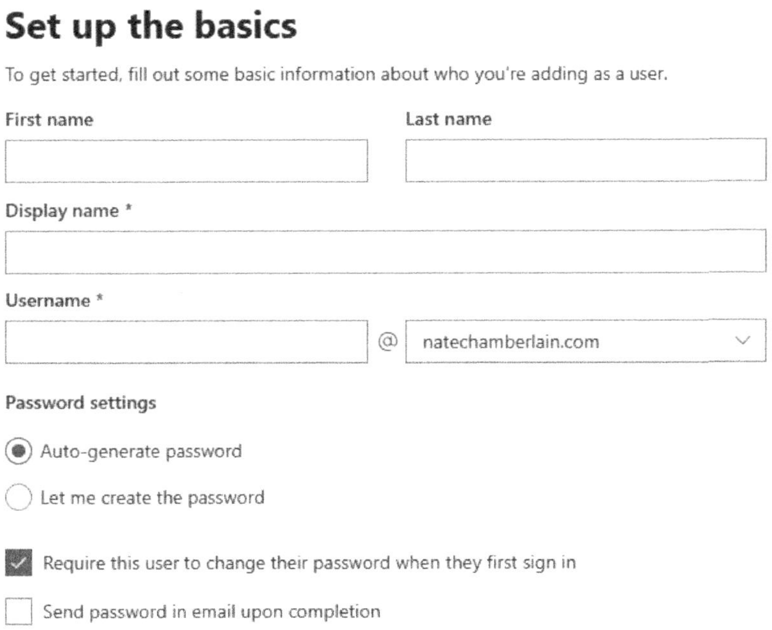

Set up the basics

To get started, fill out some basic information about who you're adding as a user.

First name

Last name

Display name *

Username *

@   natechamberlain.com   ⌄

Password settings

(●) Auto-generate password

( ) Let me create the password

[✓] Require this user to change their password when they first sign in

[ ] Send password in email upon completion

Figure 2.1 – Fields and options for setting up a new user in Office 365

In the **Password settings** section, it is recommended to allow the tenant to set a temporary password by leaving the default selections checked. You may check **Send password in email upon completion** and add an email address, or when the setup is complete, you will have a chance to copy the user's credentials.

Click **Next** to move to the **Product licenses** section.

5. As discussed in *Chapter 1, Office 365 Setup and Basic Administration*, select the appropriate location and license. Additionally, you can select the **Create user without product license (not recommended)** option if you would like to assign licenses later:

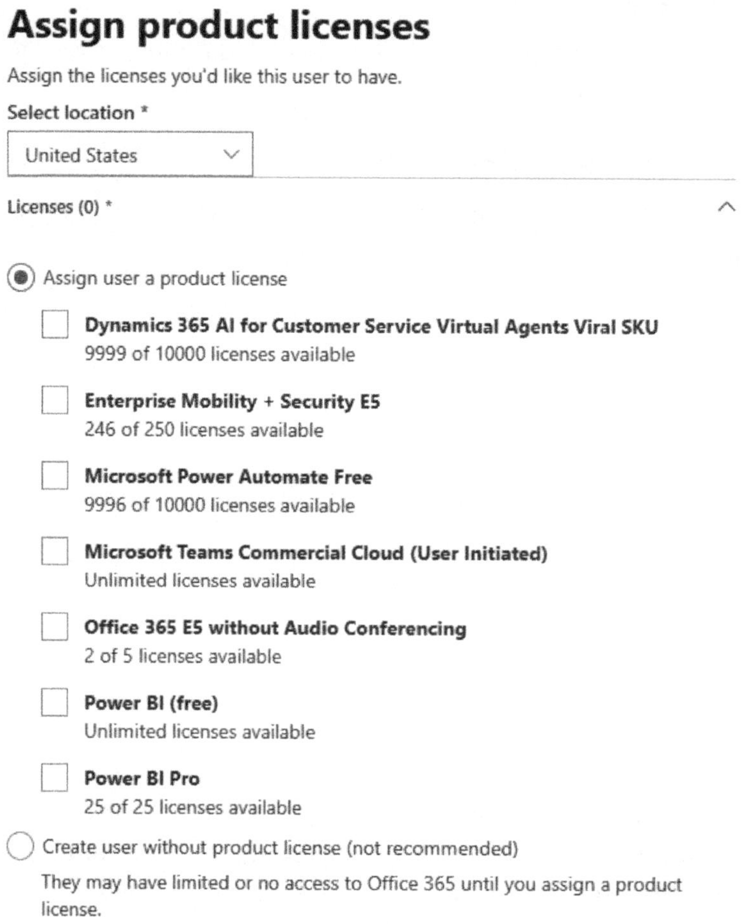

Assign product licenses

Assign the licenses you'd like this user to have.

Select location *

| United States | ∨ |

Licenses (0) *   ∧

● Assign user a product license

☐ **Dynamics 365 AI for Customer Service Virtual Agents Viral SKU**
9999 of 10000 licenses available

☐ **Enterprise Mobility + Security E5**
246 of 250 licenses available

☐ **Microsoft Power Automate Free**
9996 of 10000 licenses available

☐ **Microsoft Teams Commercial Cloud (User Initiated)**
Unlimited licenses available

☐ **Office 365 E5 without Audio Conferencing**
2 of 5 licenses available

☐ **Power BI (free)**
Unlimited licenses available

☐ **Power BI Pro**
25 of 25 licenses available

○ Create user without product license (not recommended)

They may have limited or no access to Office 365 until you assign a product license.

Figure 2.2 – License options when adding a new user

Click **Next** to move to the **Optional settings** section.

From here, you can assign an admin or elevated rights role to the user, or you can add in additional profile information for the user.

6. Select the appropriate option by expanding the section and filling in the details:

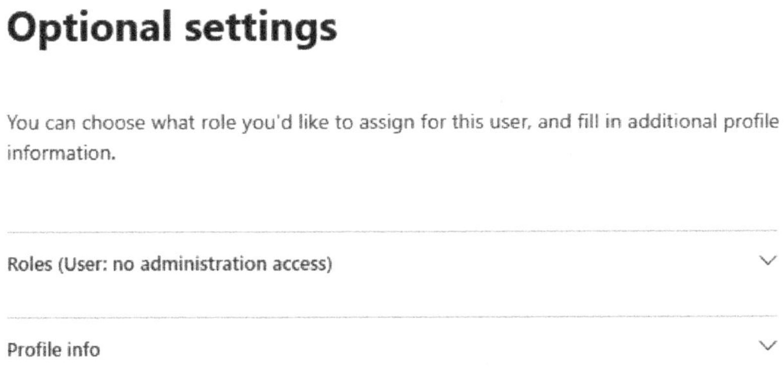

Optional settings

You can choose what role you'd like to assign for this user, and fill in additional profile information.

Roles (User: no administration access)   ⌄

Profile info   ⌄

Figure 2.3 – Optional role and profile information for a new user

7. Click **Next** to move to the **Finish** section.

8. Your user is not yet created. Review the information and click **Finish adding**:

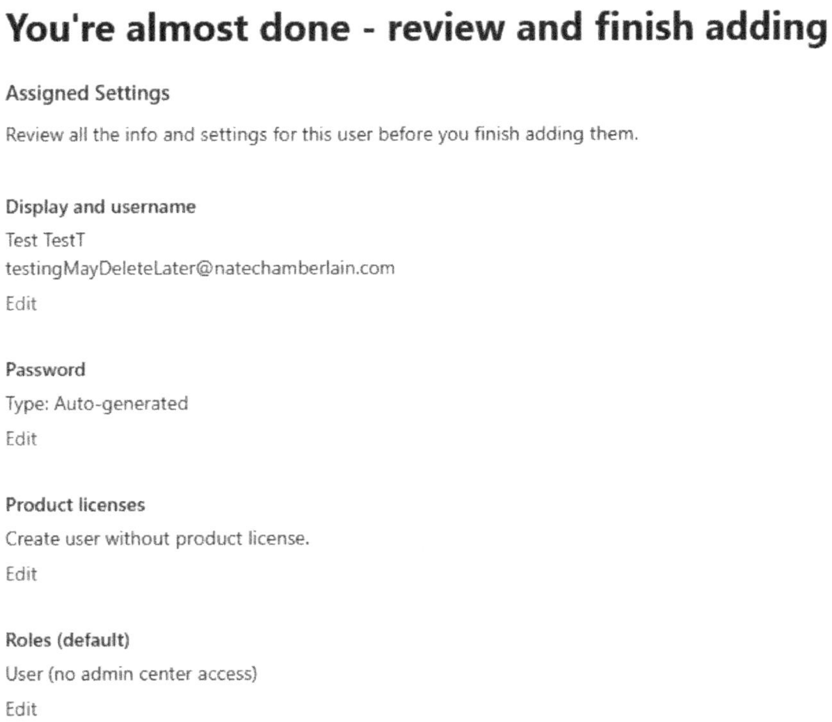

You're almost done - review and finish adding

Assigned Settings

Review all the info and settings for this user before you finish adding them.

Display and username

Test TestT

testingMayDeleteLater@natechamberlain.com

Edit

Password

Type: Auto-generated

Edit

Product licenses

Create user without product license.

Edit

Roles (default)

User (no admin center access)

Edit

Figure 2.4 – Confirmation screen for reviewing the details of a new user

9. From this screen, you can copy the **User details** and provide those to the user:

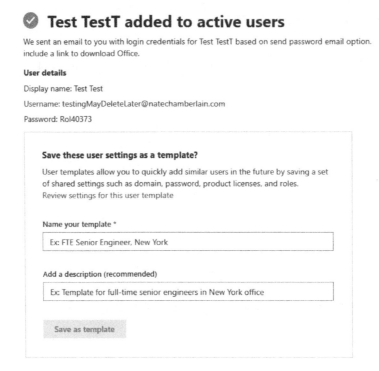

Figure 2.5 – Optional ability to save a new user's configuration as a template for future new users

How it works...

In this recipe, you created a new user from scratch. User management starts with this action of creating a new user. Once the user has been created and appropriate product licenses applied, the user will have the ability to sign in.

Importing users in bulk

Adding users one at a time can become quite laborious in a large organization. This recipe provides a method for importing a file and adding users in bulk. Additionally, this can be done through PowerShell, which will be covered in *Chapter 3, Administering Office 365 with PowerShell*.

Getting ready

The user creating the account must be either a global or user administrator.

How to do it...

1. Go to the Microsoft 365 Admin Center at `http://admin.microsoft.com`.
2. Select **Users** > **Active users**.
3. Select **Add multiple users**.
4. Click **Add multiple users**:

Active users
Add a user
User templates
Add multiple users

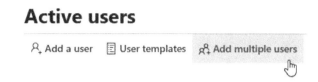

Figure 2.6 – The Add multiple users button of the Active users page

5. The **Import multiple users** panel will open. From here, you can download a sample **comma-separated values** (**CSV**) file, enter your user information according to the column headings in the download, and then upload it to your tenant:

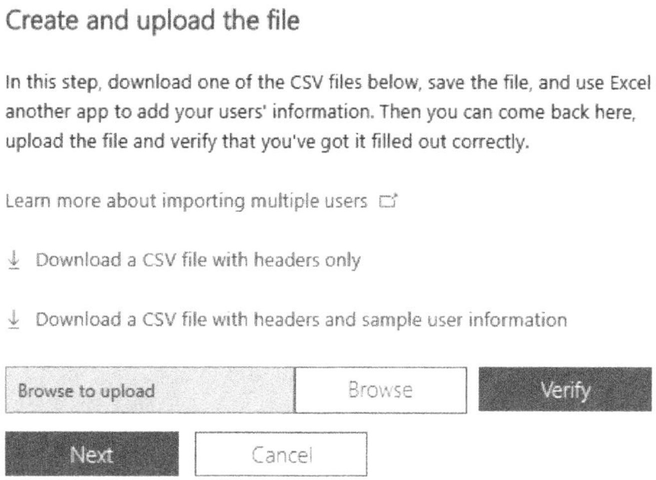

Create and upload the file
In this step, download one of the CSV files below, save the file, and use Excel or another app to add your users' information. Then you can come back here, upload the file and verify that you've got it filled out correctly.
Learn more about importing multiple users
Download a CSV file with headers only
Download a CSV file with headers and sample user information
Browse to upload
Browse
Verify
Next
Cancel

Figure 2.7 – The upload file dialog for downloading templates of and importing CSV files of new users

6. The CSV file must include all the exact column headings that are found in the sample. If you move the headings, the upload may not work appropriately.

   Data must be entered into the username and display name columns for each user.

7. Click **Next** to move to the **Set user options** section.

8. From this screen, you can set the **Sign-in status** and select product licenses for the bulk loaded users:

Figure 2.8 – Dialog options for allowing sign-in and assigning product licenses upon import

9. Click **Next** to move to the **View your result** section.

10. On the **View your result** screen, you can choose to send the results to an email address, check how many users were created, and download the results. Note that the results will include plaintext passwords. The results will help show how many users were successfully created and maybe illustrate a need for licensing adjustment to meet the number of users:

Figure 2.9 – Confirmation of created users with the option to email a result file to users

11. Click **Send and close** to finish the process.

How it works...

You just imported a CSV file with many users' data to create new users in Office 365 more efficiently. This behind-the-scenes method is functionally the same as manually adding users. However, it applies those selections in bulk and then creates a downloadable file with the login information.

See also

- Learn more about using a CSV file to import users at `https://docs.microsoft.com/en-us/Office365/enterprise/add-several-users-at-the-same-time#more-information-about-how-to-add-users-to-microsoft-365`.

Creating a new Office 365 group

Groups in Office 365 are a great way to manage people with similar tasks, access needs, or users within the same team or department. Groups are an essential component to the Office 365 ecosystem, and when an admin gets groups right, the admin's job becomes much easier to manage. In this recipe, you'll create an Office 365 group.

Getting ready

The user creating the group must be either a global or user administrator.

How to do it...

1. Go to the Microsoft 365 Admin Center at `http://admin.microsoft.com`.
2. Select **Groups** > **Add a group**.
3. Select the group type you wish to create, and then click **Next**.
4. In the **Set up the basics** section, enter a group name and description, then click **Next**.

5. From the **Edit settings** page, assign the group a unique email address, choose if the group is public or private, and determine if the group should have a Microsoft Teams team:

Edit settings

Office 365 group
Allows teams to collaborate by giving them a group email and a shared workspace for conversations, files, and calendars.

Group email address *

	@natechamberlain.com

Privacy

(●) Public - Anyone can see group content

( ) Private - Only members can see group content

Add Microsoft Teams to your group

[ ] Create a team for this group

> (i) Some settings like Allow External Senders, or Send Copies of Group Conversations to Members' Inboxes can only be set after the group is created. Learn more about this setting

Figure 2.10 – New Office 365 group creation dialog

6. Click **Next** to move to the **Owners** section.

7. In the **Owners** box, select two users who will have ownership of the group.

8. Your group is not yet created. On the **Review and finish adding group** screen, review your selections and click **Create group** to complete the process:

New group created

This group will appear in your list of groups within 5 minutes.

Now that the group has been created, you can change these settings:

* Send copies of group conversations and events to group members inboxes
* Let people outside the organization email this group

Would you like to know more?

Using groups to collaborate effectively

Figure 2.11 – Confirmation of a newly created Office 365 group

How it works...

In this recipe, you created an Office 365 group. Groups are a foundational component to many of the advanced features and products available with your tenant. Groups segment users for ease of administration and collaboration between those users. Understanding how and when to use a group is a vital component to successfully setting up a tenant and may require forward thinking on how and why a group needs to be created.

There's more...

Creating a group is only the first step. Next, you need to assign users to the group. This is done by navigating to the **Groups** section, searching for the correct group, and going to the **Members** tab. Select **View all and manage members**, and then add or remove members.

See also

- Understanding the group types: `https://docs.microsoft.com/en-US/ microsoft-365/admin/create-groups/compare-groups`

- Managing a group: `https://docs.microsoft.com/en-us/ microsoft-365/admin/create-groups/manage-groups?view=o365- worldwide`

- Adding guests to a group: `https://support.office.com/en-us/ article/adding-guests-to-office-365-groups-bfc7a840-868f- 4fd6-a390-f347bf51aff6`

Enabling Security Defaults (MFA)

Security Defaults are a set of rules and identify security mechanisms preconfigured by Microsoft, but the rules are left disabled by default. Enabling these defaults will impact your entire tenant. Admins and users will be required to start using MFA (adding an additional layer of security upon sign-in), better protecting your tenant and the data within from exposure through phishing and other identity-related attacks.

The *See also* section of this recipe includes a link to user training as well as additional resources you should read before enabling the Security Defaults, to ensure you are clear on the impact to your organization.

Getting ready

Only an admin with the **Global Admin** role can make these changes to the tenant security settings. These steps are based on the "new" admin center (released for preview in 2018-2019).

This process assumes you are working from a recently created tenant (2017 or newer). If you are using an older tenant and have set up baseline policies, you will need to disable those policies and move to the new Security Defaults. Additionally, you may need to activate modern authentication in your tenant (the *See also* section of this recipe has instructions on how to verify this). This is not required for recently created tenants (2017 or newer).

How to do it...

1. Sign in to the Microsoft 365 Admin Center at `http://admin.microsoft.com`.

2. Go to the Azure AD **Properties** page at `https://portal.azure.com/#blade/Microsoft_AAD_IAM/ActiveDirectoryMenuBlade/Properties`.

3. Select **Manage Security defaults** at the bottom of the page.

4. The **Enable Security defaults** panel will load:

Figure 2.12 – Information about and ability to Enable Security defaults

5. Toggle the **Enable Security defaults** selector to **Yes**.

6. Click **Save**.

How it works...

You've just enabled MFA, among other security enhancements, by toggling on **Enable Security defaults**. Security defaults are rules, or conditional access policies, which are set by default to help control how users and admins interact with Office 365.

See also

- User training on how to download and use Microsoft Authenticator with Office 365: `https://support.office.com/en-us/article/use-microsoft-authenticator-with-office-365-1412611f-ad8d-43ab-807c-7965e5155411?ui=en-US&rs=en-US&ad=US#ID0EAADAAA=_Step_1`

- Verify if your tenant is set up with modern authentication (typically applies to tenants older than 2017): `https://docs.microsoft.com/exchange/clients-and-mobile-in-exchange-online/enable-or-disable-modern-authentication-in-exchange-online`

- Understanding the new Security Defaults and the impact to your users and tenant: `https://docs.microsoft.com/en-us/azure/active-directory/fundamentals/concept-fundamentals-security-defaults`

Exporting users

As a tenant admin, you will be asked for reports and information about the users in your tenant. One of the basic requests is around the number of users. A basic user export provides all this information and much more. In this recipe, we'll obtain that from the Microsoft 365 Admin Center.

Getting ready

The user creating the account must be an admin with the appropriate role (such as **Global Admin**, **User Admin**, and so on).

How to do it...

1. Go to the Microsoft 365 Admin Center at `http://admin.microsoft.com`.

2. Select **Users** > **Active users**.

3. Click **Export Users**:

Active users

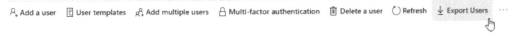

Figure 2.13 – The Export Users button in the Active users top menu

4. A dialog box will appear—click **Continue** or **No**.

5. A CSV file that provides several columns of information on each user will download to your PC.

How it works...

You used the **Export Users** button to pull down a CSV report of active users that can be sorted, filtered, or shared.

Managing guest users

When guests are added to your tenant directly by an admin or by a user in Teams, SharePoint, or other apps, those guests are stored in the Micosoft 365 admin center and can be viewed and deleted there. In this recipe, we'll cover the steps required to search for and manage guest users.

Getting ready

Guest users must be allowed in your tenant for any to appear in the admin center once invited by Team or group owners.

How to do it...

1. Go to the Microsoft 365 Admin Center at `http://admin.microsoft.com`.

2. Select **Users** > **Guest Users**.

3. Use the search bar to search for specific guest(s).

4. Use the ellipsis menu on any user's name when viewing and searching the main listing to delete a user:

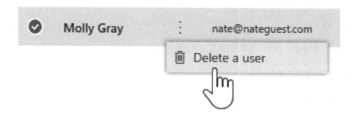

Figure 2.14 – Delete a user option on the ellipsis menu for a user

5. You can also select a user's name to view or edit contact information and O365 group memberships. You can use the trash icon under the user's name and email to delete the user:

General
_____

Display name   Email

Molly Gray   nate@nateguest.com

Department   Job title

Contact information   Groups

First Name   O365 Group Demo
Last Name   Manage groups
Phone number
Manage contact information

Figure 2.15 – User detail panel that appears when a user is selected from Active users

How it works...

In this recipe, you found guest users in your tenant and explored the details for one of them. The **Guest Users** screen of the Microsoft 365 admin center allows viewing, editing, and deleting of all invited guests.

There's more...

You can only delete one guest user at a time from the **Users** > **Guest Users** screen. Go to the **Users** > **Active users** screen to delete guest users in bulk. You'll just need to filter the **Active users** screen to **Guest users** first, as seen here:

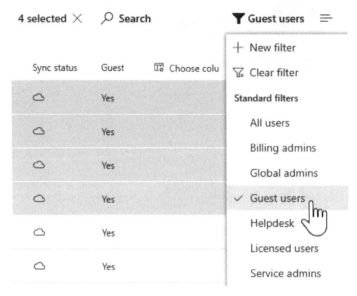

Figure 2.16 – Active user view filter options with Guest users selected

See also

- Learn more about managing O365 guests at `https://support.office.com/en-us/article/Adding-guests-to-Office-365-Groups-bfc7a840-868f-4fd6-a390-f347bf51aff6`.

- Find ways to work with guest user accounts using PowerShell at `https://docs.microsoft.com/en-us/microsoft-365/admin/create-groups/manage-guest-access-in-groups`.

Creating a user template

User templates save user administrators time by applying pre-selected licenses, applications, assigned domains, and metadata (such as Office information) to users created using that template. In this recipe, we'll cover the steps to creating a user template.

Getting ready

You must be an O365 administrator to manage users and user templates.

How to do it...

1. Go to the Microsoft 365 Admin Center at `http://admin.microsoft.com`.

2. Select **Users** > **Active users**.

3. Select **User Templates** > **Add template** from the ribbon menu:

Figure 2.17 – Add template option available upon clicking User templates in the Active users page

4. Name your template (this appears on the **User templates** menu as an option later) and give it a clear description. Click **Next**:

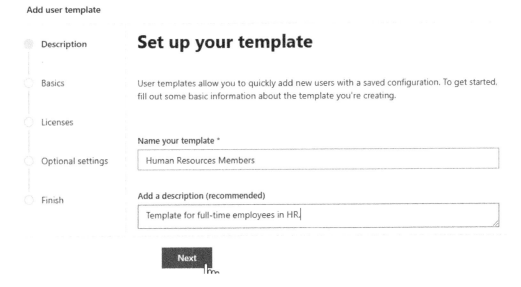

Figure 2.18 – The first screen of creating a user template including name and description fields

5. Choose to which domain users under this template should be added. This is useful when your organization encompasses multiple business units or company names operating under different domains or even subdomains. Also, choose whether these users will have an autogenerated or standard password and if that should be changed by the user on their first sign-in. Click **Next**:

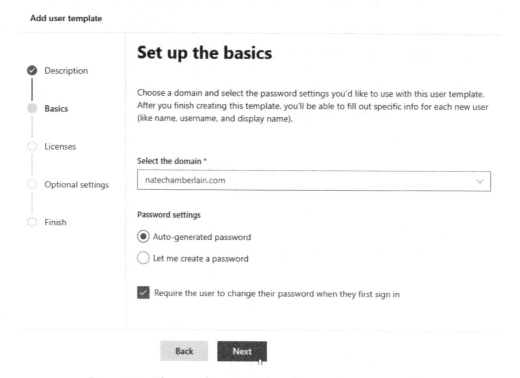

Figure 2.19 – The second screen, Basics, when creating a user template

6. Choose which location and licenses will be applied to these users, then scroll down to the next section **Licenses**:

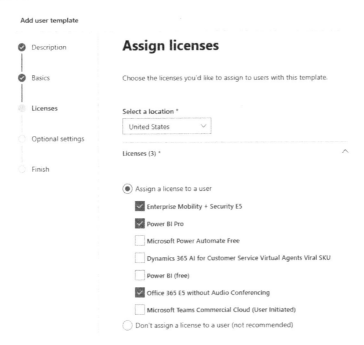

Figure 2.20 – The third screen, Licenses, when creating a user template

7. All the apps within each of the licenses you selected in the preceding screenshot appear automatically, allowing you to choose specific apps to enable/disable for users created with this template. When satisfied, click **Next**:

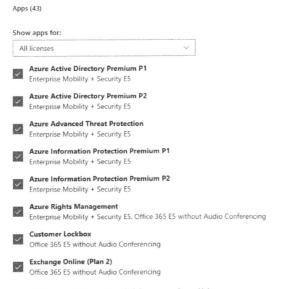

Figure 2.21 – Available apps for all licenses

8. On the **Optional settings** page, choose which (if any) administrator roles to apply to these users, then complete the **Profile info** section with info that should be applied by default to all users created using this template. Click **Next** when finished to review your template:

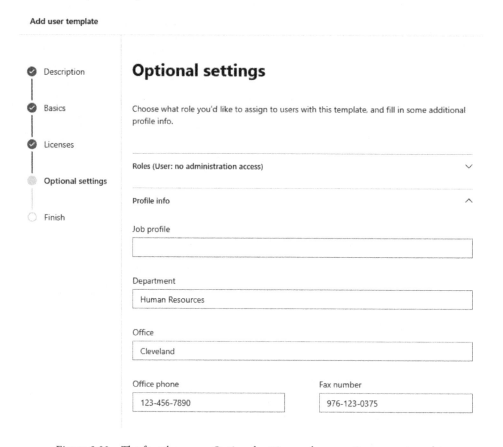

Figure 2.22 – The fourth screen, Optional settings, when creating a user template

9. If satisfied with the template, choose **Finish adding**; otherwise, choose **Edit** in the respective section to make changes first:

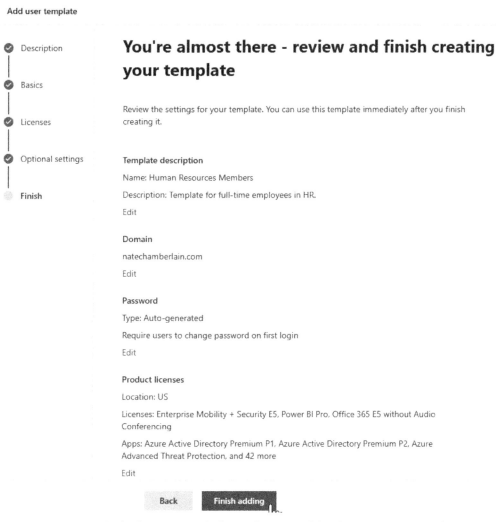

Figure 2.23 – The final screen, Finish, for confirmation of details in a new user template

10. Your template will show a confirmation message. Close this when finished:

Figure 2.24 – The confirmation message with optional Next steps after creating a user template

11. Now, when you go to create new users, you'll be able to save time by selecting the template to pre-fill much of the data:

Figure 2.25 – A newly created user template now available for selection

12. When selected, you'll have minimal information to complete for adding the new user under that template. As seen here, it's basically just name, display name, and username:

Human Resources Members

Fill out the required fields to add a user from this template.

First name

Test

Last name

HRUser

Display name *

Test HRUser

Username *

testhr   @ natechamberlain.com

Password (Auto-generated) *

You'll see the new password as soon as you finish adding this user.

☐ Send password in email upon completion

Template details

Name

Human Resources Members   ⌄

Description

Template for full-time employees in HR.

Add user

Figure 2.26 – Screen shown once the existing user template is selected for creating a new user

How it works...

In this recipe, you configured a user template to save you time when creating additional users who will have very similar, if not identical, profile parameters such as office location, department, and so on.

User templates are saved configurations for certain user types that allow administrators to apply consistent licenses, app permissions, domains, and office contact information to users belonging to a common group or role.

Once a template, such as **Human Resources Members**, is created, it simply needs to be selected the next time an HR employee is onboarded. The new user's name is entered and all the preconfigured settings for the template are applied, making the process much more efficient.

There's more...

You cannot edit a user template later. Once it's created, that template remains the same until it is deleted and potentially replaced by a new template. This helps ensure consistency of the users created with the template throughout its life cycle.

See also

- Check out Lori Craw's article on user templates on *TechCommunity*: `https://techcommunity.microsoft.com/t5/microsoft-365-blog/new-to-admin-center-templates-for-adding-users-faster/ba-p/856424`

Restricting users from creating new O365 groups

By default, anyone in your tenant can create their own O365 groups. This can happen when a user creates a new Team in Microsoft Teams, a plan in Planner, and several other apps that use O365 groups at the core. In this recipe, we'll use PowerShell to restrict users from self-provisioning their own O365 groups (whether intentionally or incidentally when creating other resources).

Getting ready

You'll need to be able to create security groups (not just O365 groups) and have the latest version of the `AzureADPreview` module for PowerShell installed. This can be installed by running SharePoint Online Management Shell as administrator and entering the following command:

```
Install-Module AzureADPreview
```

There's currently no way to do this without PowerShell.

How to do it...

1.   Go to the Microsoft 365 Admin Center at `http://admin.microsoft.com`.

2.   Select **Groups** > **Groups**.

3.   Select **Add a group**.

4.   Choose **Security** and **Next**:

⦿ Security

Controls access to OneDrive and SharePoint and can be used for Mobile Device
Management for Microsoft 365

Next

Figure 2.27 – Security groupt type selected

5.   Name and describe the group (we're using **O365 Group Creators** as our example). Click **Next**:

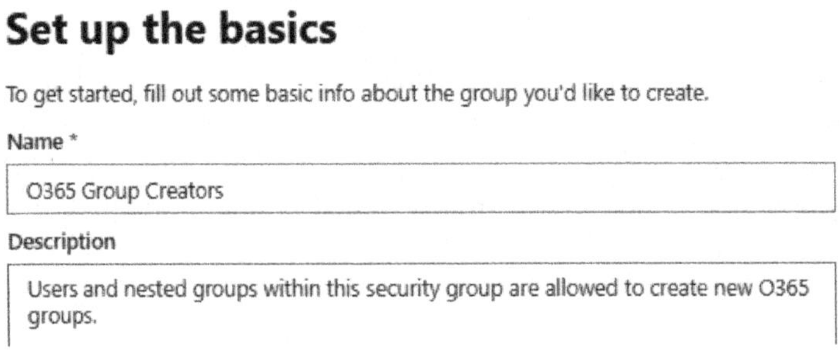

Set up the basics

To get started, fill out some basic info about the group you'd like to create.

Name *

O365 Group Creators

Description

Users and nested groups within this security group are allowed to create new O365
groups.

Figure 2.28 – Group name and description fields when creating a new group

6. Click **Create group** to confirm details and create the group. Close the panel.

7. Copy the following script from here (if you're reading the e-book) or from `https://docs.microsoft.com/en-us/microsoft-365/admin/create-groups/manage-creation-of-groups`:

```
$GroupName = "<SecurityGroupName>"
$AllowGroupCreation = "False"


Connect-AzureAD


$settingsObjectID = (Get-AzureADDirectorySetting | Where-
object -Property Displayname -Value "Group.Unified" -EQ).
id
if(!$settingsObjectID)
{
        $template = Get-AzureADDirectorySettingTemplate |
Where-object {$_.displayname -eq "group.unified"}
    $settingsCopy = $template.CreateDirectorySetting()
    New-AzureADDirectorySetting -DirectorySetting
$settingsCopy
    $settingsObjectID = (Get-AzureADDirectorySetting |
Where-object -Property Displayname -Value "Group.Unified"
-EQ).id
}


$settingsCopy = Get-AzureADDirectorySetting -Id
$settingsObjectID
$settingsCopy["EnableGroupCreation"] =
$AllowGroupCreation


if($GroupName)
{
    $settingsCopy["GroupCreationAllowedGroupId"] =
(Get-AzureADGroup -SearchString $GroupName).objectid
}
  else {
$settingsCopy["GroupCreationAllowedGroupId"] = $GroupName
}
```

```
Set-AzureADDirectorySetting -Id $settingsObjectID
-DirectorySetting $settingsCopy
(Get-AzureADDirectorySetting -Id $settingsObjectID).
Values
```

8. Paste the script into Notepad (or similar text editor). Change `<SecurityGroupName>` in *line 1* to the name of your security group. In our example, *line 1* would resemble the following:

```
$GroupName = "O365 Group Creators"
```

9. Open SharePoint Online Management Shell (as administrator).

10. Copy the text from your open Notepad application and paste into PowerShell. Hit *Enter*:

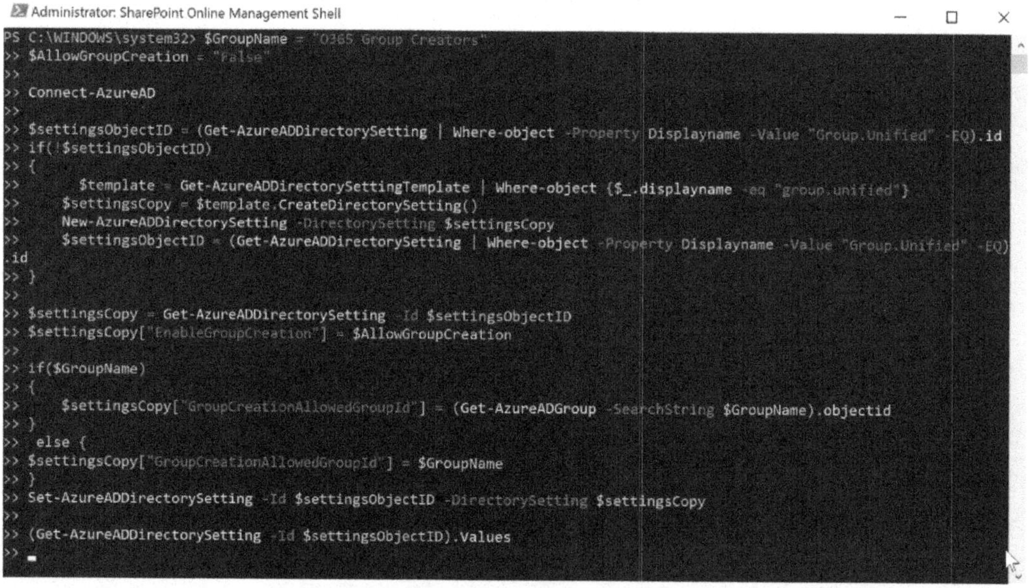

Figure 2.29 – PowerShell screen with pasted script adjusted with our "allowed" group name

11. A **sign-in** dialog will appear, requesting your administrator credentials to complete the change:

Figure 2.30 – Sign-in dialog presented as part of executing the PowerShell script

12. The script will take a moment to complete, and when finished will show the following:

```
Name  : EnableGroupCreation
Value : False
```

Figure 2.31 – Confirmation message in PowerShell

How it works...

You have just executed a PowerShell script that will restrict creation of additional O365 groups to members of a specific security group. Don't forget to add members to the new security group once it's created.

Once the script has run, users who are not global admins or members of a qualifying group or role will be unable to create new groups immediately. They can still create new plans and channels associated with existing groups, but will see a message letting them know they cannot create new groups when the opportunity would have traditionally been available:

Figure 2.32 – Message that appears to Planner users when group creation is disabled for them

Another example would be a user without permission trying to create a new team in Teams. They can click **Join or create a team** as usual, but the option to create a new group/team will not exist:

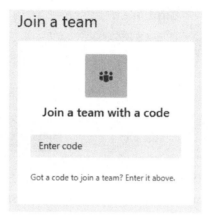

Figure 2.33 – Teams screen that appears for users who cannot create new teams (therefore, groups)

A final example would be a user creating a new SharePoint team site. They can still create team sites in SharePoint using the new or classic team template, where the classic team site template wouldn't create an associated group anyway. The only change would be the new team site template not being able to create an associated O365 group as would otherwise be normal. If they create the site first and later try to connect it to a new group separately, they will receive the following notice:

Figure 2.34 – Message that appears when users in SharePoint attempt to associate a site with a new group

> **Tip**
> Consider utilizing a training course (digital or in person) for users to "earn" the ability to create O365 groups (by getting added to your new security group) after taking the time to understand the implications and best practices.

See also

- Find more information and depth on this process at `https://docs.microsoft.com/en-us/microsoft-365/admin/create-groups/manage-creation-of-groups`.

- Gregory Zelfond has written an excellent blog post encouraging extra consideration of the landscape of modern collaboration before disabling group creation: `https://sharepointmaven.com/why-you-should-never-disable-team-site-creation-in-office-365/`

Assigning the User Administrator admin role in Azure AD

User management is usually assigned to helpdesk resources, and not a global admin. This recipe outlines the steps to assigning user management admin roles to users. This role provides its members an appropriate level of permission to manage users, but not all the access and abilities granted to the global admin role. Let's assign the **User Administrator** admin role to a user.

Getting ready

You'll need access to Azure AD and the **Global administrator** or **Privileged Role** administrator role to assign other admin roles.

How to do it...

1. Go to Azure AD at `https://aad.portal.azure.com`.

2. Select **Azure Active Directory** from the left navigation menu:

Figure 2.35 – Azure Active Directory highlighted in the left-hand navigation menu in the Azure AD admin center

3. Select **Roles and administrators** from beneath the **Manage** header:

Figure 2.36 – Roles and administrators highlighted in the Manage section

4. Search or scroll the list until you locate **User administrator**, then select it:

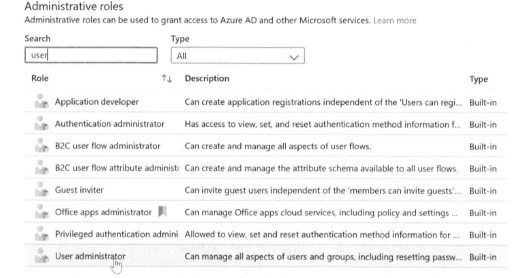

Figure 2.37 – User administrator role highlighted in Administrative roles search results

5. Select **Add assignments**:

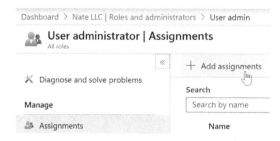

Figure 2.38 – Add assignments option in the Assignments screen of the User administrator role details

6. Select each shared service account or individual user you want added to this role group. The search bar can help find specific accounts more quickly. When finished, select **Add**:

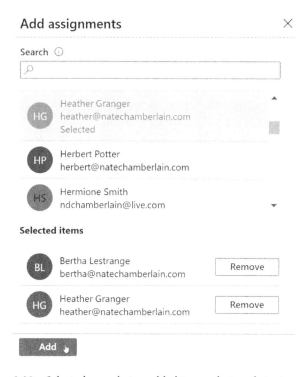

Figure 2.39 – Selected users being added to an admin role in Azure AD

7. You may now exit Azure AD:

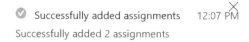

Figure 2.40 – The confirmation notification that appears once users are successfully assigned

How it works...

You've just used Azure AD to assign the User Administrator admin role. Users and accounts assigned to the user management role can reset passwords, create and manage users and groups, filter and manage service requests, and monitor service health. Azure AD is the preferred method of assigning roles because you can assign to multiple accounts at once. As you'll see in the next recipe, the Microsoft 365 Admin Center only allows one account to be assigned at a time.

> **Tip**
> Use shared service accounts (for example, `helpdesk@`
> `natechamberlain.com`) to minimize the administrative tasks involved
> during employee turnover and onboarding.

See also

- Learn more about this role, and all others available in Azure AD, at `https://` `docs.microsoft.com/en-us/azure/active-directory/users-` `groups-roles/directory-assign-admin-roles`.

Managing admin roles in the Microsoft 365 admin center

In the previous recipe, *Assigning the User Administrator admin role in Azure AD*, we covered assigning a specific admin role via Azure AD. In this recipe, we'll do the same, but from within the Microsoft 365 admin center.

Getting ready

You must be a global administrator or privileged role administrator to assign other admin roles.

How to do it...

1. Go to the Microsoft 365 Admin Center at `https://admin.microsoft.com/`.

2. Select **Users** > **Active users**:

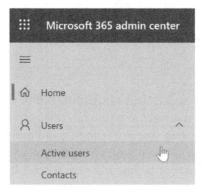

Figure 2.41 – Active users link in the left-hand navigation pane of the Microsoft 365 admin center

3. Search or scroll to select the account to which you're assigning the admin role(s). Then, use the ellipses to select **Manage roles**:

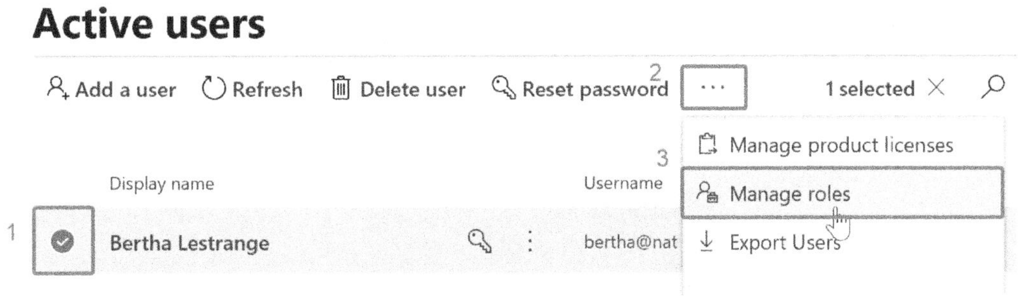

Active users

| R+ Add a user | ⟳ Refresh | 🗑 Delete user | ⚷ Reset password | ··· | 1 selected ✕ | ⊙ |

		🗐 Manage product licenses
Display name		Username	🔒 Manage roles
✓ Bertha Lestrange	⚷ ⋮	bertha@nat	↓ Export Users

Figure 2.42 – Manage roles option available on the ellipsis menu when a user is selected

4. Select/deselect the role(s) you're assigning or unassigning:

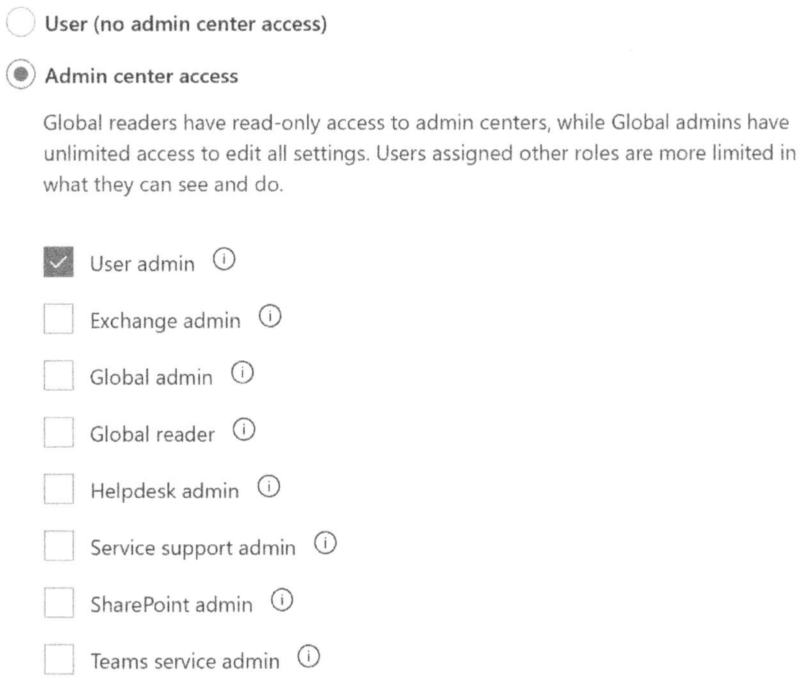

  ◯ User (no admin center access)

  ⦿ Admin center access

  Global readers have read-only access to admin centers, while Global admins have unlimited access to edit all settings. Users assigned other roles are more limited in what they can see and do.

  ☑ User admin ⓘ

  ☐ Exchange admin ⓘ

  ☐ Global admin ⓘ

  ☐ Global reader ⓘ

  ☐ Helpdesk admin ⓘ

  ☐ Service support admin ⓘ

  ☐ SharePoint admin ⓘ

  ☐ Teams service admin ⓘ

Figure 2.43 – Admin center access options, with User admin selected

5. You'll also notice there's an expandable **Show all by category** section for more (less common) admin roles not shown in the previous screenshot. These are divided into **Collaboration**, **Devices**, **Global**, **Identity**, **Other**, **Read-only**, and **Security & Compliance** categories. You can see some of the options in the following screenshot:

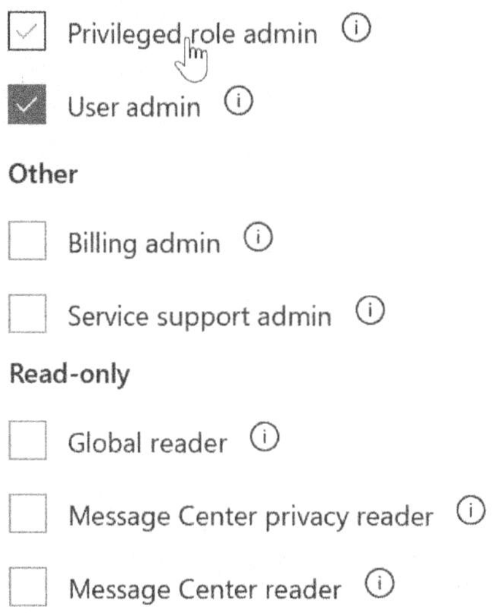

☑ Privileged role admin ⓘ

☑ User admin ⓘ

Other

☐ Billing admin ⓘ

☐ Service support admin ⓘ

Read-only

☐ Global reader ⓘ

☐ Message Center privacy reader ⓘ

☐ Message Center reader ⓘ

Figure 2.44 – Role options shown by category instead

6. When finished selecting/deselecting, click **Save changes**. If successful, you'll see **Admin roles updated**:

✓ Admin roles updated

Figure 2.45 – Confirmation message once admin roles have been added

How it works...

In this recipe, you assigned the User Admin role via the Microsoft 365 admin center. Like how you'd assign product licenses to users, the Microsoft 365 Admin Center's **Active users** blade allows you to assign admin roles as well from this singular, central location.

> **Important note**
>
> If you try to select more than one user at a time using this method, you will not get the **Manage roles** option. That's a limitation of the Microsoft 365 Admin Center and one reason you may wish to manage administrator roles using Azure AD instead.

See also

- Learn more about admin roles in the Microsoft 365 Admin Center at `https://docs.microsoft.com/en-us/microsoft-365/admin/add-users/about-admin-roles`.

3

Administering Office 365 with PowerShell

PowerShell can be used to perform administrative tasks not available through admin centers and the **graphical user interface** (**GUI**). Even for tasks that are available through the GUI, PowerShell can often perform tasks more quickly in fewer clicks and can be scheduled to perform routine tasks (such as updating exported reports regularly). In this chapter, we look at a few specific PowerShell recipes to enhance Office 365 admins' abilities and efficiency.

We'll cover the following recipes in this chapter:

- Getting a list of all available commands
- Creating a user
- Disabling a user
- Changing user settings or profile information
- Getting a list of all users with user properties
- Changing a user password

- Connecting via PowerShell to SharePoint Online

- Creating a SharePoint site collection

- Adding a new site collection admin to all SharePoint Online sites

- Restoring a deleted OneDrive site

- Hiding Office 365 groups from the Global Address List

- Preventing external senders from emailing internal Office 365 groups

Technical requirements

To start, an admin must have PowerShell installed, either the command line, black screen version or an **Integrated Scripting Environment (ISE)**. The user must have valid credentials and have an appropriate admin role (such as **Global Admin).**

As PowerShell for Office 365 has advanced, additional tools are available to minimize the past troubles of making a connection to your tenant. For this, you must download the Microsoft Online Services Sign-In Assistant (`https://www.microsoft.com/en-us/Download/details.aspx`). Download the files and install it on your PC.

The first time you connect to your Office 365 tenant, you'll want to set the `ExecutionPolicy` to `RemoteSigned`. This is done by opening a PowerShell window with elevated rights (**Run as administrator**) and executing the following code:

```
Set-ExecutionPolicy RemoteSigned
```

Once prompted, press *Y* and hit *Enter*.

Additionally, you will need to execute and install the following PowerShell modules:

```
Install-Module MSOnline
```

You may be prompted that the NuGet provider is required in order to continue. Type *Y* and press *Enter* to continue. As it downloads, you may see an additional warning regarding an untrusted repository. The repository is Microsoft and is trusted, so type *Y* and click *Enter* to continue.

Once this basic setup is complete, you will need to connect to the Office 365 tenant via the code shared in the *Setting up the PowerShell environment* recipe in *Chapter 1, Office 365 Setup and Basic Administration*. Connecting to your tenant is required every time you wish to use PowerShell commands. For reference, that code is as follows:

```
$credential = Get-Credential
connect-MsolService -Credential $credential
```

If you're using **multi-factor authentication** (**MFA**), you'll want to remove the first line (`$credential`) and remove the `credential` parameter from the second line. This will prompt you to use the Azure **Active Directory** (**AD**) login screen instead, which supports MFA.

Getting a list of all available commands

PowerShell is a growing library of tools that admins and developers can use to directly interact with the "backend" of an Office 365 tenant. Knowing which options are available is critical to using the most up-to-date and capable function to accomplish your task. In this recipe, we'll request a list of all available commands by PowerShell.

Getting ready

Using the skills learned in the *Setting up the PowerShell environment* recipe from *Chapter 1, Office 365 Setup and Basic Administration*, connect to your Office 365 tenant via PowerShell.

The module name in the command string can be replaced by the name of the PowerShell module you'd like to query (for example, `MsOnline` for basic commands; `AzureAD` for Azure AD-specific commands). The example that follows shows `MsOnline`, which provides many basic commands. However, advanced users will need to install and run more advanced modules, including Azure AD, Teams, SharePoint Online, and others.

How to do it...

To see all available commands available as part of the MSOnline module, follow these two simple steps:

1. Run PowerShell as an administrator.

2. Enter the following command into your PowerShell or ISE window:

```
Get-Command -module MSOnline
```

The following screenshot shows the output of the preceding command:

```
get-command -module msonline

CommandType     Name                                        Version      Source
-----------     ----                                        -------      ------
Cmdlet          Add-MsolAdministrativeUnitMember            1.1.183.57   MSOnline
Cmdlet          Add-MsolForeignGroupToRole                  1.1.183.57   MSOnline
Cmdlet          Add-MsolGroupMember                         1.1.183.57   MSOnline
Cmdlet          Add-MsolRoleMember                          1.1.183.57   MSOnline
Cmdlet          Add-MsolScopedRoleMember                    1.1.183.57   MSOnline
Cmdlet          Confirm-MsolDomain                          1.1.183.57   MSOnline
Cmdlet          Confirm-MsolEmailVerifiedDomain             1.1.183.57   MSOnline
Cmdlet          Connect-MsolService                         1.1.183.57   MSOnline
Cmdlet          Convert-MsolDomainToFederated               1.1.183.57   MSOnline
Cmdlet          Convert-MsolDomainToStandard                1.1.183.57   MSOnline
Cmdlet          Convert-MsolFederatedUser                   1.1.183.57   MSOnline
Cmdlet          Disable-MsolDevice                          1.1.183.57   MSOnline
Cmdlet          Enable-MsolDevice                           1.1.183.57   MSOnline
Cmdlet          Get-MsolAccountSku                          1.1.183.57   MSOnline
Cmdlet          Get-MsolAdministrativeUnit                  1.1.183.57   MSOnline
Cmdlet          Get-MsolAdministrativeUnitMember            1.1.183.57   MSOnline
Cmdlet          Get-MsolCompanyAllowedDataLocation          1.1.183.57   MSOnline
Cmdlet          Get-MsolCompanyInformation                  1.1.183.57   MSOnline
Cmdlet          Get-MsolContact                             1.1.183.57   MSOnline
Cmdlet          Get-MsolDevice                              1.1.183.57   MSOnline
Cmdlet          Get-MsolDeviceRegistrationServicePolicy     1.1.183.57   MSOnline
Cmdlet          Get-MsolDirSyncConfiguration                1.1.183.57   MSOnline
Cmdlet          Get-MsolDirSyncFeatures                     1.1.183.57   MSOnline
Cmdlet          Get-MsolDirSyncProvisioningError            1.1.183.57   MSOnline
Cmdlet          Get-MsolDomain                              1.1.183.57   MSOnline
Cmdlet          Get-MsolDomainFederationSettings            1.1.183.57   MSOnline
Cmdlet          Get-MsolDomainVerificationDns               1.1.183.57   MSOnline
Cmdlet          Get-MsolFederationProperty                  1.1.183.57   MSOnline
Cmdlet          Get-MsolGroup                               1.1.183.57   MSOnline
Cmdlet          Get-MsolGroupMember                         1.1.183.57   MSOnline
```

Figure 3.1 – Screenshot showing available commands in the MSOnline module

How it works...

You've just generated a list of all available commands you can utilize in the administration of your tenant. If you've connected to your tenant, you're able to utilize any of these. The other recipes in this chapter show several of these operations, but this is a starting point for an admin becoming familiar with the various possibilities.

Creating a user

Most tenant admins and other IT professionals prefer to automate the creation of new users in a tenant. This requires passing certain values between whatever Human Resources or onboarding system is being used to PowerShell. However, even if you are not looking to automate this process and are tired of clicking through a ton of screens to enter information, this recipe provides admins an easy method of getting a user provisioned.

Getting ready

Using the skills learned in the *Setting up the PowerShell environment* recipe from *Chapter 1, Office 365 Setup and Basic Administration*, connect to your Office 365 tenant via PowerShell.

How to do it...

1. Enter the following command into your PowerShell or ISE window, replacing the details of `UserPrincipalName`, `DisplayName`, `FirstName`, and `LastName` as appropriate:

```
New-MsolUser -UserPrincipalName test@natechamberlain.
onmicrosoft.com
-DisplayName "Test Account" -FirstName "Test" -LastName
"Account"
```

2. The script will return the user's password and license status data.

How it works...

You used the `New-MsolUser` cmdlet, part of the `MsOnline` module, to set up a new user and set user attributes or details. It is important to note that using this cmdlet to set user attributes through PowerShell parameters is only valid during user creation. If you attempt to use this script again, after a user has been created (meaning a `UserPrincipalName` has been generated), the script will fail. To make updates, refer to the *Changing user settings or profile information* recipe later in this chapter.

There's more...

The `New-MsolUser` cmdlet allows an admin to set many more parameters than what was presented in the preceding code snippet. Here is a partial list of additional parameters that can be passed to the Office 365 tenant as part of a new user creation script:

- `BlockCredential <Boolean>`
- `City <String>`
- `Country <String>`
- `Department <String>`
- `PhoneNumber <String>`

- AlternateEmailAddresses <String[]>
- Password <String>
- ForceChangePassword <Boolean>

Disabling a user

When a user's access needs to be temporarily disabled so that the user cannot access Office 365 with those credentials but the data and user setup are not lost, an admin does not need to completely remove or unlicense a user. Instead, simply blocking the user's credentials will suffice. Let's disable a user in this recipe.

Getting ready

Using the skills learned in the *Setting up the PowerShell environment* recipe from *Chapter 1, Office 365 Setup and Basic Administration*, connect to your Office 365 tenant via PowerShell.

How to do it...

Update the UserPrincipalName parameter to the appropriate user, and then run the following code snippet:

```
Set-MsolUser -UserPrincipalName testingMayDeleteLater@
natechamberlain.com -BlockCredential $true
```

How it works...

You've just disabled a user in a single step. The BlockCredential property on a user's profile will stop a user from being able to gain access with the blocked credentials. This does not unlicense or delete the user, nor does it reset the user's password; it simply makes the user account inaccessible.

There are times where a blocked account is a more appropriate solution, rather than resetting the password or deleting a user. Temporary blocks are often used in cases where a user is on leave.

Changing user settings or profile information

Name changes, office moves, password reset requests, and other updates are frequent requests from users. An admin must be able to make these updates quickly and easily within a system. While it is possible to accomplish these tasks within the tenant user interface, having the ability to script these changes (or even automate them) is the dream of any admin. This recipe covers several possibilities for making updates to a user's settings or profile information via PowerShell.

Getting ready

Using the skills learned in the *Setting up the PowerShell environment* recipe from *Chapter 1*, *Office 365 Setup and Basic Administration*, connect to your Office 365 tenant via PowerShell.

The `UserPrincipalName` parameter is a required parameter to identify which user should be impacted by the change you are making.

How to do it...

The following two examples are PowerShell snippets that show how to make user updates.

Use this to update a user's display name:

```
Set-MsolUser -UserPrincipalName "test@natechamberlain.
onmicrosoft.com"
-DisplayName "Testing Account"
```

Use this to update a user's office, title, and department:

```
Set-MsolUser -UserPrincipalName "test@natechamberlain.
onmicrosoft.com"
-Office "Kansas City" -Title "Accounts Payable Manager"
-Department "Finance"
```

How it works...

The key here is in the cmdlet being used, `Set-MsolUser`. While there are a variety of other commands that can be used to accomplish the changes (including using cmdlets and functions from other PowerShell admin modules), learning how to use `Set-MsolUser` is foundational when working with PowerShell in an Office 365 tenant.

Getting a list of all users with user properties

The Get-MsolUser cmdlet in the MsOnline PowerShell module is a very flexible and useful tool for any admin's toolkit. The cmdlet gives an admin instant access to all user properties within a tenant, but can also be restricted to specific users or even users of a certain type.

Generating reports of users and groups of users is a common task for any tenant admin. This recipe focuses on how to pull that data with only a few lines of code.

Let's practice generating a list of all users with properties.

Getting ready

Using the skills learned in the *Setting up the PowerShell environment* recipe from *Chapter 1, Office 365 Setup and Basic Administration*, connect to your Office 365 tenant via PowerShell.

How to do it...

1. Enter the following command into your PowerShell or ISE window to return a list of all Office 365 users:

```
Get-MsolUser
```

This will give the following output:

```
UserPrincipalName                    DisplayName         IsLicensed
-----------------                    -----------         ----------
nate@natechamberlain.com             Nate Chamberlain          True
richard@natechamberlain.com          Richard Weasley           True
bertha@natechamberlain.com           Bertha Lestrange          True
```

Figure 3.2 – PowerShell screen showing all Office 365 users retrieved using Get-MsolUser

By default, the UserPrincipalName and isLicensed attributes are returned.

2. Retrieving a list of properties for a user is when Get-MsolUser really becomes handy to tenant admins. This can be done by using the following code snippet:

```
Get-MsolUser -UserPrincipalName "bertha@natechamberlain.
com" | Select-Object * |Format-List
```

This can be seen as follows:

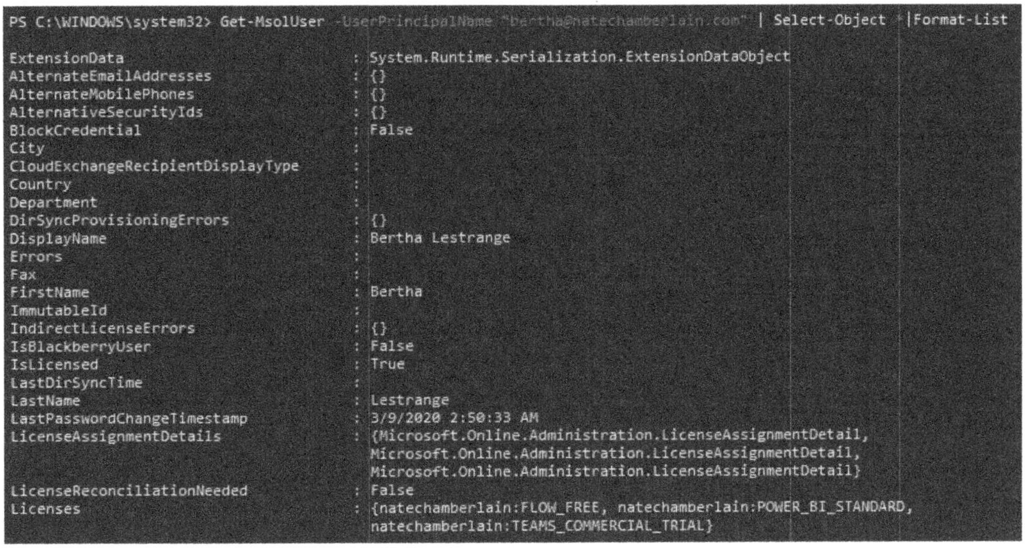

```
PS C:\WINDOWS\system32> Get-MsolUser -UserPrincipalName "bertha@natechamberlain.com" | Select-Object |Format-List

ExtensionData                    : System.Runtime.Serialization.ExtensionDataObject
AlternateEmailAddresses          : {}
AlternateMobilePhones            : {}
AlternativeSecurityIds           : {}
BlockCredential                  : False
City                             :
CloudExchangeRecipientDisplayType :
Country                          :
Department                       :
DirSyncProvisioningErrors        : {}
DisplayName                      : Bertha Lestrange
Errors                           :
Fax                              :
FirstName                        : Bertha
ImmutableId                      :
IndirectLicenseErrors            : {}
IsBlackberryUser                 : False
IsLicensed                       : True
LastDirSyncTime                  :
LastName                         : Lestrange
LastPasswordChangeTimestamp      : 3/9/2020 2:50:33 AM
LicenseAssignmentDetails         : {Microsoft.Online.Administration.LicenseAssignmentDetail,
                                   Microsoft.Online.Administration.LicenseAssignmentDetail,
                                   Microsoft.Online.Administration.LicenseAssignmentDetail}
LicenseReconciliationNeeded      : False
Licenses                         : {natechamberlain:FLOW_FREE, natechamberlain:POWER_BI_STANDARD,
                                   natechamberlain:TEAMS_COMMERCIAL_TRIAL}
```

Figure 3.3 – PowerShell screen showing user details for a specific user

A lot of detail and data is returned, most of it system generated information that is not useful for the average situation. However, you can limit what information is returned:

```
Get-MsolUser -UserPrincipalName "bertha@natechamberlain.
com" | Select-Object UserPrincipalName, DisplayName,
Department, Title, Office
```

Additionally, you can use the same snippet of code, with a slight change, to export the data as a **comma-separated values** (**CSV**) file:

```
Get-MsolUser -UserPrincipalName "bertha@natechamberlain.
com" |Select-Object UserPrincipalName, DisplayName,
Department, Title, Office |Export-CSV c:\userlist.csv
```

Finally, you do not need to limit this functionality to a single user. An admin can pull a list of all users and export the data into a CSV file:

```
Get-MsolUser | Select-Object UserPrincipalName,
DisplayName, Department, Title, Office| Export-CSV c:\
userslist.csv –NoTypeInformation
```

How it works...

In this recipe, you generated a list of all users with properties, and if you tried additional options, you may have also exported that list to a file. Combining the MSOnline module with other standard PowerShell capabilities (such as piping data from one cmdlet into another function, Format-List, or using Export-CSV to generate a report) allows an admin expanded access and extensibility of an Office 365 tenant.

There's more...

When using PowerShell to generate user reports with Get-MsolUser, admins often have some filtering criteria in mind. This can be easily accomplished as part of the script, saving you time once the report is generated.

The following code snippet shows how filtering can be used with Get-MsolUser to generate cleaner reports:

```
Get-msoluser | Where {$_.Department -eq "Finance"}
```

This returns a list of all users who have a department equal to Finance.

Changing a user password

While it is typically best to allow a user to set their own password, there are times where an admin needs to take over and set a user's password on their behalf (for example, service accounts, terminated users, or a new user who is struggling to get their password properly set).

While it is a typical best practice to have a user immediately change their password once set, this recipe focuses on the admin setting the password and not forcing the user to reset the password upon the next login.

Getting ready

Using the skills learned in the *Setting up the PowerShell environment* recipe from *Chapter 1, Office 365 Setup and Basic Administration*, connect to your Office 365 tenant via PowerShell.

How to do it...

Enter the following command into your PowerShell or ISE window to change the password of a specific Office 365 user:

```
Set-MsOlUserPassword -UserPrincipalName "bertha@
natechamberlain.com" -NewPassword "Password1" -
ForceChangePassword $false
```

Should an admin wish to require a user to change the password upon next login, simply change the `ForceChangePassword` parameter's value of `$false` to `$true`.

How it works...

Instead of logging in to the Office 365 Admin center, an admin can quickly set a password through PowerShell and require whether a user resets that password upon next login or not.

Connecting via PowerShell to SharePoint Online

SharePoint Online administration, as with basic tenant administration, can be simplified when using PowerShell commands to complete common or repetitive tasks. This recipe provides the steps to set up your PowerShell console to use SharePoint Online cmdlets and functions.

Getting ready

Using the skills learned in the *Setting up the PowerShell environment* recipe from *Chapter 1, Office 365 Setup and Basic Administration*, connect to your Office 365 tenant via PowerShell.

To access SharePoint Online PowerShell cmdlets and functions, you must download and install the SharePoint Online Management Shell (link included in the *See also* section of this recipe).

How to do it...

There are a set of numbered, sequential tasks that the reader needs to perform in order to complete the recipe:

1. Download and install the SharePoint Online Management Shell.

2. Import the module using the following code snippet:

```
Import-Module Microsoft.Online.SharePoint.PowerShell
-DisableNameChecking
```

This can be seen as follows:

```
PS C:\WINDOWS\system32> Import-Module Microsoft.Online.SharePoint.PowerShell
WARNING: The names of some imported commands from the module 'Microsoft.Online.SharePoint.PowerShell' include
unapproved verbs that might make them less discoverable. To find the commands with unapproved verbs, run the
Import-Module command again with the Verbose parameter. For a list of approved verbs, type Get-Verb.
PS C:\WINDOWS\system32> Import-Module Microsoft.Online.SharePoint.PowerShell -DisableNameChecking
```

Figure 3.4 – PowerShell warning when -DisableNameChecking isn't used

The preceding screenshot shows the various steps, and warns that the -DisableNameChecking parameter is required if wanting to use commands inclusive of those that have unapproved verbs.

> **Important note**
> If your PowerShell console or ISE is already open after installing the SharePoint Online Management Shell, you should close and reopen the console.

3. Next, connect your PowerShell console session to your SharePoint Online tenant. This is done by using the Connect-SPOService cmdlet, which needs your SharePoint Online tenant admin site **Uniform Resource Locator (URL)**.

An example of an admin site URL is https://<your tenant name>-admin. sharepoint.com.

For this example, we will use https://natechamberlain-admin. sharepoint.com.

Use the following code snippet:

```
Connect-SPOService -url https://natechamberlain-admin.
sharepoint.com
```

4. To check if you are connected, you can run the following code snippet:

```
Get-SPOSite | Select Title, Url
```

This can be seen as follows:

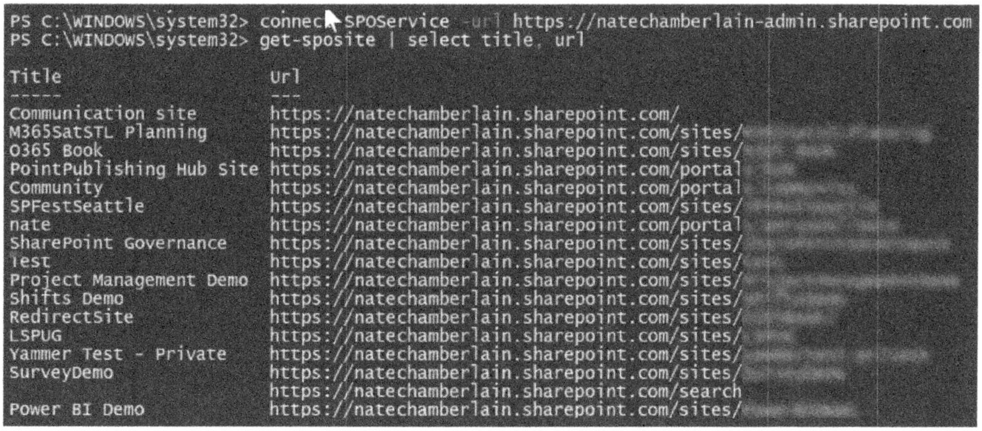

Figure 3.5 – PowerShell screen showing all SharePoint sites returned when using Get-SPOSite

How it works...

You've just connected to SharePoint Online. Importing the SharePoint Online Management Shell gives an admin access to a comprehensive list of commands available for SharePoint administration. Connecting to the tenant in this manner is a required step each time a console is opened or if a console has been inactive for a long period.

See also

- SharePoint Online Management Shell can be downloaded at `https://www.microsoft.com/en-us/download/details.aspx?id=35588` if you don't already have it.

Creating a SharePoint site collection

Creating a new SharePoint site collection is a basic SharePoint administration task. This recipe covers how to complete that task with a few lines of PowerShell.

Getting ready

Using the skills learned in the *Setting up the PowerShell environment* recipe from *Chapter 1*, *Office 365 Setup and Basic Administration* and the *Connecting via PowerShell to SharePoint Online* recipe in this chapter, connect to your Office 365 tenant via PowerShell.

How to do it...

1. Update the `URL`, `Owner`, and `Title` parameters as appropriate, then run the following code snippet:

```
New-SPOSite -Url https://natechamberlain.sharepoint.
com/sites/PowerShell -Owner bertha@natechamberlain.com
-StorageQuota 1000 -Title "PowerShell Site"
```

2. The site will be generated, but this can take some time. Wait until the PowerShell console has completed the task.

3. To verify that the site has been created, use the `Get-SPOSite` cmdlet learned in the previous recipe:

```
Get-SPOSite | Select Title, Url
```

How it works...

Using the `New-SPOSite` PowerShell cmdlet, a SharePoint site collection can be quickly generated. Passing parameters and values such as storage quota and owner allows an admin to simply the task of building a new site collection.

There's more...

Additional parameters can be passed when using `New-SPOSite`, including site template and time zone.

Adding a new site collection admin to all SharePoint Online sites

Administration of sites requires having a certain level of access for a site collection. Users with the SharePoint **Admin** role have full control access to all sites, but there may be a reason to give a user without an **Admin** role elevated SharePoint access (for example, a site developer). This recipe explains how to give an admin access to all SharePoint Online sites. However, it can be amended to give such access to specific site collections, or a single site collection.

Getting ready

This recipe will utilize the skills learned in the *Setting up the PowerShell environment* recipe in *Chapter 1, Office 365 Setup and Basic Administration,* and the *Connecting via PowerShell to SharePoint Online* recipe in this chapter, and require that you are a global or SharePoint admin.

How to do it...

Update the -LoginName parameter, and then run the following code snippet:

```
$Sites = Get-SPOSite -Limit ALL
Foreach ($Site in $Sites)
{Write-host "Adding Site Collection Admin for:"$Site.URL
Set-SPOUser -site $Site -LoginName bertha@natechamberlain.
com -IsSiteCollectionAdmin $True}
```

How it works...

The $Sites variable in the script is calling all SharePoint sites within the tenant. This is where you could enter a specific URL, or use a where clause to find sites of a specific type. Write-host is mostly for show so that the admin can see where the script is in making the requested change. Finally, the real power of the code comes from the Set-SPOUser cmdlet.

This function is calling every site listed in the $Sites variable and setting the Site Collection Admin property to true.

Restoring a deleted OneDrive site

When a user is deleted from an Office 365 tenant, that user's OneDrive site is also deleted (depending on the retention policy set by the tenant admins). This recipe will explain how to recover that deleted OneDrive site.

Getting ready

Using the skills learned in the *Setting up the PowerShell environment* recipe in *Chapter 1, Office 365 Setup and Basic Administration,* and the *Connecting via PowerShell to SharePoint Online* recipe in this chapter, connect to your Office 365 tenant via PowerShell.

The admin restoring the OneDrive site must be assigned the Global admin or SharePoint admin role.

Finally, the admin must have the URL of the deleted OneDrive site. This can be found by checking the **Deleted Sites** recycle bin with the following code snippet:

```
Get-SPODeletedSite -IncludeOnlyPersonalSite | FT url
```

You can verify you have the correct URL with the following code snippet:

```
Get-SPODeletedSite -Identity "https://natechamberlain.
sharepoint.com/personal/testingMayDeleteLater_com"
```

How to do it...

Restore the deleted site by updating the -Identity parameter with the deleted OneDrive site URL, and then run the following code snippet:

```
Restore-SPODeletedSite -Identity "https://natechamberlain.
sharepoint.com/personal/testingMayDeleteLater_com"
```

> **Important note**
> If you receive an **Unable to find the deleted site** error message, check the URL. Do not include the final / at the end of the URL string.

How it works...

You've just restored a deleted OneDrive site. Note that when a OneDrive site is deleted, it is sent to a recycle bin. Depending on your tenant configuration, the site can still be restored for 93 days. After that time period, you may need to submit a service request to see if it's possible to still be recovered by Microsoft.

Hiding Office 365 groups from the Global Address List

Managing data and access to that data is a core component of tenant administration. In Office 365, groups have become a critical component of effective collaboration. However, this means the list of Office 365 groups can become long and, at times, confusing for users.

Trimming which groups show in the **Global Address List** (**GAL**) can help users find and connect with the right people in their organization. Additionally, some groups may require additional security or confidentiality even around its existence (for example, merger and acquisition projects, executive committees, and so on).

In this recipe, we'll restrict certain Office 365 groups from the GAL.

Getting ready

Using the skills learned in the *Setting up the PowerShell environment* recipe in *Chapter 1, Office 365 Setup and Basic Administration*, connect to your Office 365 tenant via PowerShell.

The cmdlets for interacting with Office 365 groups are found within the `ExchangeOnlineManagement` module. Use the following steps to install, import, and connect to the Exchange Online Management shell:

1. Start by installing the `ExchangeOnlineManagement` module:

    ```
    Install-Module -Name ExchangeOnlineManagement
    ```

2. Import the module and load it to your PowerShell console:

    ```
    Import-Module ExchangeOnlineManagement; Get-Module
    ExchangeOnlineManagement
    ```

3. The following step is required every time you wish to use cmdlets in the `ExchangeOnlineManagement` module, just as you must connect to other admin modules (for example, `SharePoint`, `AzureAD`, and so on):

    ```
    Connect-ExchangeOnline -Credential $UserCredential
    ```

How to do it...

Update the `-Identity` parameter with the display name of the group you wish to hide, and then run the following code snippet:

```
Set-UnifiedGroup -Identity "Test"
-HiddenFromAddressListsEnabled $true
```

How it works...

`UnifiedGroup` is PowerShell "lingo" for Office 365 groups. You used this command to hide the specified group from the GAL. Setting the hidden property is as simple as changing a user's office location, or any other property.

Preventing external senders from emailing internal Office 365 groups

This recipe will cover how an admin can prevent external parties from emailing internal Office 365 groups, which can have their own email address and shared mailbox.

Getting ready

You must be a global admin to perform these steps.

How to do it...

Update the `-Identity` parameter with the display name of the group you wish to change, and then run the following code snippet:

```
Set-UnifiedGroup -Identity "Test"
-RequireSenderAuthenticationEnabled $true
```

How it works...

You've just protected an Office 365 group's inbox from unwanted external emails. Setting the `-RequireSenderAuthenticationEnabled` property on a group allows only internal users to send an email to that group. If external users send a message to the group's email address, that message will be rejected. Internal users are still able to send externally, unless other restrictions are put in place.

4
Managing Exchange Online

If your chosen subscription includes mail from Outlook, you'll be working with Exchange to configure the user experience and security of your mail environment. We'll cover the basics of getting started, as well as a few security features to decrease the likelihood of malicious content reaching your users via Exchange.

We will cover the following recipes in this chapter:

- Creating a user mailbox
- Creating a mail-enabled security group
- Creating a shared mailbox without an O365 group
- Creating a distribution list
- Creating a dynamic distribution list
- Assigning permissions and roles
- Creating an Exchange-specific retention policy
- Creating a mail flow rule

- Configuring spam filter policies
- Creating room and equipment resources
- Enabling **advanced threat protection (ATP)** features

Technical requirements

There are no technical requirements specific to this chapter, other than needing an **Office 365 (O365)** subscription and appropriate administrative roles assigned. In most cases, you'll need to be a global or Exchange admin.

Creating a user mailbox

When a user is licensed in O365 under a subscription that includes Exchange, they're automatically allocated a mailbox. This recipe covers how to create a user mailbox through licensing.

How to do it...

1. Go to the Microsoft 365 admin center at `https://admin.microsoft.com`.

2. Select **Users | Active users** from the left-hand navigation pane.

3. Select the ellipsis next to an unlicensed user's name and choose **Manage product licenses**:

Figure 4.1 – A selected user and the Manage product licenses option from the ellipsis menu

4. Choose a location for the user and check a subscription option (such as E3 or E5) that includes **Exchange**. Click on **Save changes**:

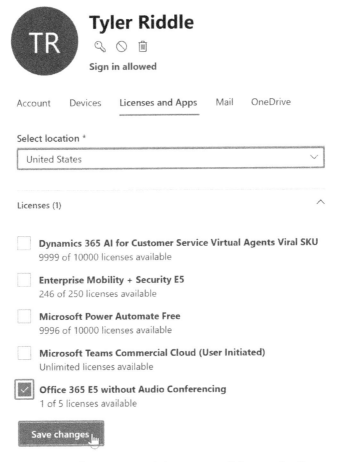

Figure 4.2 – The Licenses and Apps screen of the user details page

How it works...

You've just created a user mailbox by assigning the user a license for O365. Exchange Online is included in most O365 subscriptions, and users assigned O365 licenses will automatically be allocated a mailbox.

> **Important note**
> Do note, however, that mailboxes that are provisioned can take up to 24 hours to become available, so administrators should plan for this delay when preparing for employee onboarding.

There's more

If you're unsure whether a subscription includes **Exchange**, you can check what's included during *step 4* before you click on **Save changes**. Just scroll down to the **Apps** section and see whether **Exchange** is one of the sub-products included in the subscription you've selected:

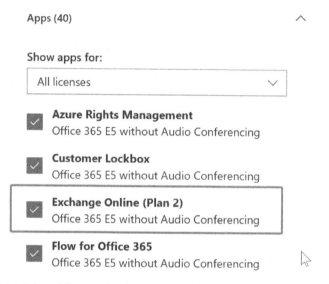

Figure 4.3 – Selected licenses for the user; checking whether Exchange is included

See also

- Learn how to create a user mailbox via PowerShell at `https://docs.microsoft.com/en-us/exchange/recipients-in-exchange-online/create-user-mailboxes`.

> **Important note**
> You must still license the user with an Exchange Online plan or the mailbox you provision with PowerShell will be disabled after a 30-day grace period.

Creating a mail-enabled security group

Mail-enabled security groups can be used to assign permissions to their members and provide a shared mailbox for the group. You can create a mail-enabled security group in several locations throughout Microsoft 365, including the Microsoft 365 admin center, Azure **Active Directory** (**AD**), and the Exchange admin center. For this recipe, we'll use the Exchange admin center.

Getting ready

You must have an available license from a subscription that includes Exchange to assign to a user.

Getting ready

You'll need to be an Exchange admin, a global admin, or have the Organization Management or Recipient Management roles to complete this recipe's steps.

How to do it...

1. Go to the classic Exchange admin center at `https://outlook.office.com/ecp/`.

2. Choose **groups** from beneath the **recipients** header:

Figure 4.4 – The groups link in the recipients section

3. Select the drop-down arrow next to the **New Office 365 group** button and select **Mail-enabled security group**:

Figure 4.5 – Additional group type options available when using the arrow next to New Office 365 group

4. A dialog opens, prompting you to provide basic group information. Enter the following fields:

-- **Display name**: For the address book and To/CC lines.

-- **Alias**: For the email address.

--**Email address**: This is automatically populated with the value of Alias, but select the proper domain if this is not defaulted.

-- **Notes**: So that others know the purpose and function of the group when browsing/searching or assigning permissions to it:

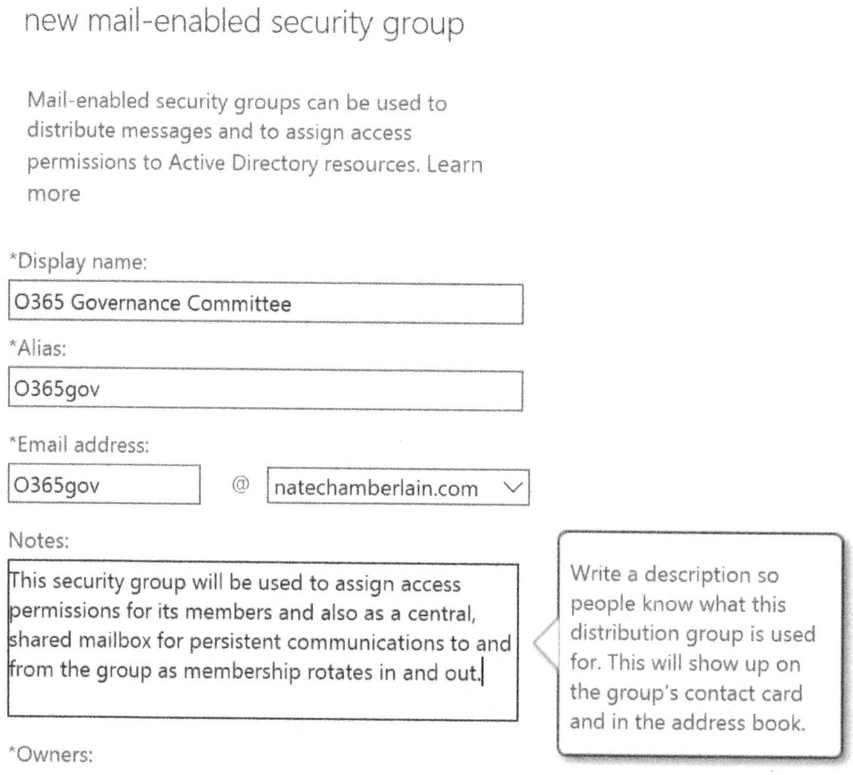

new mail-enabled security group

Mail-enabled security groups can be used to distribute messages and to assign access permissions to Active Directory resources. Learn more

*Display name:

> O365 Governance Committee

*Alias:

> O365gov

*Email address:

> O365gov   @   natechamberlain.com   ⌄

Notes:

> This security group will be used to assign access permissions for its members and also as a central, shared mailbox for persistent communications to and from the group as membership rotates in and out.

Write a description so people know what this distribution group is used for. This will show up on the group's contact card and in the address book.

*Owners:

Figure 4.6 – Mail-enabled security group details

Scroll down and enter/change the group owners and members and choose whether owners must approve new members. owners must approve new members:

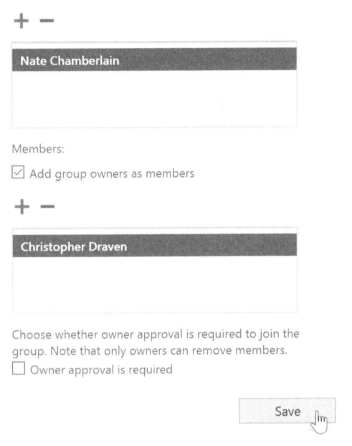

Figure 4.7 – Owners and members of the mail-enabled security group being created

5. Click **Save**. A dialog confirming the group's creation appears. Click **OK**.

How it works...

You've just created a mail-enabled security group using the Exchange admin center, and its members can now share an address and be granted permissions as appropriate.

See also

- Learn how to manage mail-enabled security groups at `https://docs.microsoft.com/en-us/exchange/recipients-in-exchange-online/manage-mail-enabled-security-groups`.

Creating a shared mailbox without an O365 group

An O365 group can easily be granted access to several products for the group's usage, such as a Teams team, a SharePoint site collection, and a Planner plan. But sometimes, you just need a shared mailbox for a group of people without any additional applications for collaboration. This recipe outlines the steps to achieving this via the Exchange admin center.

Getting ready

You'll need to be an Exchange admin, global admin, or have the Organization Management or Recipient Management roles to create shared mailboxes.

How to do it...

1. Go to the new Exchange admin center at `https://admin.exchange.microsoft.com/`.

2. Select **Recipients | Mailboxes**.

3. Choose **Add a shared mailbox**:

Mailboxes

          Add a shared mailbox   ↻ Refresh

Figure 4.8 – The Add a shared mailbox button available on the Mailboxes screen

4. Give the shared mailbox a display name (for the address book and email **To** lines), an email address, and an alias:

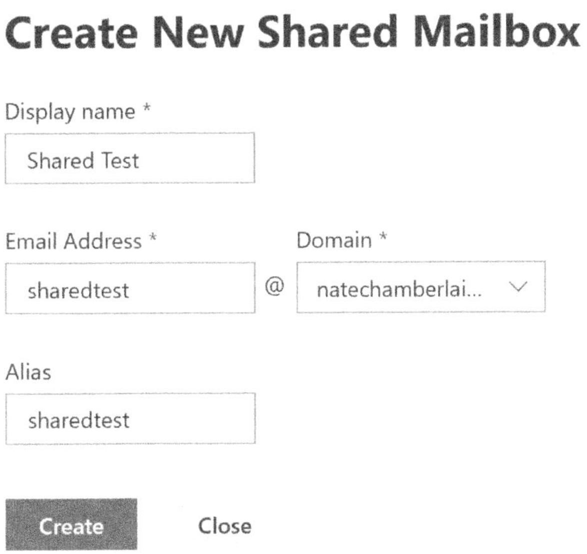

Create New Shared Mailbox

Display name *

Shared Test

Email Address *   Domain *

sharedtest   @   natechamberlai...   ∨

Alias

sharedtest

Create   Close

Figure 4.9 – Shared mailbox configuration details

5. Click on **Create** and wait while the mailbox is provisioned.

6. Once finished, choose **View details**:

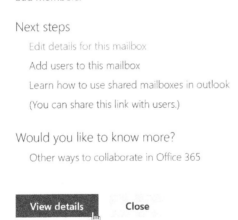

The shared mailbox was created. It may take a few minutes before you can add members.

Next steps

Edit details for this mailbox

Add users to this mailbox

Learn how to use shared mailboxes in outlook

(You can share this link with users.)

Would you like to know more?

Other ways to collaborate in Office 365

View details   Close

Figure 4.10 – Next steps presented once the mailbox is created with the View details option

7. Now, you're viewing the shared mailbox management pane, where you have several options, including managing its permissions (both read/manage and send as), automatic replies, and more:

Mailbox   Account

Email addresses

sharedtest@natechamberlain.com

Manage email address types

Mail flow settings

Default message size and delivery setting are applied

Manage mail flow settings

Mailbox permissions

Manage mailbox permissions

Mailbox policies

Default mailbox policies are applied for the organization

Manage mailbox policies

More actions

Convert to regular mailbox

Manage litigation hold

Manage mailbox archive

Set recipient limit

Automatic replies

Manage automatic replies

Figure 4.11 – Details of the new shared mailbox that we created

How it works...

You've just created a shared mailbox. Creating an explicit shared mailbox prevents unnecessary resources, such as SharePoint sites and Teams teams, from being created. It simply provides a shared mailbox for a group of people to manage incoming and outcoming messages from a single shared identity.

See also

- Learn more about creating a shared mailbox at `https://docs.microsoft.com/en-us/microsoft-365/admin/email/create-a-shared-mailbox?view=o365-worldwide`.

Creating a distribution list

Create an email account that does not have a shared email inbox but receives and distributes all incoming mail to a static list of users' individual inboxes. You could also use an O365 group, but in some cases, you may not want the additional features or apps that come with that. In this recipe, you'll create a distribution list.

Getting ready

You'll need to be an Exchange admin, global admin, or have the Organization Management or Recipient Management roles to create distribution groups.

How to do it...

1. Go to the classic Exchange admin center at `https://outlook.office.com/ecp/`.

2. Choose **groups** from beneath the **recipients** header:

Figure 4.12 – The groups link in the recipients section

3. Select **Distribution list** from the drop-down menu next to the **New Office 365 group** button:

Figure 4.13 – Additional group type options available when using the arrow next to
New Office 365 group

4. Enter a display name (for the address book and the **To** lines), an alias, an email address with a domain, a description, the owners, and the members of the distribution list:

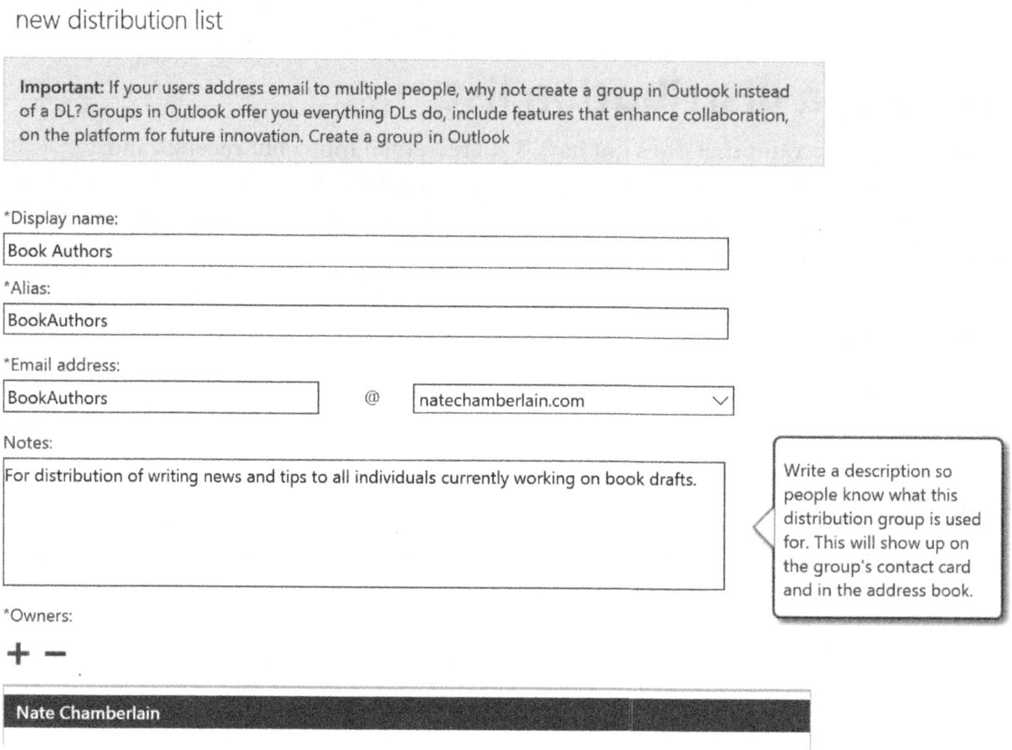

new distribution list

> **Important:** If your users address email to multiple people, why not create a group in Outlook instead of a DL? Groups in Outlook offer you everything DLs do, include features that enhance collaboration, on the platform for future innovation. Create a group in Outlook

*Display name:

Book Authors

*Alias:

BookAuthors

*Email address:

BookAuthors   @   natechamberlain.com

Notes:

For distribution of writing news and tips to all individuals currently working on book drafts.

> Write a description so people know what this distribution group is used for. This will show up on the group's contact card and in the address book.

*Owners:

+ −

Nate Chamberlain

Figure 4.14 – The new distribution list dialog for configuring basic details

5. Scroll down and enter members. You should also choose whether people who want to join or leave the group must have approval from the group owner, or whether members can join and leave without approval. When finished, click **Save**:

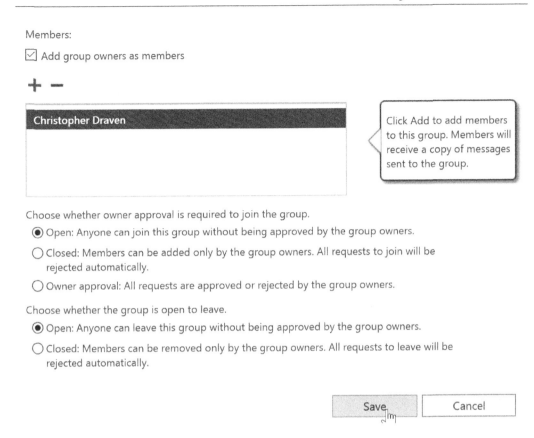

Figure 4.15 – The options under the Members section for requiring approval and allowing members to opt-out of the group.

6. When the confirmation dialog appears, click **OK**.

How it works...

You've just created a distribution list. Once the distribution list is created, the email address you entered (BookAuthors@natechamberlain.com, in this recipe's example) can be emailed and it will send any received messages individually to those listed as members.

See also

- Learn more about distribution groups in Exchange at https://docs. microsoft.com/en-us/exchange/recipients-in-exchange-online/manage-distribution-groups/manage-distribution-groups.

Creating a dynamic distribution list

Create an email account that does not have a shared email inbox, but instead sends all incoming mail to a dynamically generated list of users that updates itself based on specified criteria, such as users listed under a specific department. In this recipe, we'll create a dynamic distribution list.

Getting ready

You'll need to be an Exchange admin or have the Organization Management or Recipient Management roles to create distribution groups.

How to do it...

1. Go to the classic Exchange admin center at `https://outlook.office.com/ecp/`.

2. Choose **groups** from beneath the **recipients** header:

Figure 4.16 – The groups link under the recipients section

3. Select **Dynamic distribution list** from the drop-down menu next to the **New Office 365 group** button:

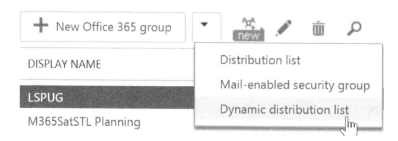

Figure 4.17 – Additional group type options available when using the arrow next to New Office 365 group

4. Enter the display name, the alias, notes, and the owner of the dynamic distribution list:

new dynamic distribution list

*Display name:

LSPUG Members

*Alias:

LSPUG

Notes:

All staff and members of LSPUG in the natechamberlain.com tenant.

Owner:

NateChamberlain   ✕   Browse...

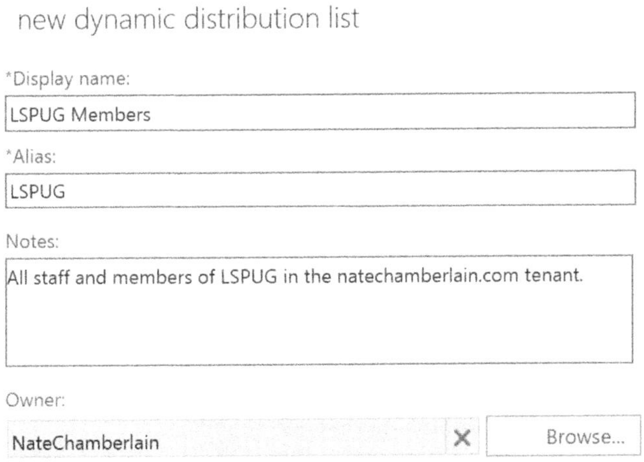

Figure 4.18 – The new dynamic distribution list dialog for basic details

5. Choose what types of recipients you want to include in the group:

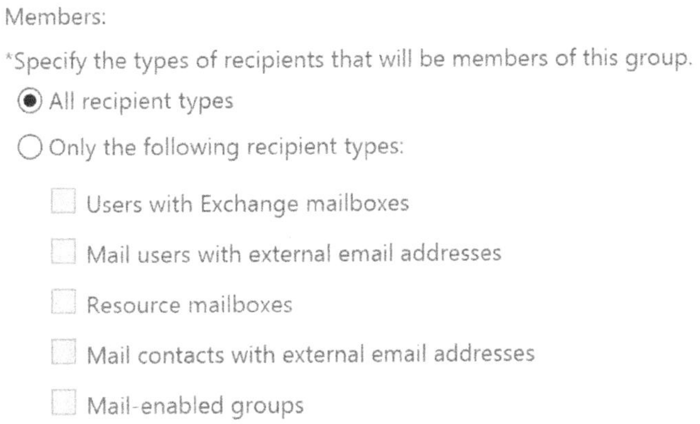

Members:

*Specify the types of recipients that will be members of this group.

◉ All recipient types

○ Only the following recipient types:

☐ Users with Exchange mailboxes

☐ Mail users with external email addresses

☐ Resource mailboxes

☐ Mail contacts with external email addresses

☐ Mail-enabled groups

Figure 4.19 – The filter options available for the types of recipients to be included in the list

6. Select **add a rule**:

Membership in this group will be determined by the rules you set up below.

Figure 4.20 – The add a rule button

7. Expand the **Select one** menu and choose **Department** (or another attribute to filter by):

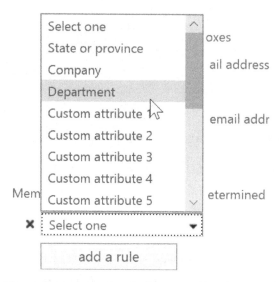

Figure 4.21 – The attribute options by which you can filter dynamic group members

8. Enter words or phrases to search for in the selected attribute:

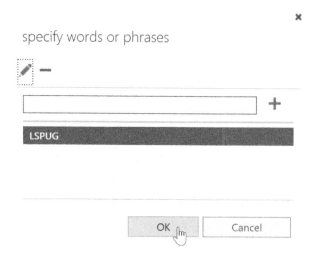

Figure 4.22 – Words or phrases to look for in the selected attribute

9. Click **OK** once you've entered all the words or phrases to look for.

10. Click **Save** unless you need to add additional rules, then repeat *steps 7–9*.

11. Click **OK** on the confirmation dialog.

How it works...

In this recipe, you created a dynamic distribution list from the Exchange admin center. Now, when new users are added to the LSPUG department (or whenever their attribute values match your criteria), they'll receive messages sent to the dynamic distribution list without having to be manually added. The list is "rebuilt" every time a message is sent to it, so it's always up to date.

See also

- Learn more about dynamic distribution lists at `https://docs.microsoft.com/en-us/exchange/recipients-in-exchange-online/manage-dynamic-distribution-groups/manage-dynamic-distribution-groups`.

Assigning permissions and roles

In this recipe, you'll learn how to manage a user's ability to access, read, edit, or own an inbox, distribution list, shared inbox, O365 group, and more. We'll accomplish this by utilizing the classic Exchange admin center's **permissions** blade.

Getting ready

You'll need to be an Exchange admin or have the Organization Management or Recipient Management roles to manage permissions and roles in the classic Exchange admin center.

How to do it...

1. Go to the classic Exchange admin center at `https://outlook.office.com/ecp/`.

2. Click on **permissions** in the left-hand navigation menu:

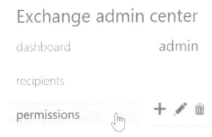

Figure 4.23 – The permissions menu link in the Exchange admin center

3. Double-click on any admin role (such as **Discover Management**) to see its details and the specific sub-roles (such as **Legal Hold** and **Mailbox Search**) included in the main role. You can modify the included sub-roles and add or remove members here as well:

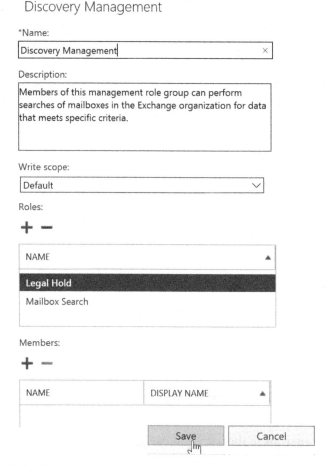

Figure 4.24 – Details for the Discovery Management admin role, including its sub-roles and members

4. Click **Save** when you have finished making changes.

How it works...

There are several admin roles that come out of the box in Exchange. Each of these contains sub-roles or specific roles that its members can perform. You can also create custom roles, combining any specific sub-roles you wish, or modify the default roles themselves (not recommended).

See also

- Learn about permissions and roles in Exchange Online at `https://docs.microsoft.com/en-us/exchange/permissions-exo/permissions-exo`.

Creating an Exchange-specific retention policy

This recipe will show how you can create a retention policy on specific user inboxes or security groups' inboxes via the O365 Security & Compliance Center.

Getting ready

You'll need access to the O365 Security & Compliance Center and, if you're not a global admin, one of the following roles:

- Compliance Management
- Organization Management
- Records Management

How to do it...

1. Go to the O365 Security & Compliance Center at `https://protection.office.com`.

2. Select **Information governance | Retention** from the left-hand navigation menu:

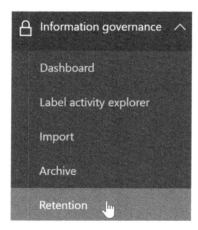

Figure 4.25 – The Retention link under Information governance in the
O365 Security & Compliance Center's left-hand navigation menu

3. Select **Create**:

Figure 4.26 – The Create button

4. Name and describe your retention policy:

Figure 4.27 – The retention policy's name and description

5. Choose the length of time, or retention period, for the inbox's contents. Click **Next**:

Figure 4.28 – Retention period configuration options

6. Select **Let me choose specific locations** if not selected by default. Turn off the toggle switch for every location except **Exchange email**. Then, click **Choose recipients**:

The policy will apply to content that's stored in the locations you choose.

○ Apply policy only to content in Exchange email, public folders, Office 365 groups, OneDrive and SharePoint documents.

◉ Let me choose specific locations. ⓘ

Status	Location	Include	Exclude
	Exchange email	All	None
		Choose recipients	Exclude recipients
	SharePoint sites		

Figure 4.29 – Retention policy applicable locations

7. Select **Choose recipients** again.

8. Search for or select each security group and/or individual to whom this retention policy should apply, and then click **Choose**:

Exchange email

Choose which recipients to choose from the list below.

Search	🔍

Distribution lists and mail-enabled security groups will be expanded so the policy will apply to all the mailboxes in the group. Only the mailboxes that are currently members of these groups will be covered by the policy. Mailboxes added to these groups later won't be covered, but ones that are removed later will still be covered.

⌄ Added (0)

⌃ Recipients (5)

☐ Name ⌄	Email
☐ O365 Governance Committee	O365gov@natechamberlain.com
☐ Nate Chamberlain	nate@natechamberlain.com
☐ Book Authors	BookAuthors@natechamberlain.com

Figure 4.30 – Dialog for choosing users to whom the retention policy will apply

9. When you have finished selecting the users whose inboxes will be held to this retention policy, you'll see your new members listed for confirmation, and then you can click **Done**.

10. Choose **Next**.

11. Note the warning that it will take up to 1 day to apply the retention policy to the selected recipients. Click **Create this policy**.

How it works...

This recipe took us beyond the Exchange admin center to create a retention policy for Exchange content. The O365 Security & Compliance Center features robust retention and data loss prevention options to help make sure sensitive and important data is retained and protected according to policies and industry standards. In the example used in this recipe, we created a retention policy on user inboxes—administrators specifically—to make sure that the organization would have access to the inbox's contents for 2 years after creation.

See also

- Read more about creating retention policies in Exchange Online at `https://docs.microsoft.com/en-us/Exchange/security-and-compliance/messaging-records-management/apply-retention-policy`.

Creating a mail flow rule

While users can create their own rules to apply to messages upon delivery, mail flow rules set by administrators take effect on messages in transit before they're delivered. In this recipe, we'll create a mail flow rule to help identify and report outgoing mail containing credit card numbers.

> **Important note**
> Mail flow rules are also known as transport rules.

Getting ready

You should be a global admin or have the Organization Management role as part of your assigned permissions to be able to complete the steps in this recipe.

How to do it...

1. Go to the classic Exchange admin center at `https://outlook.office.com/ecp/`.

2. Select **mail flow** from the left-hand side navigation menu.

3. Choose the plus sign (+) to create a new rule:

Figure 4.31 – The plus button for creating a new rule

4. In this recipe, we'll select **Generate an incident report when sensitive information is detected**:

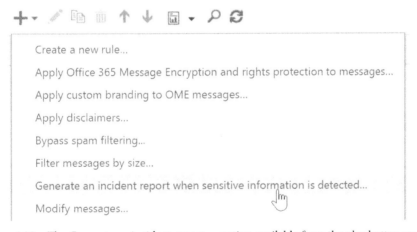

Figure 4.32 – The Generate an incident report… option available from the plus button menu

5. Name the rule and choose **Select sensitive information types…**:

Name:

| Prevent credit card data from leaving organization |

*Apply this rule if…

| The message contains any of these sensitive information types…   ▼ | *Select sensitive information types…

| add condition |

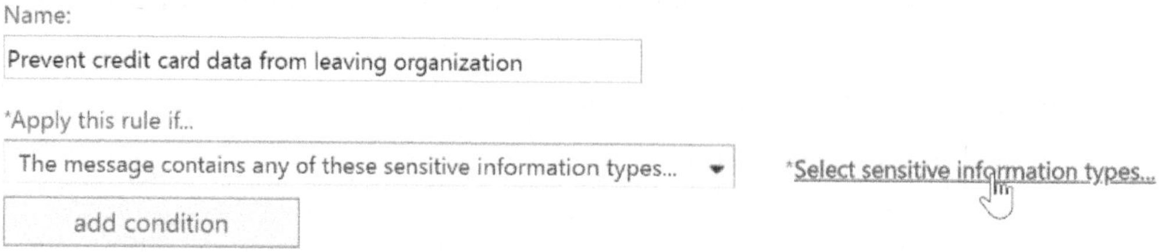

Figure 4.33 – The Name and sensitive information types… configuration for the rule

6. Select the plus sign (+) to add a sensitive information type.

7. Double-click on **Credit Card Number** and then click **OK**:

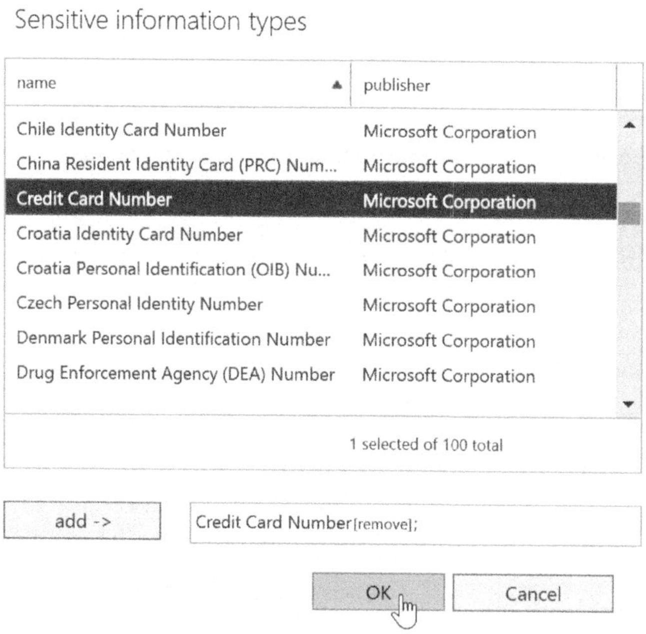

Sensitive information types

name ▲	publisher	
Chile Identity Card Number	Microsoft Corporation	▲
China Resident Identity Card (PRC) Num…	Microsoft Corporation	
Credit Card Number	Microsoft Corporation	
Croatia Identity Card Number	Microsoft Corporation	
Croatia Personal Identification (OIB) Nu…	Microsoft Corporation	
Czech Personal Identity Number	Microsoft Corporation	
Denmark Personal Identification Number	Microsoft Corporation	
Drug Enforcement Agency (DEA) Number	Microsoft Corporation	▼

1 selected of 100 total

| add -> | | Credit Card Number[remove]; |

| OK | | Cancel |

Figure 4.34 – The Sensitive information types selection dialog

8. Click **OK** again.

9. Next to **Send incident report to:**, click **Select one…**:

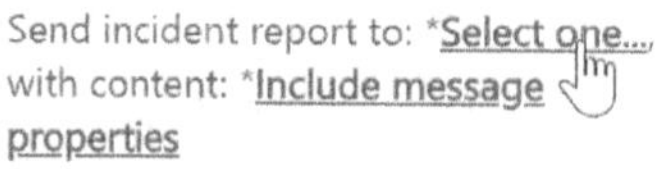

Send incident report to: *Select one….
with content: *Include message
properties

Figure 4.35 – The Select one… link for the selection of incident report recipients

10. Chose a recipient or group and click **OK**.

11. Click **Include message properties**.

12. Choose **Select all** and then **OK**:

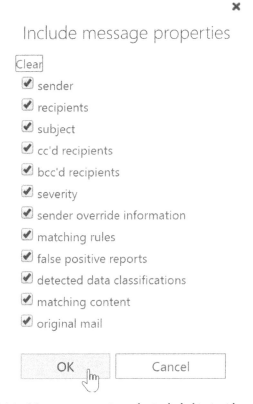

Figure 4.36 – Message properties to be included in incident reports

13. Choose **Add condition**, then **The recipient… | is external/internal**:

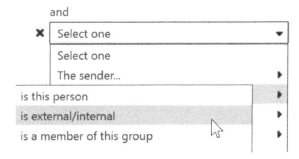

Figure 4.37 – Conditions for the mail flow rule

14. Change the recipient location to **Outside the organization** and click **OK**:

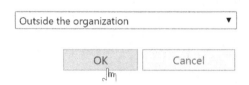

Figure 4.38 – The recipient location dropdown

15. Configure any other settings you wish, then choose **Save** at the bottom of the dialog.

16. Confirm that the rule details match your expectations:

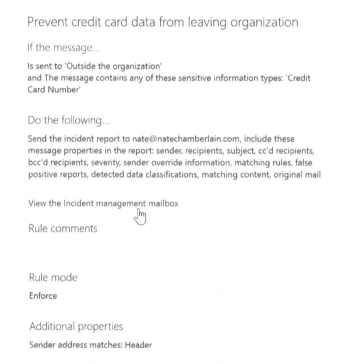

Figure 4.39 – Details of the mail flow rule, with a link to View the Incident management mailbox

How it works...

In this recipe, you created a mail flow rule. This mail flow rule monitors mail being sent to external recipients and notifies an administrator or group whenever a message is sent externally and appears to contain credit card information.

> **Important note**
> There are infinite combinations of conditions, exceptions, actions, and properties to configure for each rule. Take some time to get to know some of the other possibilities to enhance the security and compliance of your organization's Exchange environment.

See also

- Learn more about mail flow rules at `https://docs.microsoft.com/en-us/exchange/security-and-compliance/mail-flow-rules/mail-flow-rules`.

Configuring spam filter policies

Configure spam filter policies to allow or reject mail sent by specific domains or users, and apply complex logic to incoming mail to ensure spam is handled appropriately. In this recipe, we'll create a spam filter policy that blocks incoming mail from specific domains that we specify.

Getting ready

To complete the steps in this recipe, you should be a global admin, Exchange admin, or have a role that includes the Organization Management or Hygiene Management roles.

How to do it...

1. Go to the classic Exchange admin center at `https://outlook.office.com/ecp/`.

2. Click on **Protection** in the left-hand navigation menu.

3. Select **spam filter** from the top navigation menu:

malware filter   connection filter   spam filter

Figure 4.40 – The spam filter link in the Exchange admin center

4. Choose the plus sign (+) to create a new spam filter policy:

New
NAME

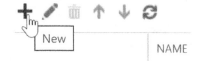

Figure 4.41 – The plus button for adding a new policy

5. Give the policy a name and description:

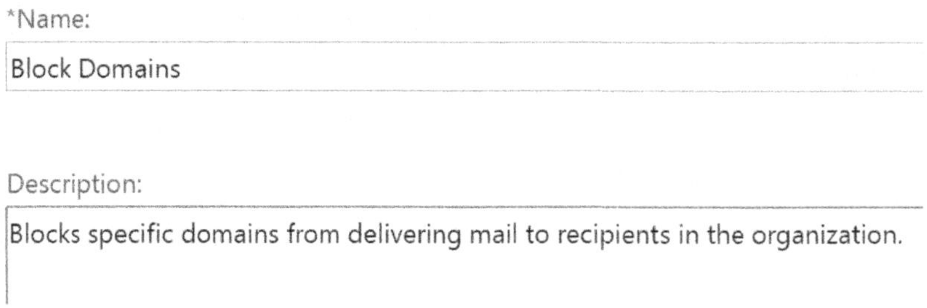
*Name:
Block Domains
Description:
Blocks specific domains from delivering mail to recipients in the organization.

Figure 4.42 – Name and description configuration for a new policy

6. Scroll down to the **Domain block list** section and choose the plus sign (+):

Domain block list
Always mark email from the following domains as spam.
BL
Add
DOMAIN

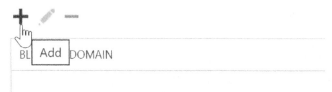

Figure 4.43 – The plus button for adding a new domain to block

7. Enter semicolon-delimited domains to block, but do not enter an ending semicolon after the last domain to block. Then, click **OK**:

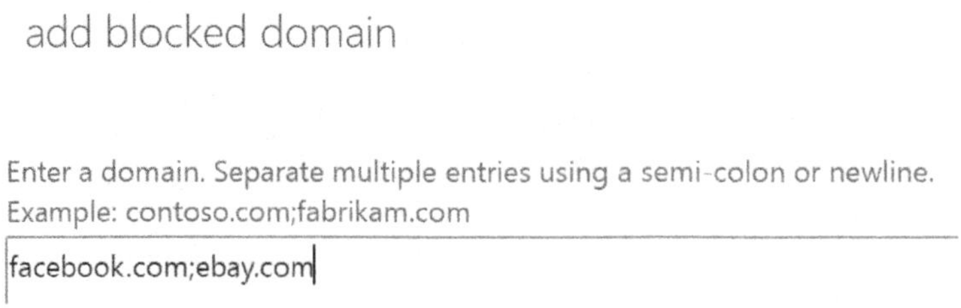
add blocked domain
Enter a domain. Separate multiple entries using a semi-colon or newline.
Example: contoso.com;fabrikam.com
facebook.com;ebay.com

Figure 4.44 – Domains to block separated by semicolons

8. Scroll down to near the bottom and change the **Applied To** section's **If...** section option to **The recipient domain is**. A dialog appears. Add your user's domain(s) and click **OK**:

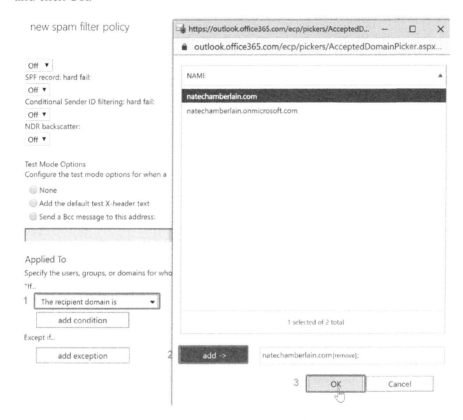

Figure 4.45 – The Applied To condition configuration dialog

9. Scroll down to the bottom and select **Save**.

How it works...

With a customized spam policy in place, you're able to more granularly control the incoming and outgoing mail in your organization. This helps with your organization's security and compliance and helps enable your users to be more productive since they're spending less time weeding through distracting (and sometimes malicious) emails.

Tip

You can also create anti-spam policies from the O365 Security & Compliance Center. You'll find these under **Threat management** | **Policy** > **Anti-spam**.

Creating room and equipment resources

In this recipe, we'll establish a conference room or equipment resource that users can utilize in Outlook. Most commonly, users would **invite** the room or piece of equipment to a meeting to reserve it.

Getting ready

To create room and equipment resources, you need to be a global or Exchange admin, or at least have the Organization Management or Recipient Management role assigned to you.

How to do it...

1. Go to the new Exchange admin center at `https://admin.exchange.microsoft.com/`.

2. Select **Recipients | Resources**:

Figure 4.46 – The Resources link in the left-hand navigation menu of the new
Exchange admin center

3. Click on **Add a resource**:

Resources

Figure 4.47 – The Add a resource button on the Resources page

4. Choose **Room** or **Equipment** and fill in the basic information for it, including the email address it should have. Then, click **Next**:

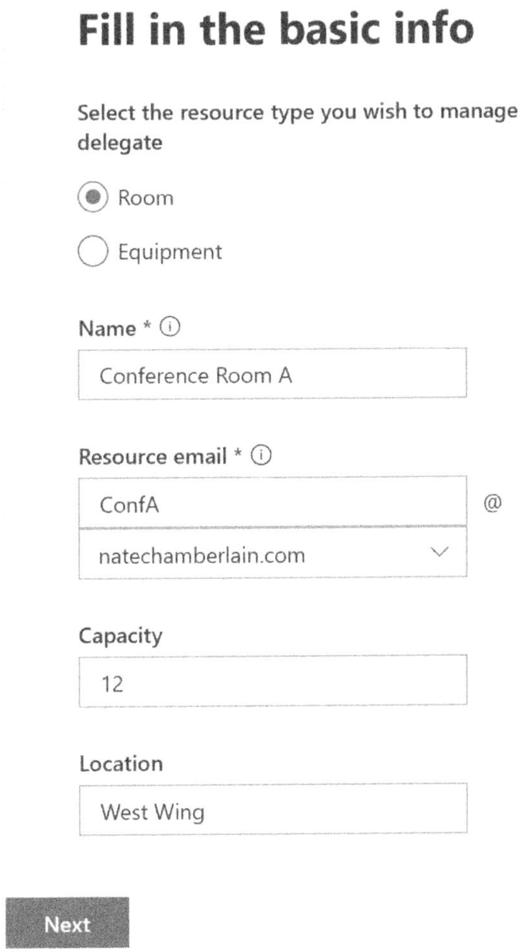

Fill in the basic info

Select the resource type you wish to manage through email or delegate

(•) Room

( ) Equipment

Name * ⓘ

| Conference Room A |

Resource email * ⓘ

| ConfA | @

| natechamberlain.com ⌄ |

Capacity

| 12 |

Location

| West Wing |

Next

Figure 4.48 – Basic information for a new room or equipment resource in Exchange

5. Enter a department, company, and address information if applicable and click **Next**.

6. Choose the conditions under which the room can be reserved, such as whether recurring meetings are allowed and whether there should be a human delegate who approves or whether requests are approved on a first-come, first-served basis. Click **Next**:

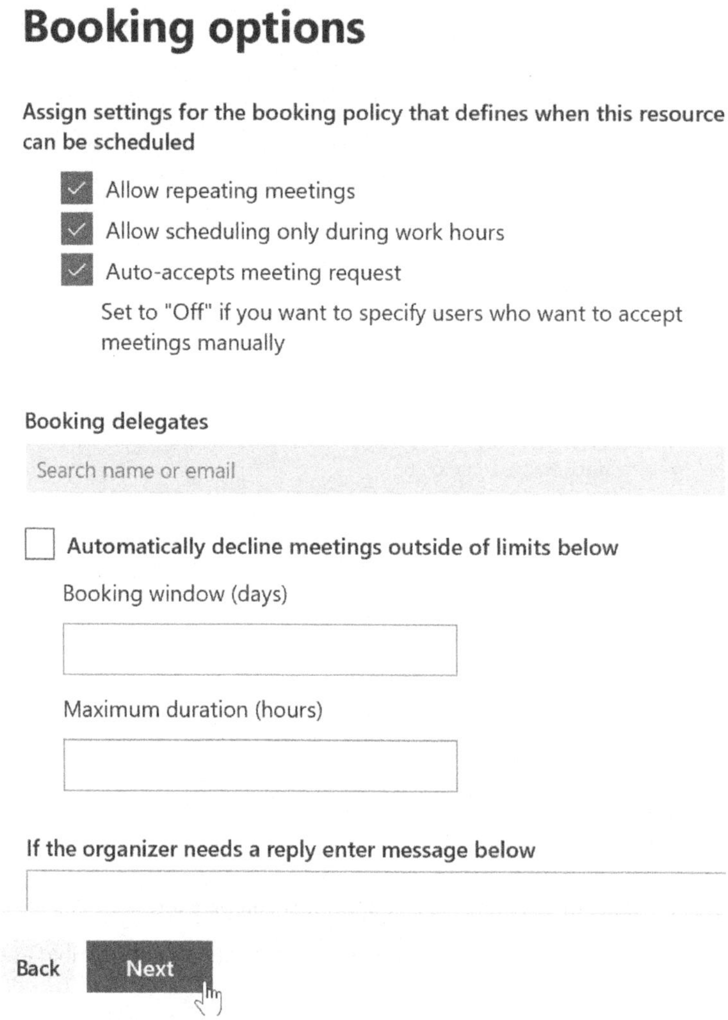

Booking options

Assign settings for the booking policy that defines when this resource can be scheduled

☑ Allow repeating meetings

☑ Allow scheduling only during work hours

☑ Auto-accepts meeting request

Set to "Off" if you want to specify users who want to accept meetings manually

Booking delegates

Search name or email

☐ **Automatically decline meetings outside of limits below**

Booking window (days)

Maximum duration (hours)

If the organizer needs a reply enter message below

Back   Next

Figure 4.49 – Booking options for a room resource

7. Review the resource you've configured and when satisfied, click **Create**:

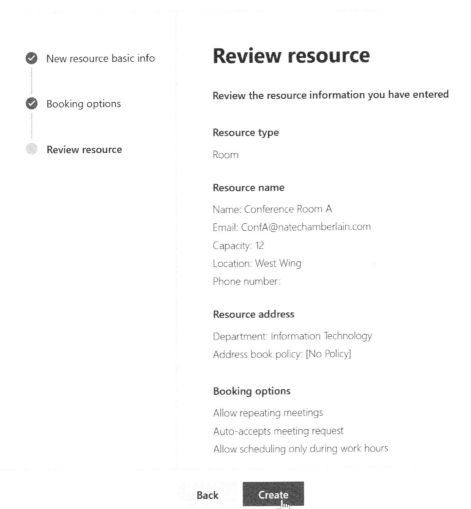

Figure 4.50 – The Review resource screen when creating a new resource mailbox

8. Wait a minute or two until you get the green success message, then click **Done**:

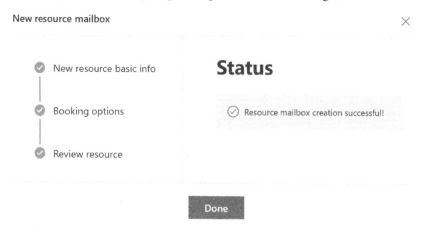

Figure 4.51 – The confirmation screen with the creation status when creating a new resource mailbox

How it works...

Creating a resource is a bit like creating a user mailbox. The major difference is in how users are meant to interact with the account. Should requests be auto-accepted? Does a human need to be involved in approvals for, say, an administrative board room reservation?

Enabling advanced threat protection (ATP) features

This final recipe will cover the steps needed to configure safe attachments and safe links settings in the Exchange admin center. These settings empower administrators to take steps to minimize vulnerabilities and improve the organization's overall data security.

Getting ready

You'll need access to the O365 Security & Compliance Center and, if you're not a global admin, one of the following roles:

- Compliance Management
- Organization Management
- Records Management

How to do it...

1. Go to the O365 Security & Compliance Center at `https://protection.office.com`.

2. Select **Threat management | Policy**:

Figure 4.52 – The Threat management Policy link in the
O365 Security & Compliance Center's left-hand navigation menu

3. Select **ATP safe attachments**.

4. Click on the plus sign (+) in the **Protect email attachments** section.

5. Name and describe your safe attachments policy. Then, choose a malware response method. In this recipe, we'll choose **Dynamic Delivery** to reduce the delay in email delivery while still scanning attachments for malware:

*Name:

Safe Attachments Policy

Description:

This policy will deliver messages immediately, but remove and scan attachments for malware before reattaching to the original message.

Safe attachments unknown malware response

Select the action for unknown malware in attachments.Learn more

Warning
Monitor, Replace and Block actions may cause significant delay to email delivery. Learn more
Dynamic Delivery is only available for recipients with hosted mailboxes. Learn more

- ○ Off - Attachment will not be scanned for malware.
- ○ Monitor - Continue delivering the message after malware is detected; track scan results.
- ○ Block - Block the current and future emails and attachments with detected malware.
- ○ Replace - Block the attachments with detected malware, continue to deliver the message.
- ● Dynamic Delivery - Deliver the message without attachments immediately and reattach once scan is complete.

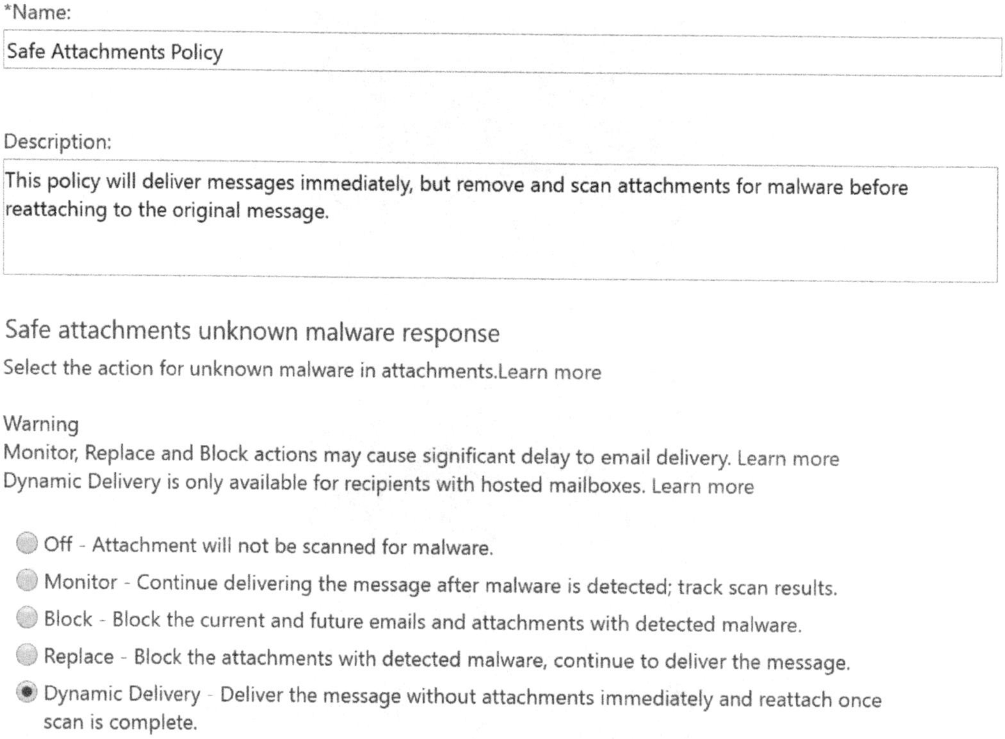

Figure 4.53 – The ATP safe attachments policy configuration fields and options

6. Scroll down to the **Applied To** section and set the policy to apply to all recipients within your domain(s):

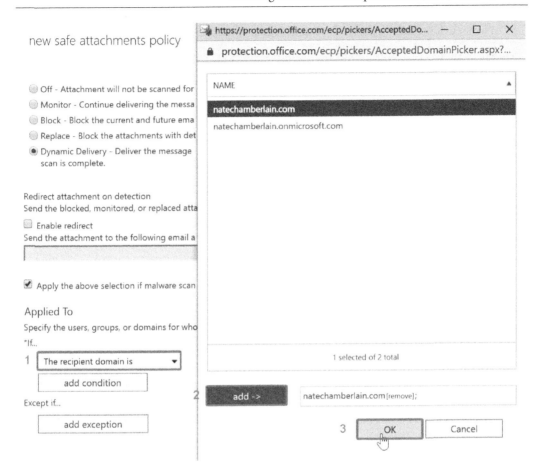

Figure 4.54 – The Applied To configuration and dialog

7. Click **Save** and then **OK** after reading the warning dialog(s):

Warning

Dynamic Email Delivery is for O365 hosted mailboxes only. If this action is chosen for a recipient with a non-hosted mailbox, then a Replace action will be taken for that recipient.

Figure 4.55 – Warning for non-O365-hosted mailboxes

8. Now, click on **safe links** in the top navigation menu.

9. Click on the plus sign (+) in the **Policies that apply to specific users** section.

10. Name and describe your new policy, and turn on any features you'd like:

new safe links policy

*Name:

Safe Links Policy

Description:

This policy will rewrite all URLs in messages and check Teams URLs against known malicious links but not rewrite them.

Select the action for unknown potentially malicious URLs in messages.

○ Off

◉ On - URLs will be rewritten and checked against a list of known malicious links when user clicks on the link.

Select the action for unknown or potentially malicious URLs within Microsoft Teams.

○ Off

◉ On - Microsoft Teams will check against a list of known malicious links when user clicks on a link; URLs will not be rewritten.

☑ Apply real-time URL scanning for suspicious links and links that point to files.
  ☑ Wait for URL scanning to complete before delivering the message.

☑ Apply safe links to email messages sent within the organization.

Figure 4.56 – The new safe links policy configuration fields and options

11. Scroll down and repeat *step 6* to choose the users to whom this policy applies. In this case, we'll again choose all recipients within our domain(s). Click **Save** when finished.

12. Choose **OK** on the success message when it appears.

How it works...

You utilized the O365 Security & Compliance Center in this recipe to create a safe attachments policy. Creating a safe attachments policy for emails in Exchange makes sure any attached files moving within, into, and out of your organization are safe before completing their transit.

Safe links policies can rewrite URLs in email messages to make sure they're checked when being clicked on for malicious intent.

> **Important note**
>
> The **Monitor**, **Block**, and **Replace** options are alternatives to **Dynamic Delivery** for emails with attachments. Consider choosing one of them instead for certain groups/conditions.

See also

- Learn more about O365 ATP Safe Attachments policies at `https://docs.microsoft.com/en-us/microsoft-365/security/office-365-security/atp-safe-attachments`.

- Check out more information on O365 ATP Safe Links at `https://docs.microsoft.com/en-us/microsoft-365/security/office-365-security/atp-safe-links`.

5
Setting Up and Configuring Microsoft Search

Microsoft Search is an enterprise-wide search solution that simplifies finding resources from all locations from a single search experience. We'll cover some basic setup and configuration tasks, such as adding bookmarks and Q&A results, as well as utilizing data to improve and enhance the user experience.

We'll specifically cover the following topics in this chapter:

- Creating an acronym
- Creating a bookmark
- Importing bookmarks in bulk from CSV
- Importing SharePoint promoted results as bookmarks
- Adding a location
- Adding a floor plan
- Adding a Q&A result

- Assigning the **Search Admin** and **Search Editor** roles
- Setting up the usage of Microsoft Search in Bing
- Using Search Insights dashboard reports

Technical requirements

This chapter is entirely based in the Microsoft Search admin center. There are no technical requirements beyond access as a global or search admin for completing all the recipes in this chapter.

Creating an acronym

Acronyms in Search allow your users to become familiar with the acronyms, or abbreviated terminology, specifically used in your organization. Since different organizations may use the same acronym for different things (for example, **SPD** could be **SharePoint Designer** or **Sterile Processing Department**), this can be helpful for users who may otherwise use Google and find the wrong meaning for your organization's context. In this recipe, we'll set **HR** as an acronym that expands to **Human Resources**.

Getting ready

You must be a global admin, search admin, or search editor to complete the steps in this recipe.

How to do it...

1. Go to the Microsoft Search admin center at `https://admin.microsoft.com/Adminportal/Home#/MicrosoftSearch` or by selecting **All Admin Centers | Microsoft Search** from the left-side navigation menu of the Microsoft 365 admin center.

2. Select **Answers | Acronyms** from the top and left-side navigation menus, respectively:

Microsoft Search

Figure 5.1 – The Answers | Acronyms options in the Microsoft Search navigation menus

3. Click **Add**.

4. Enter the acronym and its meaning, as well as a description and source or reference URL, if applicable. As you type, you'll see a preview of the result card that will be shown to users who search HR:

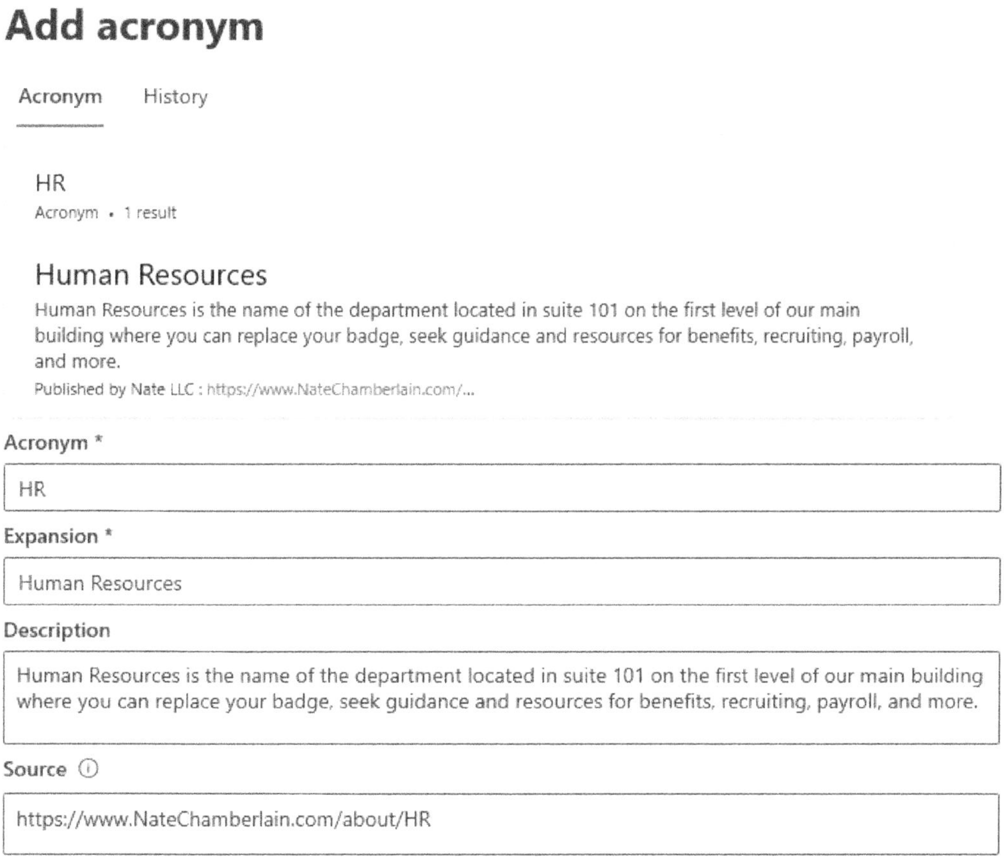

Add acronym

Acronym   History

HR
Acronym · 1 result

Human Resources

Human Resources is the name of the department located in suite 101 on the first level of our main building where you can replace your badge, seek guidance and resources for benefits, recruiting, payroll, and more.

Published by Nate LLC : https://www.NateChamberlain.com/...

Acronym *

> HR

Expansion *

> Human Resources

Description

> Human Resources is the name of the department located in suite 101 on the first level of our main building where you can replace your badge, seek guidance and resources for benefits, recruiting, payroll, and more.

Source ⓘ

> https://www.NateChamberlain.com/about/HR

Figure 5.2 – Acronym configuration fields

5. Click **Publish**.

How it works...

We just added an acronym to Microsoft Search. Once imported or published, it could take up to 3 days before results are shown to users who search the acronyms you've added.

There's more

After *step 2*, you could also select **Import** to import acronyms in bulk, rather than one at a time. Once selected, you'll be able to download a template to use for proper formatting, then click **Browse** to upload your completed CSV file:

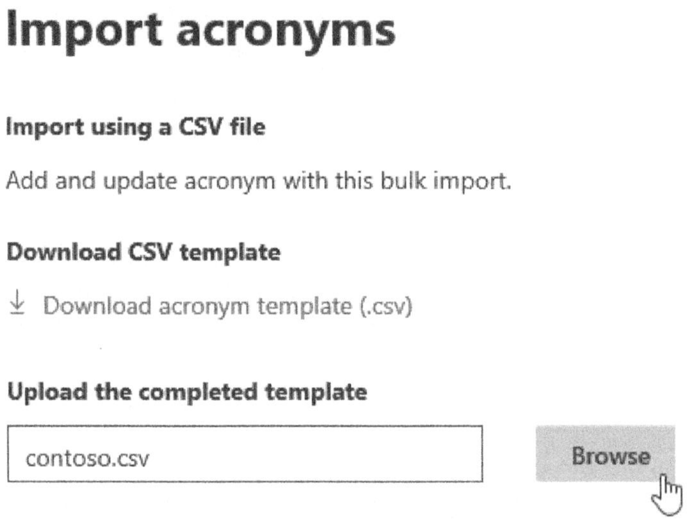

Import acronyms

Import using a CSV file

Add and update acronym with this bulk import.

Download CSV template

↓ Download acronym template (.csv)

Upload the completed template

| contoso.csv | Browse |

Figure 5.3 – The Import acronyms dialog

See also

- Learn more about acronyms in the Microsoft Search admin center at `https://docs.microsoft.com/en-us/microsoftsearch/manage-acronyms`.

Creating a bookmark

Bookmarks can be used to easily direct users to third-party apps and services at other URLs or top resources within your Office 365 environment. In this recipe, we'll create a bookmark to an external HR portal that will appear for users searching for `PTO Request`.

Getting ready

You must be a global admin, search admin, or search editor to complete the steps in this recipe.

How to do it...

1. Go to the Microsoft Search admin center at `https://admin.microsoft.com/Adminportal/Home#/MicrosoftSearch` or by selecting **All Admin Centers | Microsoft Search** from the left-side navigation menu of the Microsoft 365 admin center.

2. Select **Answers | Bookmarks** from the top and left-side navigation menus, respectively:

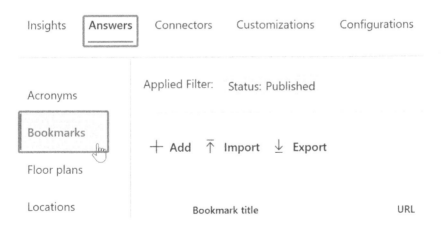

Figure 5.4 – The Answers | Bookmarks options in the Microsoft Search navigation menus

3. Click **Add**.

4. Enter a title, a URL, a bookmark description, keywords, and reserved keywords (unique to this result). You'll notice that the preview of the result card updates as you type:

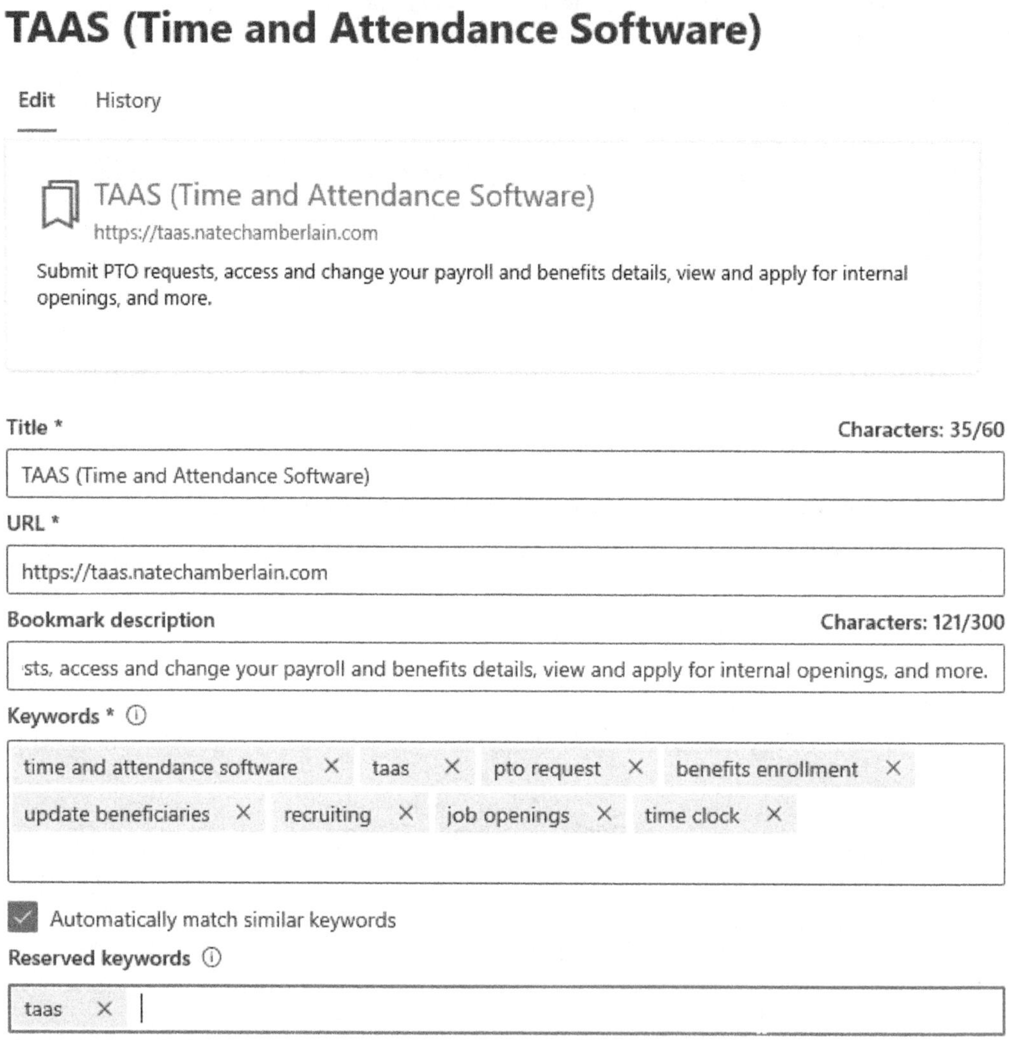

TAAS (Time and Attendance Software)

Edit   History

TAAS (Time and Attendance Software)
https://taas.natechamberlain.com

Submit PTO requests, access and change your payroll and benefits details, view and apply for internal openings, and more.

Title *   Characters: 35/60

TAAS (Time and Attendance Software)

URL *

https://taas.natechamberlain.com

Bookmark description   Characters: 121/300

sts, access and change your payroll and benefits details, view and apply for internal openings, and more.

Keywords * ⓘ

time and attendance software ✕   taas   ✕   pto request ✕   benefits enrollment ✕

update beneficiaries ✕   recruiting ✕   job openings ✕   time clock ✕

☑ Automatically match similar keywords

Reserved keywords ⓘ

taas ✕ |

Figure 5.5 – New bookmark configuration fields and options

5. Scroll down and configure any additional (optional) settings for the bookmark, such as the following:

    --**Dates**: Is there only a certain relevant time that this result should be displayed?

    --**Country or region**: Should the result be restricted to users in certain geographic locations?

    --**Groups**: Should the result be restricted to certain groups, such as managers?

    --**Device & OS**: Will this result be accessible and relevant from all devices and OSes?

    --**Targeted variations**: Adjust the result based on the user's device/OS and geography.

    --**PowerApp**: Embed a PowerApp in the search results for convenience of completion:

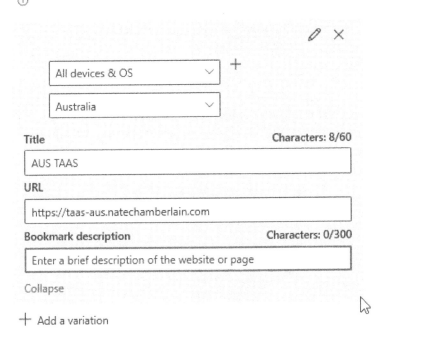

Figure 5.6 – The Targeted variations options

6. Click **Publish**.

How it works...

In this recipe, you added a bookmark to Microsoft Search via the admin center. For bookmarks and Q&A results, the search index is refreshed almost immediately. Once a new bookmark result is added or modified, the change will be visible to users querying matching keywords and phrases quite soon.

See also

- Learn more about managing bookmarks via the Microsoft Search admin center at `https://docs.microsoft.com/en-us/microsoftsearch/manage-bookmarks`.

Importing bookmarks in bulk from CSV

The previous recipe showed how to add a single bookmark to Microsoft Search. This recipe will show how you can import several at once using a CSV import.

Getting ready

You must be a global admin, search admin, or search editor to complete the steps in this recipe.

How to do it...

1. Go to the Microsoft Search admin center at `https://admin.microsoft.com/Adminportal/Home#/MicrosoftSearch` or by selecting **All Admin Centers | Microsoft Search** from the left-side navigation menu of the Microsoft 365 admin center.

2. Select **Answers | Bookmarks** from the top and left-side navigation menus, respectively:

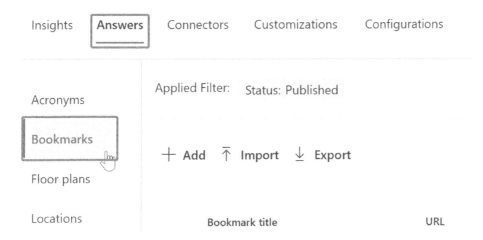

Figure 5.7 – The Answers | Bookmarks options in the Microsoft Search navigation menus

3. Select **Download bookmarks template (.csv)** to get a CSV file with proper headings to complete. Open the downloaded file:

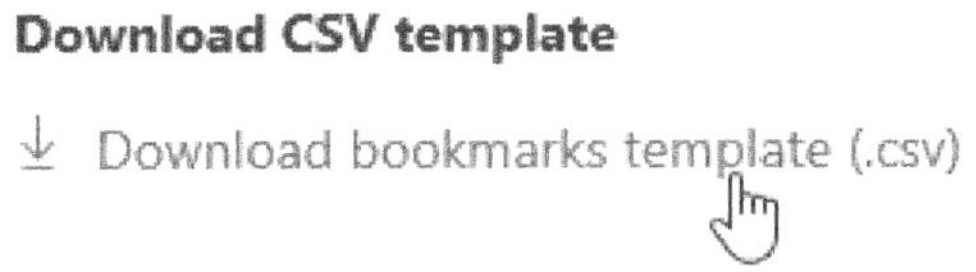

Download CSV template

↓ Download bookmarks template (.csv)

Figure 5.8 – The Download bookmarks template link

4. Enter the details for each bookmark you intend to import:

	A	B	C	D	E
1	Title	Url	Keywords	State	Description
2	Outlook Web Access	https://outlook.office365.	outlook web access;ou	published	Manage your work e
3	Office Online	https://portal.office.com	office online;office 365	published	Collaborate for free
4	Word	https://office.live.com/sta	word online;word logi	published	Collaborate for free
5	Flow	https://flow.microsoft.cor	flow online;flow login	published	Automate tasks by i
6	Office Install Site	http://aka.ms/getoffice	install office;install off	published	Try or buy Office for
7	Microsoft Search in Bing explore	https://www.bing.com/bu	bing for business;bing	published	Explore features of

Figure 5.9 – CSV template for importing bookmarks

5. Save the file with a name and in a location that you'll remember for the next step.

6. Back in the admin center, select **Browse** and select the file you saved. Once uploaded, it'll inform you of how many bookmarks will be added:

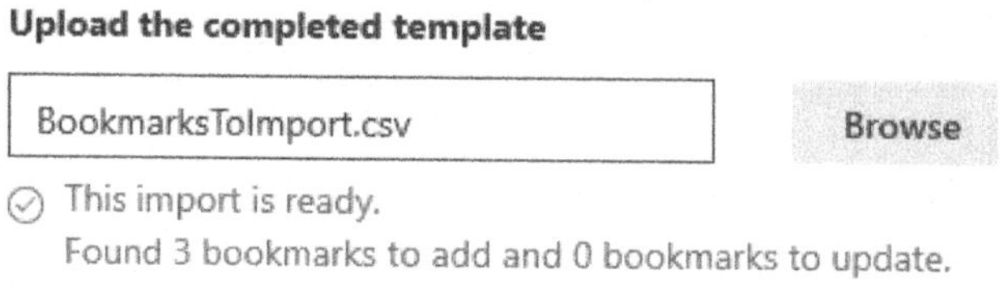

Upload the completed template

BookmarksToImport.csv	Browse

⊘ This import is ready.
  Found 3 bookmarks to add and 0 bookmarks to update.

Figure 5.10 – The import ready confirmation with the quantity of found bookmarks

7. Click **Import**.

8. Click **Done**.

How it works...

This time, you've added multiple bookmarks via a CSV import in the Microsoft Search admin center. Remember, for bookmarks and Q&A results, the search index is refreshed almost immediately. Once your new bookmarks are added or modified, the changes will be visible to users querying matching keywords and phrases quite soon.

See also

*   Learn more about specifically importing bookmarks in bulk at `https://docs.microsoft.com/en-us/microsoftsearch/manage-bookmarks#bulk-add-or-edit-bookmarks`.

Importing SharePoint promoted results as bookmarks

In the previous recipe, we imported bookmarks from a CSV file. In this recipe, we'll convert existing SharePoint promoted results into bookmarks in Microsoft Search.

Getting ready

You must be a global admin, search admin, or search editor to complete the steps in this recipe.

How to do it...

1. Go to the Microsoft Search admin center at `https://admin.microsoft.com/Adminportal/Home#/MicrosoftSearch` or by selecting **All Admin Centers | Microsoft Search** from the left-side navigation menu of the Microsoft 365 admin center.

2. Select **Answers | Bookmarks** from the top and left-side navigation menus, respectively:

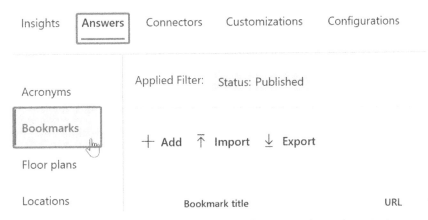

Figure 5.11 – The Answers | Bookmarks options in the Microsoft Search navigation menus

3. Click **SharePoint**, then **Import from SharePoint**:

Figure 5.12 – The Import from SharePoint option for importing promoted results as bookmarks

4. Wait for the import to complete, then refresh and return to the bookmarks pane of the Microsoft Search admin center.

5. Imported promoted results will now appear under **Suggested**. Select **Suggested**:

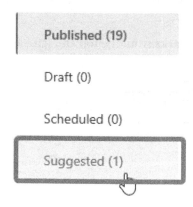

Figure 5.13 – The Suggested menu link to view imported promoted results

6. Select the promoted results you wish to import as bookmarks, then click **Publish**:

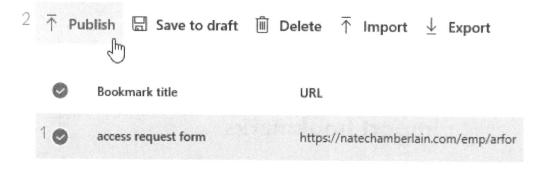

Figure 5.14 – The selected promoted results to be published as bookmarks

How it works...

We've just imported SharePoint's promoted results as suggestions in the Microsoft Search admin center's bookmarks section. Then, we chose one to publish as an actual bookmark. Your imported bookmarks are immediately available to users searching matching keywords. As seen in the following screenshot, when a user searches ar form, they are presented with the SharePoint promoted result as a Microsoft Search bookmark:

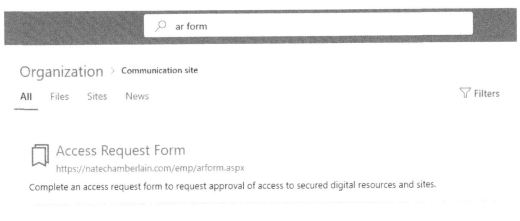

Figure 5.15 – Search results showing a successful test of the promoted result we converted into a bookmark

See also

- Learn more about specifically importing bookmarks in bulk at `https://docs.microsoft.com/en-us/microsoftsearch/manage-bookmarks#bulk-add-or-edit-bookmarks`.

Adding a location

Adding locations to Microsoft Search allows your users to search for a specific building or location and get a visual card in the search results, resembling the following:

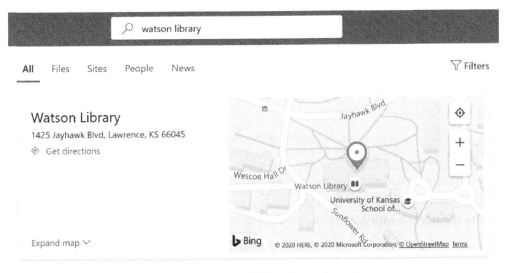

Figure 5.16 – Example location card result

In this recipe, we'll cover the steps for adding a location to Microsoft Search so that it'll show in the results.

Getting ready

You must be a global admin, search admin, or search editor to complete the steps in this recipe.

How to do it...

1. Go to the Microsoft Search admin center at `https://admin.microsoft.com/Adminportal/Home#/MicrosoftSearch` or by selecting **All Admin Centers | Microsoft Search** from the left-side navigation menu of the Microsoft 365 admin center.

2. Select **Answers | Locations** from the top and left-side navigation menus, respectively:

Figure 5.17 – The Answers | Locations options in the Microsoft Search navigation menus

3. Click **Add**.

4. Enter a location name, country, and address. As you type the address, results will be suggested for selection. If a match doesn't appear, you'll need to select **Address not in the list? Kindly specify the latitude & longitude**:

Suggested results

1301 Mississippi St, Lawrence, KS 66045

1301 Mississippi St, Monroe, LA 71202

1301 Mississippi St, St Paul, MN 55112

🔍   Address not in the list? Kindly specify the latitude & longitude.

1301 Mississippi St

Figure 5.18 – The Address field with suggested results

5. Scroll down and enter keywords that should return this location card in the search results. You can also specify reserved keywords that will override any other keywords:

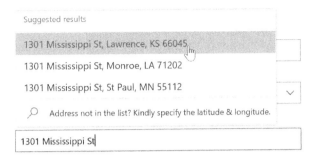

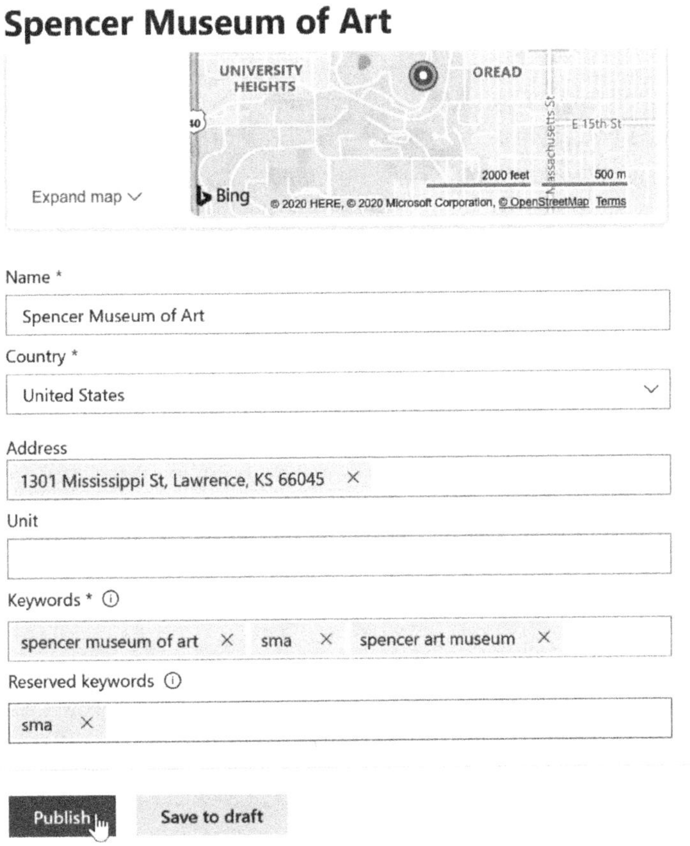

Spencer Museum of Art

Name *

Spencer Museum of Art

Country *

United States

Address

1301 Mississippi St, Lawrence, KS 66045   ✕

Unit

Keywords * ⓘ

spencer museum of art   ✕   sma   ✕   spencer art museum   ✕

Reserved keywords ⓘ

sma   ✕

Publish   Save to draft

Figure 5.19 – Location card configuration fields

6. When finished, click **Publish**.

How it works...

You've just created a location result in the Microsoft Search admin center. Once the new location result has been created, it will be crawled and added to the search index. Once the index is refreshed (which could take several hours for location results), the new location will appear to users when searched using the provided keywords.

There's more

You can bulk import locations as well, using the **Import** button on the **Locations** screen of the Microsoft Search admin center:

Import locations

Import using a CSV file

Download a copy of the locations template to make sure any items you're importing are in the correct format. When you're ready to import, come back here and upload your file.

Download CSV template

↓ Download locations template (.csv)

Upload the completed template

Figure 5.20 – The Import locations dialog

See also

- Learn more about managing locations in Microsoft Search at `https://docs.microsoft.com/en-us/microsoftsearch/manage-locations`.

Adding a floor plan

Make it easier for employees to find conference rooms, meeting locations, facilities, and departments by adding your buildings' floor plans to Microsoft Search. This recipe will demonstrate how to add a floor plan as a Microsoft Search result.

Getting ready

You must be a global admin, search admin, or search editor to complete the steps in this recipe. You must also have added locations (see the previous recipe) before you can add floor plans for them.

Your floor plans should be in DWG format with room number labels, and Microsoft recommends one for each floor or wing.

How to do it...

1. Go to the Microsoft Search admin center at `https://admin.microsoft.com/Adminportal/Home#/MicrosoftSearch` or by selecting **All Admin Centers | Microsoft Search** from the left-side navigation menu of the Microsoft 365 admin center.

2. Select **Answers | Floor plans** from the top and left-side navigation menus, respectively:

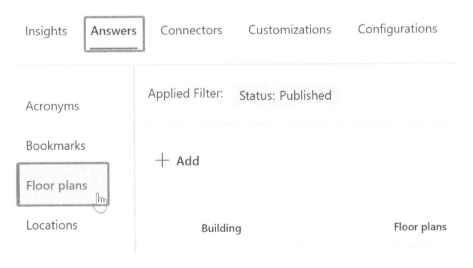

Figure 5.21 – The Answers | Floor plans options in the Microsoft Search navigation menus

3. Click **Add**.

4. Select a building from the **Location** dropdown. Click **Next** when ready:

Select your building

Can't find the building you're looking for? Select **Cancel**, and then select **+Add** from the **Locations** tab. When you're done, come back here to finish.

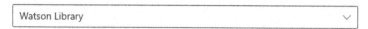

Figure 5.22 – Building dropdown containing previously created locations

5. For each file that you upload for the selected location (which must be in DWG format), indicate which floor and/or zone it represents, if applicable:

↑ **Upload files**

Figure 5.23 – Uploaded file configuration fields

6. Choose the office location data from Azure Active Directory to map to the uploaded files' contents. For each one, you'll enter the floor, wing, and room number information as well:

Specify location patterns

We need a little more information to smartly assign user office locations to rooms in the uploaded files. For each office location, identify the floor, wing or zone, and the room number.

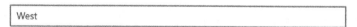

Figure 5.24 – Additional required information for the uploaded file

7. Click **Publish**.

How it works...

You've just added floor plans as results in the Microsoft Search admin center. Adding floor plans for each floor and wing of your organization's buildings allows users to search for individuals and be directed exactly to that individual's office space within the floor plan. They can also just search for a conference room or building and then conveniently find what they need without leaving your tenant.

See also

- See more about managing floor plans and formatting them correctly for Microsoft Search at `https://docs.microsoft.com/en-us/microsoftsearch/manage-floorplans`.

Adding a Q&A result

Q&A results allow search administrators to provide FAQ-type content as prominent search results. For example, you might include a question such as *When are benefits elections due?* and schedule it to provide a clearly stated date of 3/31/2021 within the search results, with a link to more info on benefits enrollment. This reduces clicks for the querying user and creates a more dynamic user experience. Let's add a Q&A result to Microsoft Search.

Getting ready

You must be a global admin, search admin, or search editor to complete the steps in this recipe.

How to do it...

1. Go to the Microsoft Search admin center at `https://admin.microsoft.com/Adminportal/Home#/MicrosoftSearch` or by selecting **All Admin Centers | Microsoft Search** from the left-side navigation menu of the Microsoft 365 admin center.

2. Select **Answers | Q&A** from the top and left-side navigation menus, respectively:

Figure 5.25 – The Answers | Q&A options in the Microsoft Search navigation menus

3. Click **Add**.

4. Enter a title (a question), URL source, and answer description for the Q&A result:

Figure 5.26 – Q&A result configuration fields

5. Scroll down and enter keywords, reserved (exclusive) keywords, start/end date(s), and the regional availability of the result:

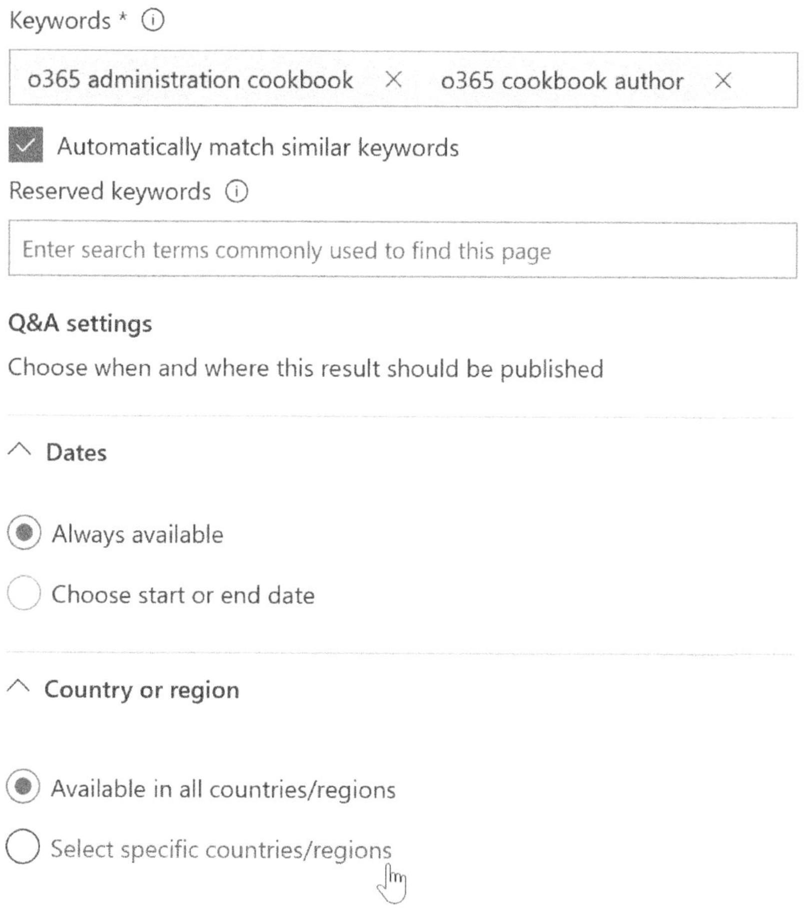

Figure 5.27 – Q&A result configuration fields

6. Choose which groups, devices, and other targeted variations the result should be visible to:

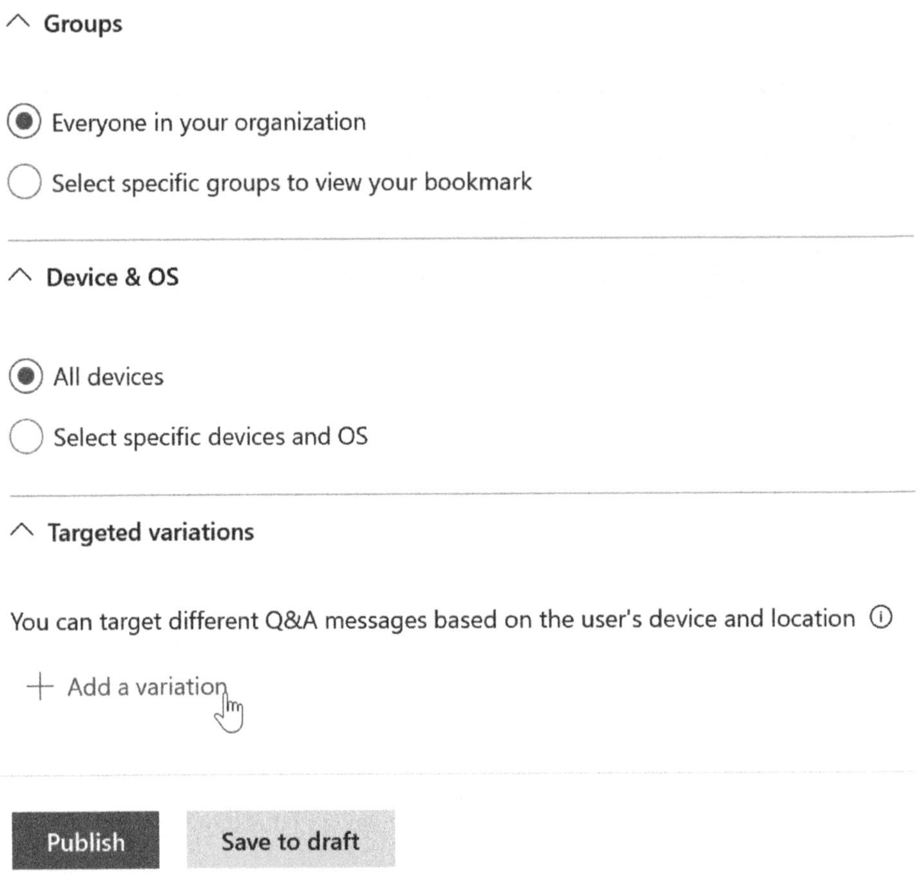

∧ **Groups**

◉ Everyone in your organization

◯ Select specific groups to view your bookmark

∧ **Device & OS**

◉ All devices

◯ Select specific devices and OS

∧ **Targeted variations**

You can target different Q&A messages based on the user's device and location ⓘ

+ Add a variation

Publish   Save to draft

Figure 5.28 – Q&A result configuration fields

7. Click **Publish**.\

How it works...

You've just added a Q&A result to Microsoft Search via its admin center. For bookmarks and Q&A results, the search index is refreshed almost immediately. Once a new Q&A result is added, reaches its scheduled start date, or is modified, the update will be visible to users querying matching keywords and phrases quite soon.

There's more

Notice how when providing an answer in a Q&A, you're able to utilize rich text features and stylings, such as bold, quote formatting, ordered lists, and additional in-line hyperlinks:

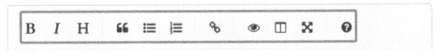

Nate Chamberlain wrote Packt's O365 Administration Cookbook in 2020.

Figure 5.29 – Rich text styling options for Q&A results

See also

- Read more about managing Q&As in Microsoft Search at `https://docs.microsoft.com/en-us/microsoftsearch/manage-qas`.

Assigning the Search Admin and Search Editor roles

Individuals assigned the **Search Admin** and **Search Editor** roles can complete the recipes in this chapter and manage Microsoft Search on a day-to-day basis. In this recipe, you'll learn how to assign the search admin role to a user, and you can follow the same steps to assign the search editor role (swapping, of course, the role selected).

Getting ready

You must be a global admin or search admin to complete the steps in this recipe.

How to do it...

1. Go to the Microsoft 365 admin center at `https://admin.microsoft.com`.
2. From the left-side navigation menu, select **Users | Active users**.

3. Search for and/or select the user to which you're assigning the search admin role, and use the top menu's ellipsis icon to select **Manage roles**:

Figure 5.30 – The Manage roles link available from the selected user's ellipsis menu

4. Expand **Show all by category**:

Figure 5.31 – The Show all by category option

5. Scroll down and select either **Search admin** or **Search editor** from beneath the **Collaboration** heading:

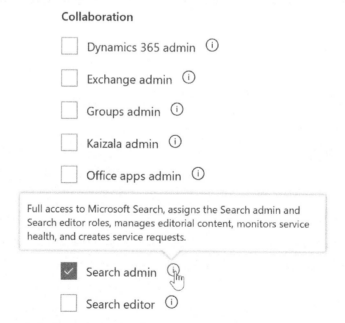

Figure 5.32 – Roles by category, specifically showing the Collaboration category options

6. Click **Save changes**.

How it works...

In this recipe, you visited the Microsoft 365 admin center to assign a user as a search admin.

Adding users as search *editors* allows those users to create/edit/delete content such as bookmarks, locations, and Q&A results in Microsoft Search as discussed in this chapter.

Adding users as search *admins* allows them to not only create/edit/delete content in Microsoft Search but also manage the assignment of search roles for others, monitor service health, and create service requests.

See also

- Learn more about assigning the search admin and editor roles at `https://docs.microsoft.com/en-us/microsoftsearch/setup-microsoft-search#step-1-assign-search-admin-and-search-editor`.

Setting up the usage of Microsoft Search in Bing

In this recipe, we'll discover how users in your organization can get internal results alongside their normal internet results when searching using Bing.

Getting ready

You must be a global admin or search admin to complete the steps in this recipe.

How to do it...

1. Go to the Microsoft Search admin center at `https://admin.microsoft.com/Adminportal/Home#/MicrosoftSearch` or by selecting **All Admin Centers | Microsoft Search** from the left-side navigation menu of the Microsoft 365 admin center.

2. Select **Configurations** from the top navigation menu.

3. Click **Edit** beneath **Change Microsoft Search in Bing settings**:

Change Microsoft Search in Bing settings

Users in your organization will be able to get work results along with internet results when searching on Bing. It may take up to 24 hours to see changes.

Edit

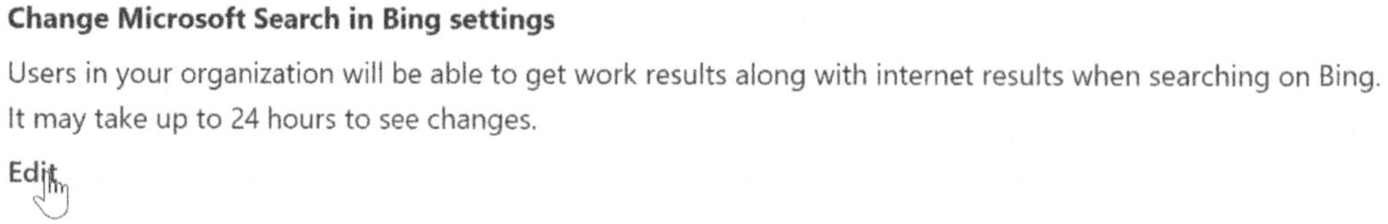

Figure 5.33 – The Change Microsoft Search in Bing settings Edit link

4. If it is not already toggled on, switch the **Allow your organization to use Microsoft Search in Bing** toggle to the on (blue) position:

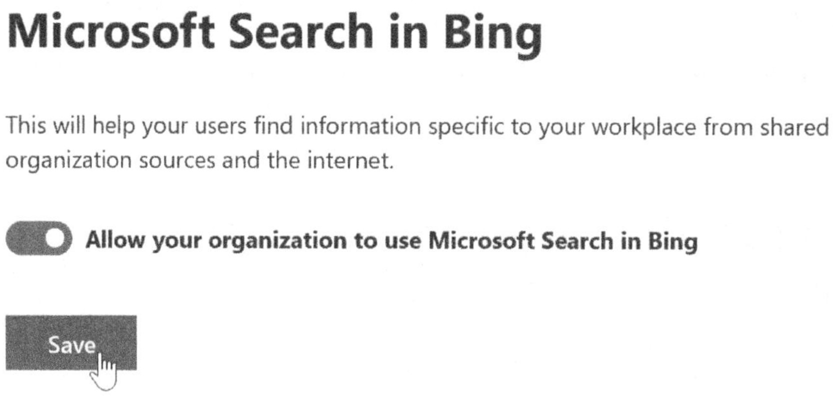

Microsoft Search in Bing

This will help your users find information specific to your workplace from shared organization sources and the internet.

🔵 **Allow your organization to use Microsoft Search in Bing**

Figure 5.34 – The Microsoft Search in Bing toggle option

5. Click **Save**.

How it works...

You've just prepared your organization for the incorporation of internal results in Bing searches.

These steps only enable your users to get organization results alongside their Bing results. Users must then follow the steps in the *There's more* section of this recipe to opt in.

There's more

Let's see how you and your organization's users can now enable Bing to show search results from your organization when searching in the browser:

1. Go to http://bing.com.

2. If you are not already signed in, select **Sign in**. Otherwise, skip to *step 4*:

Figure 5.35 – Bing loaded in a browser, showing the Sign in option

3. Sign in using your organization/work credentials:

Figure 5.36 – The sign-in screen

4. Once you search for something, click **Show results from OrganizationName**:

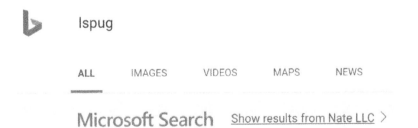

Figure 5.37 – Bing search results with a link to find results within our organization

5. If there are internal results, they will be shown in a shaded section at the top of the public Bing results:

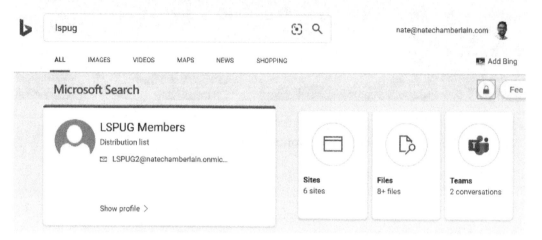

Figure 5.38 – Internal organization results shown above the public results

See also

- Learn more about Microsoft Search results in Bing at `https://support.microsoft.com/en-us/office/find-what-you-need-with-microsoft-search-in-bing-0b64be13-f20f-4e17-82b6-4deaea4940fb?ui=en-us&rs=en-us&ad=us`.

Using Search Insights dashboard reports

The Microsoft Search Insights dashboard only shows Microsoft Search in Bing data (see the previous recipe). This data can still be helpful, providing a glimpse into how your organization's users are interacting with internal results via Bing. In this recipe, we'll cover how to access this dashboard.

Getting ready

You must be a global admin, search admin, or search editor to complete the steps in this recipe.

How to do it...

1. Go to the Microsoft Search admin center at `https://admin.microsoft.com/Adminportal/Home#/MicrosoftSearch` or by selecting **All Admin Centers | Microsoft Search** from the left-side navigation menu of the Microsoft 365 admin center.

2. Your default landing screen is the Insights dashboard. Here, you can filter top searches overall or by category:

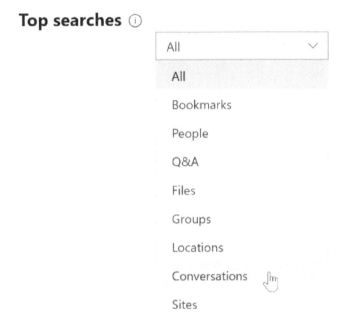

Figure 5.39 – The Microsoft Search Top searches drop-down options

3. You'll also find impression distribution by result type (seen in the dropdown in the previous step) over time along the right side of the dashboard, showing trends or spikes in activity that can potentially correlate with content creation/ management activities.

How it works...

You've discovered Search Insights in this recipe. If you've enabled Microsoft Search in Bing (see the previous recipe), your organization's users can view internal results alongside public Bing results when searching for information. Insights lets you know the clickthrough rate of your organization results on Bing result search pages.

See also

- Learn more about Insights dashboard reports at `https://docs.microsoft.com/en-us/microsoftsearch/get-insights`.

6
Administering OneDrive

OneDrive is **Office 365 (O365)**'s solution for individual users' storage space. While SharePoint is best for team file collaboration, OneDrive provides personal storage and enables productivity on a personal level. In this chapter, we will dive into important settings that enable users to remain productive and creative while still operating within secure boundaries set by administrators. We will manage the default settings and take a look at migrating data from local network locations to OneDrive.

In this chapter, we'll cover the following OneDrive recipes:

- Enabling the local syncing of files
- Restricting local syncing to PCs on specific domains
- Setting up compliance safeguards
- Providing manager access to a terminated employee's OneDrive
- Setting the default share link type
- Configuring external sharing permission levels
- Restricting sharing to specific domains

- Adjusting all users' default storage allocation and retention periods
- Restricting OneDrive access to devices on specific IP address locations
- Configuring mobile app permissions
- Migrating data using the SharePoint Migration Tool

Technical requirements

You'll need to be a SharePoint or global admin to complete the recipes in this chapter.

Enabling the local syncing of files

This recipe will demonstrate how you can allow/disallow the syncing of OneDrive files from online to local machines. Note that this affects SharePoint sync abilities as well.

Getting ready

You must be a global or SharePoint administrator to access the OneDrive admin center.

How to do it...

1. Go to https://admin.onedrive.com.
2. Select **Sync** from the left-side navigation menu:

Figure 6.1 – The Sync option in the left-hand navigation menu of the OneDrive admin center

3. Choose how you want users to be able to sync files from your organization by checking/unchecking the first box, labeled **Show the Sync button on the OneDrive website**:

Sync

Use these settings to control syncing of files in OneDrive and SharePoint.
Download the sync client
Fix sync problems

☑ Show the Sync button on the OneDrive website

☑ Allow syncing only on PCs joined to specific domains

        Enter each domain as a GUID on a new line.

☐ Block sync on Mac OS

☑ Block syncing of specific file types

        Enter each file extension on a new line.

Save

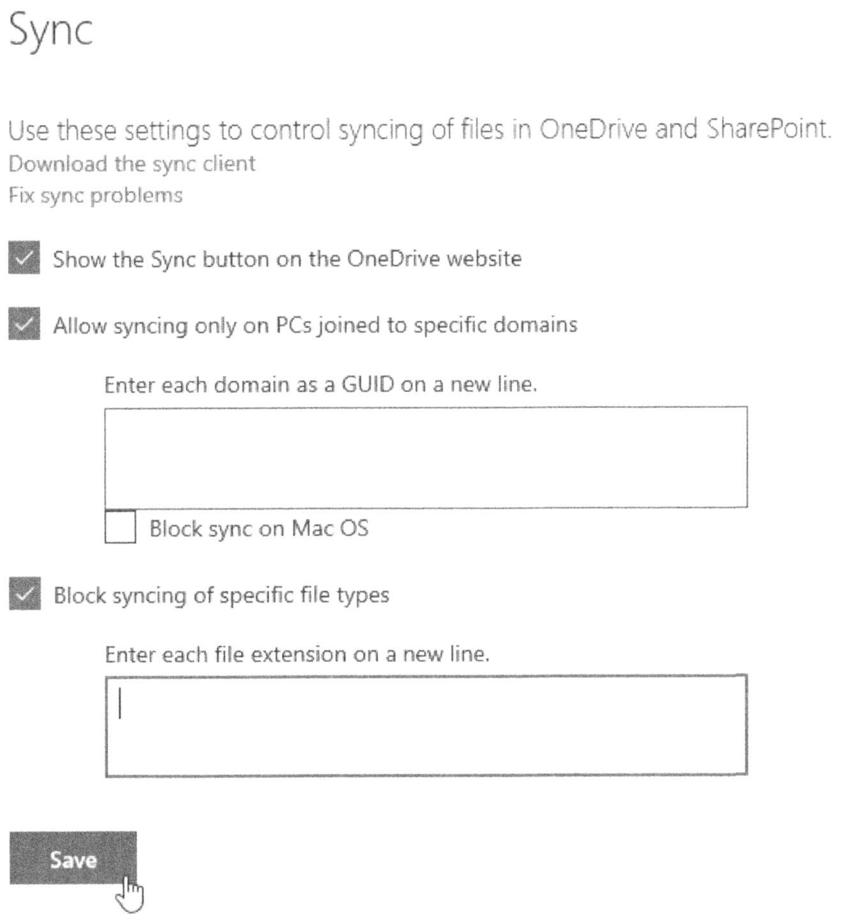

Figure 6.2 – Option to show the Sync button for OneDrive enabled

4. Click **Save**.

How it works...

You've just ensured users will see the **Sync** button on their OneDrive sites. Once you've made sure that the **Sync** button is visible for users (and device management images allow the OneDrive sync client on machines), users will be able to sync their OneDrive library to their machine. This allows convenient File Explorer access to OneDrive files both online and offline without the need to use a browser.

See also

- Read about common OneDrive sync issues at `https://support.office.com/en-us/article/fix-onedrive-sync-problems-0899b115-05f7-45ec-95b2-e4cc8c4670b2`.

- Learn much more about syncing OneDrive at `https://docs.microsoft.com/en-us/onedrive/one-drive-sync`.

Restricting local syncing to PCs on specific domains

In this recipe, we'll get more granular and make sure only users attempting to sync their OneDrive from specific domain addresses can do so. Note that this affects SharePoint sync abilities as well.

Getting ready

You must be a global or SharePoint administrator to access the OneDrive admin center.

How to do it...

1. Go to `https://admin.onedrive.com`.

2. Select **Sync** from the left-side navigation menu:

Figure 6.3 – The Sync option in the left-hand navigation menu of the OneDrive admin center

3. Check the second checkbox, labeled **Allow syncing only on PCs joined to specific domains**. Enter the GUIDs for allowed domains in the box that appears (one per line, as directed):

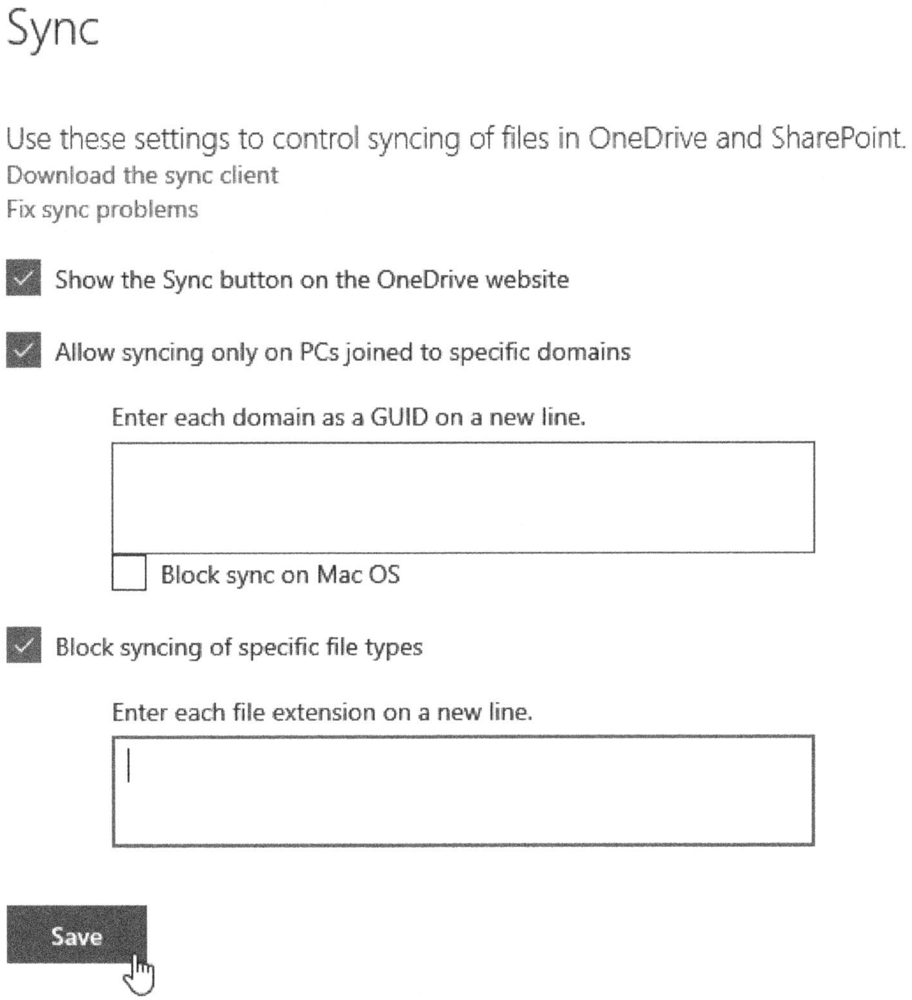

Sync

Use these settings to control syncing of files in OneDrive and SharePoint.
Download the sync client
Fix sync problems

✓ Show the Sync button on the OneDrive website

✓ Allow syncing only on PCs joined to specific domains

Enter each domain as a GUID on a new line.

☐ Block sync on Mac OS

✓ Block syncing of specific file types

Enter each file extension on a new line.

Save

Figure 6.4 – The Sync option for allowing syncing on devices joined to specific domains

4. Click **Save**.

How it works...

In this recipe, you configured the sync settings in the OneDrive admin center to only allow syncing on PCs joined to a list of domains you specified. Once those domains' GUIDs are added, users must be on one of the listed domains to be able to sync files in OneDrive and SharePoint.

See also

- Read about common OneDrive sync issues at `https://support.office.com/en-us/article/fix-onedrive-sync-problems-0899b115-05f7-45ec-95b2-e4cc8c4670b2`.

- Learn more about syncing OneDrive at `https://docs.microsoft.com/en-us/onedrive/one-drive-sync`.

Setting up compliance safeguards

Compliance is a deep and important topic that can't be covered fully in a single recipe. In this recipe, we'll simply cover accessing compliance settings and ideas relating to OneDrive specifically. Check out the final three chapters of the book for more general O365 security and compliance recipes.

Getting ready

You should be a SharePoint or global admin, and in some cases, you may need additional permissions depending on what specific compliance tasks you'd like to complete.

How to do it...

1. Go to the OneDrive admin center at `https://admin.onedrive.com`.

2. Click on **Compliance** in the left-side navigation menu.

3. Review all of the OneDrive compliance activities you can perform, shown in the following screenshot, noting that all of them will redirect you to the O365 Security & Compliance Center (`https://protection.office.com`):

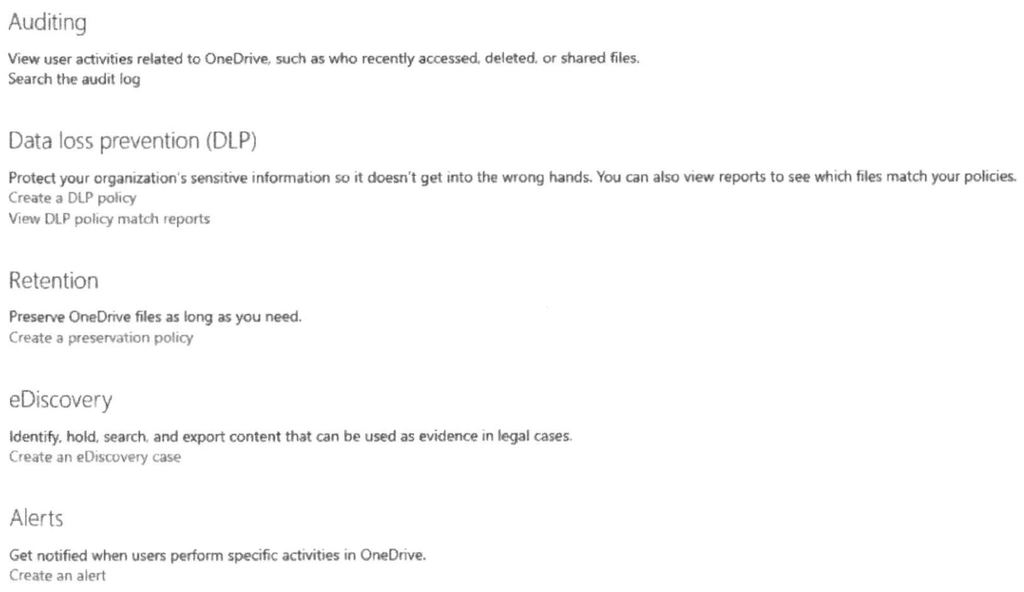

Auditing

View user activities related to OneDrive, such as who recently accessed, deleted, or shared files.
Search the audit log

Data loss prevention (DLP)

Protect your organization's sensitive information so it doesn't get into the wrong hands. You can also view reports to see which files match your policies.
Create a DLP policy
View DLP policy match reports

Retention

Preserve OneDrive files as long as you need.
Create a preservation policy

eDiscovery

Identify, hold, search, and export content that can be used as evidence in legal cases.
Create an eDiscovery case

Alerts

Get notified when users perform specific activities in OneDrive.
Create an alert

Figure 6.5 – Compliance settings linked in the OneDrive admin center

How it works...

In this recipe, you discovered where you can find quick links to the compliance settings in the O365 Security & Compliance Center. The listed settings include descriptions of how the settings can specifically apply to OneDrive. Once you click over to the O365 Security & Compliance Center, you can implement compliance safeguards specifically pertaining to OneDrive access and usage.

Providing manager access to a terminated employee's OneDrive

After an employee leaves your organization, their OneDrive is scheduled for deletion. Before it's gone, it's common to provide that employee's manager with access to their OneDrive in case there are business-critical documents or resources there that need to be relocated for others to use. In this recipe, you'll learn how to provide managers with access to their former employees' OneDrive sites.

Getting ready

You must be a global or SharePoint administrator to complete these steps within the SharePoint admin center.

How to do it...

1. Go to the SharePoint admin center at `https://YOURTENANT-admin.sharepoint.com`.

2. Select **More features** from the left-side navigation menu:

Figure 6.6 – The More features option in the SharePoint admin center's left-hand navigation menu

3. Under **User profiles**, click the **Open** button:

User profiles

Add and remove admins for a user's OneDrive, disable OneDrive creation for some users, and more. Learn more

Figure 6.7 – The Open button to access the User profiles settings

4. Under **My Site Settings**, click **Setup My Sites**:

Figure 6.8 – The Setup My Sites option on the User Profiles settings page

5. Scroll down to the **My Site Cleanup** section. Make sure the box for **Enable access delegation** is checked (automatically delegates the OneDrive site to the user's manager upon termination) and set a secondary owner (which applies to all OneDrive sites):

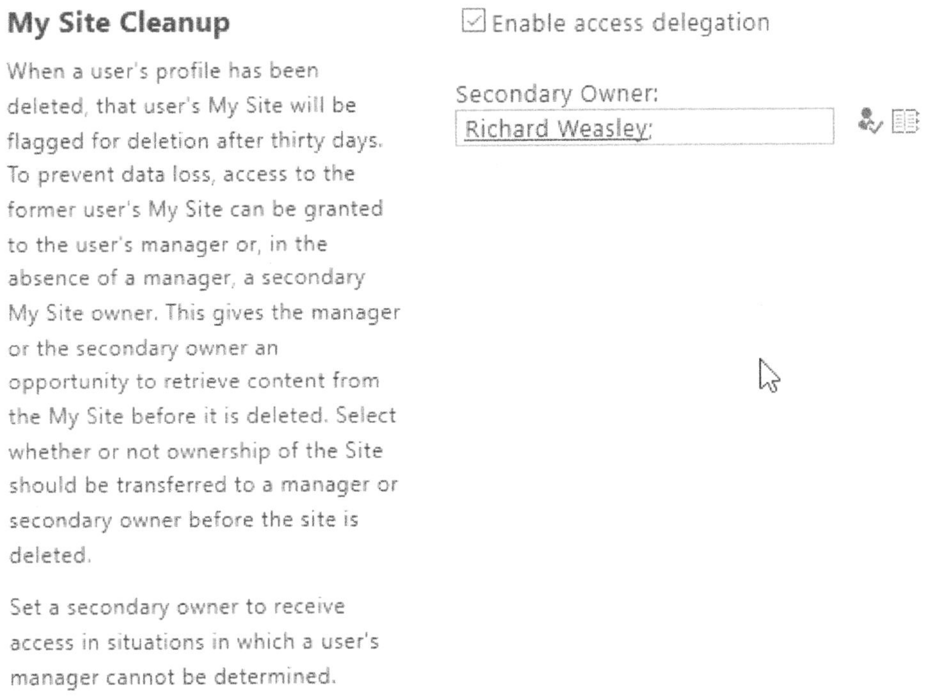

My Site Cleanup

When a user's profile has been deleted, that user's My Site will be flagged for deletion after thirty days. To prevent data loss, access to the former user's My Site can be granted to the user's manager or, in the absence of a manager, a secondary My Site owner. This gives the manager or the secondary owner an opportunity to retrieve content from the My Site before it is deleted. Select whether or not ownership of the Site should be transferred to a manager or secondary owner before the site is deleted.

Set a secondary owner to receive access in situations in which a user's manager cannot be determined.

☑ Enable access delegation

Secondary Owner:

Richard Weasley;

Figure 6.9 – The My Site Cleanup configuration options

6. Scroll down to the bottom and click **OK**.

How it works...

You've just set OneDrive sites to be automatically delegated to a user's manager when that employee leaves the company. For situations where a manager isn't configured for an employee or it is unclear, the secondary owner is granted permission. Whoever is delegated will receive an email notice of access with a link to the user's OneDrive content.

There's more

You can also do this manually, instead of automatically, by deleting a user via the Microsoft 365 admin center's **Active Users** pane. When this is done, you'll be prompted to provide another user who should have access to that user's OneDrive for 30 days. Whoever is delegated will receive an email notice of access with a link to the user's OneDrive content.

See also

- Check Microsoft's documentation on this topic at `https://docs.microsoft.com/en-us/onedrive/retention-and-deletion#configure-automatic-access-delegation`.

Setting the default share link type

When users choose to share a file from their OneDrive with other people (whether internal or external to the organization and depending on what you've allowed external sharing), they're presented with a default share link type upon clicking **Share**. You can choose what kind of link is presented to the user by default to make it easier to make the most appropriate choice for your organization's sharing habits. In this recipe, we'll set the default share link type to **Direct** so that the link that is generated and sent to others can only be opened (and possibly modified) by the intended recipients.

Getting ready

You must be a global or SharePoint administrator to access the OneDrive admin center.

How to do it...

1. Go to the OneDrive admin center at `https://admin.onedrive.com`.

2. Click on **Sharing** in the left-side navigation menu.

3. Change the radio button selection under **Links** to **Direct: Specific people**:

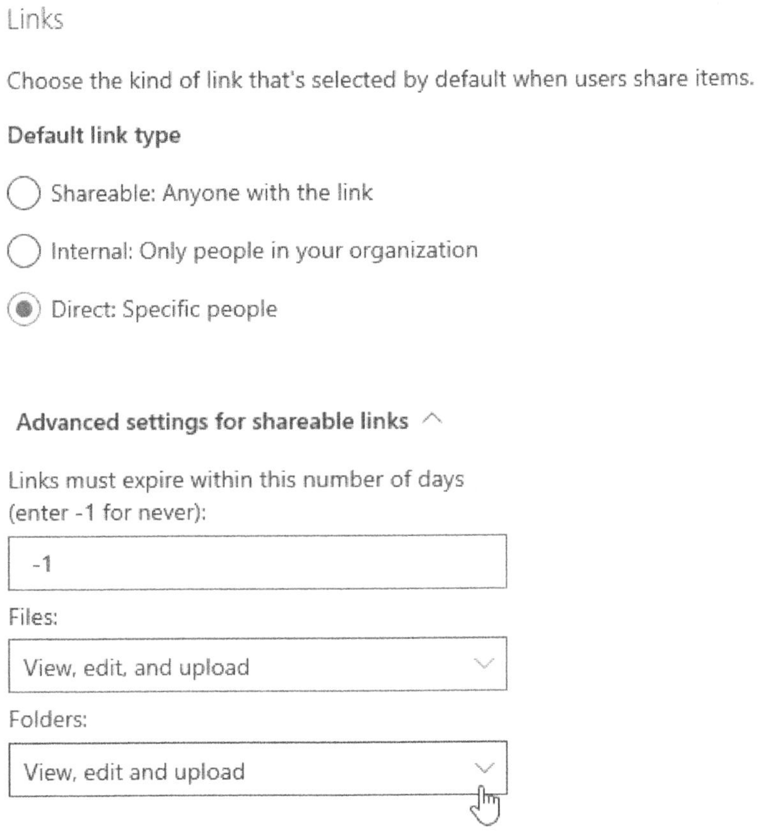

Figure 6.10 – The default share link type options

4. Click **Save**.

How it works...

You've just configured OneDrive's sharing settings so that users sharing their files and folders will be presented with a default link type when sharing that asks for specific names of individuals with whom to share the content. They can change this, but you've made it easier for them to make the preferred choice and avoid the potential risk of data loss:

Figure 6.11 – Example of a share dialog with the new default settings implemented

Configuring external sharing permission levels

External sharing in OneDrive (and SharePoint) allows your users to open access to specific documents and content to users outside your organization's directory. As an admin, you can control the level to which this is possible, including blocking anonymous sharing or requiring that the external user be added to the organization's directory before they can access the content.

In this recipe, we'll go through the steps to review and adjust the OneDrive external sharing settings from the OneDrive admin center.

Getting ready

You must be a global or SharePoint administrator to access the OneDrive admin center.

How to do it...

1. Go to the OneDrive admin center at `https://admin.onedrive.com`.

2. Select **Sharing** from the left-side navigation menu.

3. Scroll down to the **External sharing** section.

4. Slide the OneDrive slider to the desired level of allowed external sharing that you want to set, as shown in the following screenshot:

Figure 6.12 – External sharing levels for SharePoint and OneDrive

5. Expand **Advanced settings for external sharing** and select the appropriate options there for additional sharing configuration in your organization:

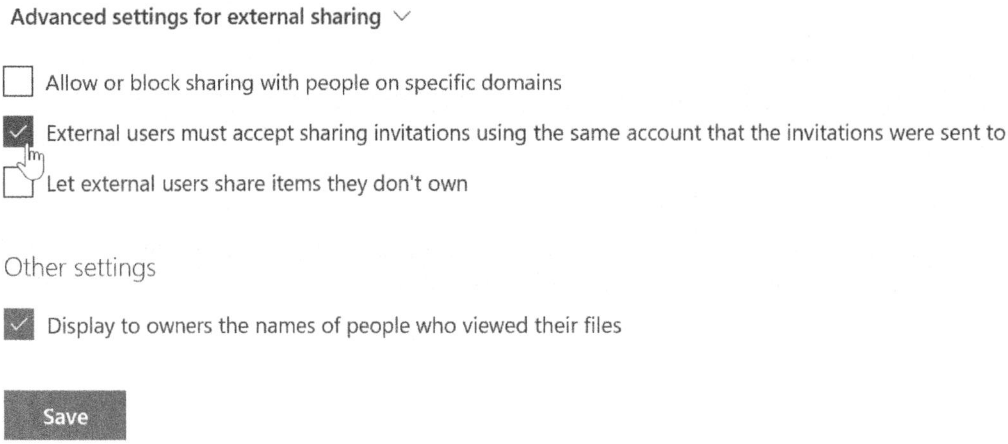

Advanced settings for external sharing ∨

☐ Allow or block sharing with people on specific domains

☑ External users must accept sharing invitations using the same account that the invitations were sent to

☐ Let external users share items they don't own

Other settings

☑ Display to owners the names of people who viewed their files

Save

Figure 6.13 – Advanced settings for external sharing

6. Click **Save**.

How it works...

We've just adjusted the organization-wide settings for all OneDrive users to help ensure the proper governance and compliance of content and communication within (and outside of) the organization's virtual boundaries.

> **Important note**
>
> These settings also apply to SharePoint. In SharePoint, site admins can apply *stricter* sharing settings, but these (at the global level) provide a baseline sharing level for *all* sites that cannot be made less restrictive at a specific site level.
>
> Your OneDrive external sharing slider level cannot be more permissive than your SharePoint external sharing slider level.

See also

*   Read more about managing sharing in OneDrive and SharePoint at https://docs.microsoft.com/en-us/onedrive/manage-sharing.

Restricting sharing to specific domains

In the previous recipe, we covered how to configure external sharing abilities within OneDrive and SharePoint. Part of doing so is considering the restriction of external sharing to people on specific domains. For example, you may wish to block users in your organization from sharing files with your top competitors' domain, or you may wish to only allow sharing with brand domains that fall under a parent company umbrella.

In this recipe, we'll cover how to restrict external sharing to specific domains we trust and know our users need to collaborate with regularly.

Getting ready

You must be a global or SharePoint administrator to access the OneDrive admin center.

How to do it...

1. Go to the OneDrive admin center at `https://admin.onedrive.com`.

2. Select **Sharing** from the left-side navigation menu.

3. Scroll down to the **External sharing** section.

4. Expand **Advanced settings for external sharing**.

5. Check the box for **Allow or block sharing with people on specific domains**:

Figure 6.14 – The Allow or block external sharing based on domain option

Since we're choosing to only *allow* sharing to specific domains, we'll leave the dropdown on allow.

6. In the **Enter each domain on a new line** box, enter a list of the allowable domains for sharing and collaboration:

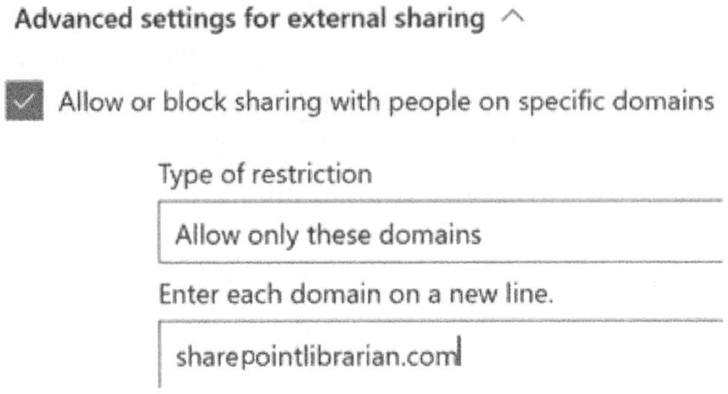

Advanced settings for external sharing ⌃

☑ Allow or block sharing with people on specific domains

Type of restriction

Allow only these domains

Enter each domain on a new line.

sharepointlibrarian.com

Figure 6.15 – Domain specification for the allow or block by domain setting in external sharing

7. Click **Save**.

How it works...

You've just used the OneDrive admin center to restrict the sharing of OneDrive files to specific domains only. Once domains have been explicitly listed for allowing or blocking, users who receive a link (including **Anyone with the link can edit link**) will have to sign in to their domain to validate that they're eligible/allowed to access the shared content.

> **Important note**
> Remember that these sharing settings also apply to SharePoint.

See also

- Check out more information on restricting the sharing of content by domain at `https://docs.microsoft.com/en-us/sharepoint/restricted-domains-sharing`.

Adjusting all users' default storage allocation and retention periods

In this recipe, we'll cover a simple but important setting in the OneDrive admin center that allows setting the default storage limit for individual users' OneDrive sites, as well as the retention period for which those sites should be kept after the associated user is marked for deletion.

Getting ready

You must be a global or SharePoint administrator to access the OneDrive admin center.

How to do it...

1. Go to the OneDrive admin center at `https://admin.onedrive.com`.

2. Select **Storage** from the left-side navigation menu.

3. Enter a number (in/GB) in the **Default storage in GB** box that represents the maximum amount all users can save in their OneDrive site. Then, enter a number (in days) in the **Days to retain files in OneDrive after a user account is marked for deletion** box that represents how long files will be kept once their associated owner is marked for deletion:

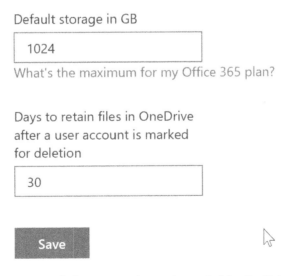

Figure 6.16 – Default storage and retention period for OneDrive sites

4. Click **Save**.

How it works...

The default storage space for users is `1024` GB, or 1 TB. You could, in many license/user scenarios, increase this up to 5 TB (`5120` GB). If you decrease the allowed space but there are users who will already have more than the new maximum, their OneDrive sites will be marked as read-only.

While the default retention period is 30 days, this can be increased to up to 10 years (3,650 days).

See also

- Learn more about setting the default storage allocation at `https://docs.microsoft.com/en-us/onedrive/set-default-storage-space`.

- Read more about adjusting the default retention period for a user's content once they've been marked for deletion at `https://docs.microsoft.com/en-us/onedrive/set-retention`.

Restricting OneDrive access to devices on specific IP address locations

Depending on your organization's industry and compliance requirements, it may be helpful to know how you can restrict OneDrive access to only those devices connecting from approved IP addresses. In this recipe, we'll specify the IP addresses from which we'll allow connections to OneDrive.

Getting ready

You must be a global or SharePoint administrator to access the OneDrive admin center.

How to do it...

1. Go to the OneDrive admin center at `https://admin.onedrive.com`.
2. Select **Device access** from the left-side navigation menu.
3. Check the box for **Allow access only from specific IP address locations**.

4. Enter the IP addresses, one per line, from which connected devices should be able to access OneDrive:

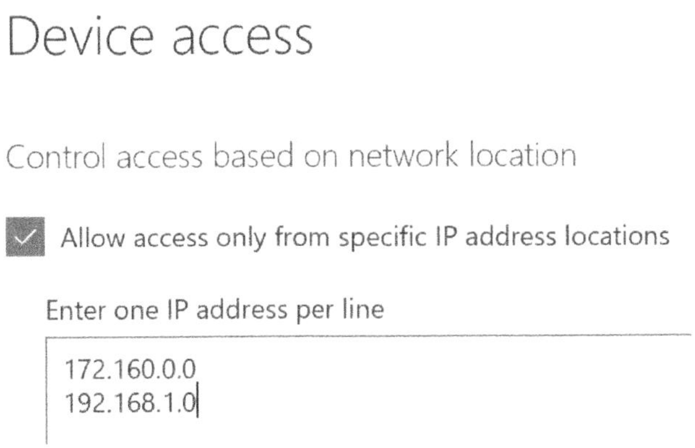

Device access

Control access based on network location

☑ Allow access only from specific IP address locations

Enter one IP address per line

172.160.0.0
192.168.1.0

Figure 6.17 – Allowed IP addresses configuration

5. Click **Save**.

How it works...

Once you've saved the list of approved IP addresses, users will receive an **Access restricted error** message when attempting to access OneDrive from an unlisted IP address. Note that this will not only prevent users from accessing OneDrive, but also the OneDrive admin center.

See also

*   Learn more about controlling access to OneDrive based on a device's IP address at `https://docs.microsoft.com/en-us/onedrive/control-access-based-on-network-location-or-app`.

Configuring mobile app permissions

You can control how users interact with organizational data via the OneDrive and SharePoint mobile apps. For example, you may wish to prevent users from taking screenshots, copying and pasting organizational data, downloading files to their device storage, or more. In this recipe, we'll specify those restrictions as a policy in the OneDrive admin center.

Getting ready

You must be a global or SharePoint administrator to access the OneDrive admin center.

How to do it...

1. Go to the OneDrive admin center at `https://admin.onedrive.com`.

2. Select **Device access** from the left-side navigation menu.

3. Scroll down to the **Mobile application management** section.

4. Check the boxes for any settings that help users adhere to the compliance and security policies deployed by your organization:

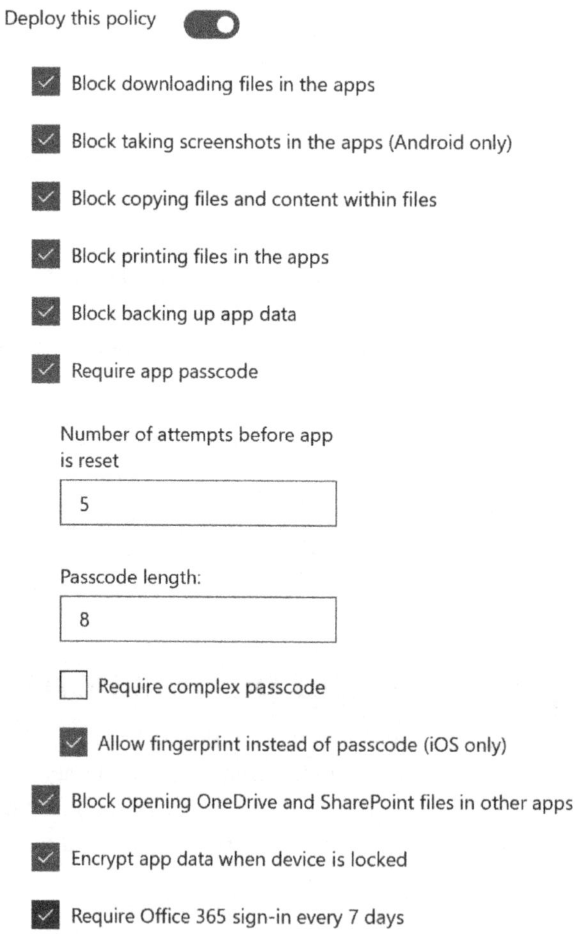

Deploy this policy

☑ Block downloading files in the apps

☑ Block taking screenshots in the apps (Android only)

☑ Block copying files and content within files

☑ Block printing files in the apps

☑ Block backing up app data

☑ Require app passcode

Number of attempts before app is reset

> 5

Passcode length:

> 8

☐ Require complex passcode

☑ Allow fingerprint instead of passcode (iOS only)

☑ Block opening OneDrive and SharePoint files in other apps

☑ Encrypt app data when device is locked

☑ Require Office 365 sign-in every 7 days

Figure 6.18 – Mobile app permissions policy settings

5. Specify a time limit after which user access should be reverified, and at which point app data should be wiped for offline devices:

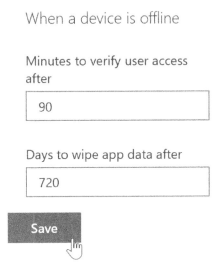

When a device is offline

Minutes to verify user access after

90

Days to wipe app data after

720

Save

Figure 6.19 – Offline device settings

6. Click **Save**.

How it works...

The policy you specify in the OneDrive admin center comes second to anything deployed via Intune (mobile device management), and will also not affect personal accounts that users may have also added to the OneDrive app. The policy we designed in this recipe will only apply to the data within our organization accessed via the OneDrive mobile app.

See also

- Read more about controlling access to particular features in the OneDrive mobile app at `https://docs.microsoft.com/en-us/onedrive/control-access-to-mobile-app-features`.

Migrating data using the SharePoint Migration Tool

You can use the SharePoint Migration Tool to migrate content from your network or local file shares to OneDrive. In this recipe, we'll do just that, migrating content from a local file to our OneDrive.

Getting ready

- You must be a global administrator to perform migrations, or at least have appropriate permissions to both source and destination sites.

- You must download and install the SharePoint Migration Tool at `https://aka.ms/spmt-ga-page`.

How to do it...

1. Launch the SharePoint Migration Tool and sign in to your O365 tenant when prompted.

2. If you haven't used the tool before, select **Start your first migration**. Otherwise, choose **Start new migration**.

3. Select **File Share** for this recipe. Note you could also prepare a CSV file to map bulk sources and destinations for bulk migration.

4. Click **Choose folder**.

5. Select a folder and click **Next**:

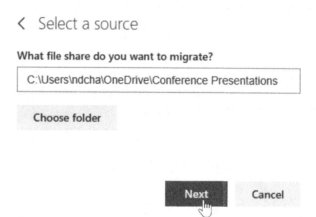

Figure 6.20 – File share location to be migrated

6. Copy and paste the URL to your OneDrive, deleting _layouts and everything that follows from the URL. **Documents** (the top-level folder of your OneDrive) is selected by default, but you could select a subfolder if you wish:

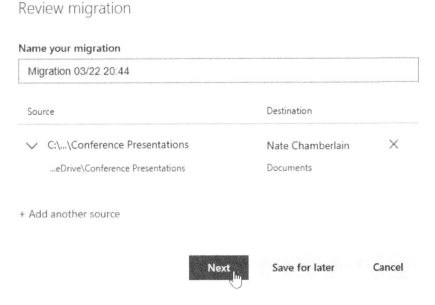

Figure 6.21 – The destination site to which the files will be migrated

7. Click **Next**.

8. You can choose to add additional sources (if you're migrating multiple folders to this single OneDrive location). Click **Next** when ready:

Review migration

Name your migration

Migration 03/22 20:44

Source	Destination
⌄ C:\...\Conference Presentations	Nate Chamberlain ✕
...eDrive\Conference Presentations	Documents

+ Add another source

Next   Save for later   Cancel

Figure 6.22 – The name migration task screen with the option to add another source

9. Review the settings and adjust if needed, then select **Migrate**:

Choose your settings
Basic settings
Only perform scanning
Off
Preserve file share permissions
Off
Migrate file version history
On
Azure Active Directory lookup
On
View all settings
Migrate
Cancel

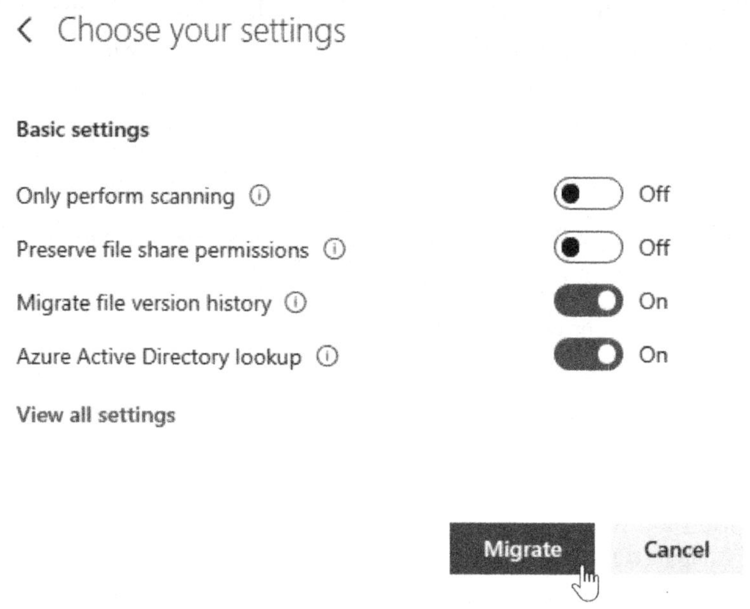

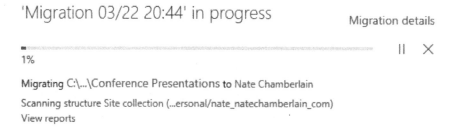

Figure 6.23 – Migration settings and migration initiation screen

10. Wait for the migration to complete:

'Migration 03/22 20:44' in progress
Migration details
1%
Migrating C:\...\Conference Presentations to Nate Chamberlain
Scanning structure Site collection (...ersonal/nate_natechamberlain_com)
View reports

Figure 6.24 – Migration status

11. Once complete, choose **Save** and close the SharePoint Migration Tool:

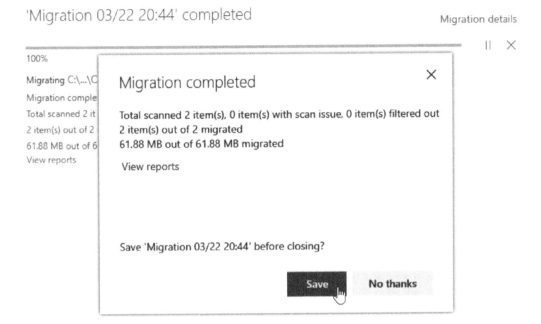

Figure 6.25 – The Migration completed dialog with the results data

How it works...

In this recipe, we used the SharePoint Migration Tool to move a local folder and its contents to our OneDrive. The SharePoint Migration Tool can help move local content from traditional file shares or network drives to OneDrive. It can, of course, be used for SharePoint migrations as well, but this recipe focuses specifically on OneDrive sites.

The migration of content doesn't delete it from the source location – it simply copies it and retains metadata (such as the last modified date) where possible. Changes made to the source file will not sync to the newly migrated (copied) file.

Because you can select multiple sources for a single destination, you can consolidate several existing locations into a single, final location in OneDrive.

> **Important note**
>
> Chances are, you won't often be migrating content to just one OneDrive site at a time. Learn how to format the JSON or CSV file for bulk migrations at `https://docs.microsoft.com/en-us/sharepointmigration/how-to-format-your-csv-file-for-data-content-migration`.

See also

Learn more about the SharePoint Migration Tool at `https://aka.ms/SPMT-LearnMore`.

7
Configuring the Power Platform

The Power Platform is an industry leader in dynamic data visualization, automation, and app experiences. They work together, and independently, to deliver innovative solutions for nearly any business problem. Power BI delivers dynamic data reporting and dashboarding. Power Automate (formerly Microsoft Flow) delivers robotic process automation and data transformation and movement based on triggers and schedules. Power Apps allows the customization of SharePoint forms and the creation of independent apps and forms.

In this chapter, we'll learn how to administer important settings for each of the Power Platform services, specifically covering the following recipes:

- Creating a new Power Platform environment
- Restricting certain connectors in Power Apps and Power Automate from accessing business data
- Installing an on-premises data gateway
- Restricting users from installing on-premises data gateways
- Auditing Power BI embed codes created by your organization
- Restricting Power BI's Publish to Web (anonymous share) ability to specific security group members
- Restricting the external sharing of Power BI reports
- Configuring a default logo, cover image, and theme for Power BI
- Creating a Common Data Service database

Technical requirements

Most of the recipes in this chapter will require you to be a global or Power Platform service administrator. You'll most likely also require licensing to Power BI, Power Apps, and/or Power Automate if you don't already have it unless you're working on a trial license.

Creating a new Power Platform environment

A Power Platform environment provides a place for your organization to centrally manage and share its data and processes. You might also use a Power Platform environment as a security boundary to separate processes and apps that require different levels of data protection. In this recipe, we'll create a new Power Platform environment with a new database by utilizing the Power Platform admin center.

Getting ready

In order to complete the steps in this recipe, you must have a Dynamics 365, Power Apps, or Power Virtual Agents plan (trial or production) and be a global or Power Platform service admin or have settings configured so that non-admins can also create environments.

You'll also need 1 GB of storage capacity to complete these steps. Learn more about capacity plans at `https://docs.microsoft.com/en-us/power-platform/admin/capacity-storage`.

How to do it...

1. Go to the Power Platform admin center at `https://admin.powerplatform.microsoft.com`.

2. Select **New**:

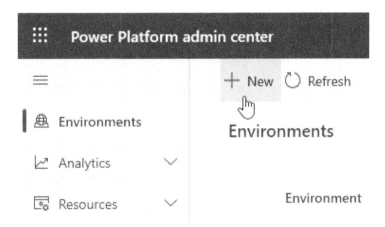

Figure 7.1 – The New button on the Environments screen of the Power Platform admin center

3. Configure the name, environment type, region, and purpose of the environment. Change **Create a database for this environment?** to the *on* position:

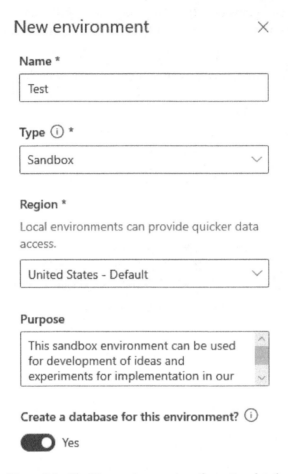

Figure 7.2 – The New environment configuration details

4. Click **Next**.

5. Configure the database-specific options available to you (**Language**, **Currency**, and so on):

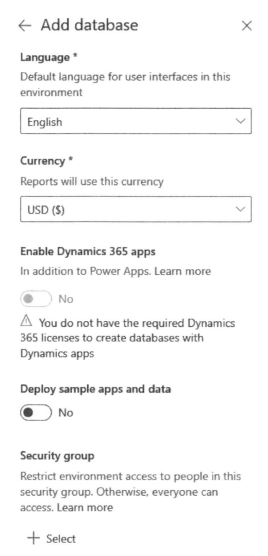

Figure 7.3 – The database configuration details for the new environment

6. Click **Save**.

How it works...

In this recipe, you created a new Power Platform environment via the Power Platform admin center. This can now be used to contain and manage apps, data, and flows.

There's more

If you wish to create a new Power Platform environment without a new database (because you have your own data store, perhaps), you'll just need to complete *steps 1–3* and click **Save**. Follow the instructions at `https://docs.microsoft.com/en-us/ power-platform/admin/create-environment#create-an-environment- without-a-database` for more assistance with this method.

See also

- For more information on creating Power Platform environments, check out `https://docs.microsoft.com/en-us/power-platform/admin/ create-environment`.

Restricting certain connectors in Power Apps and Power Automate from accessing business data

In this recipe, we'll cover the steps needed to prevent certain data connections in Power Platform apps from accessing business data.

Getting ready

You must be a global or Power Platform service administrator to complete the steps in this recipe.

How to do it...

1. Go to the Power Platform admin center at `https://admin.powerplatform.microsoft.com`.

2. Click on **Data policies** in the left-hand navigation menu:

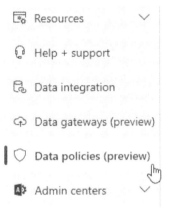

Figure 7.4 – The Data policies link in the left-hand navigation menu of the
Power Platform admin center

3. Click **New Policy**.

4. Name your policy and click **Next**:

Name your policy

Start by giving your new policy a name. You can change this later.

Figure 7.5 – The name field for the new data policy

5.   Find the connectors in the default category that should be restricted from sharing data with other connectors. We'll select **Dropbox** and then **Move to Business** for this demo:

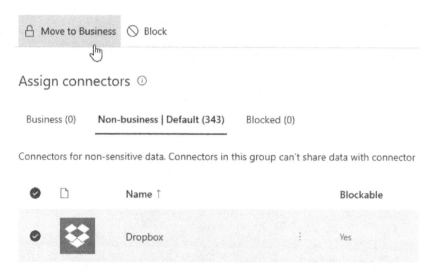

Figure 7.6 – The Dropbox connector selected and the Move to Business button highlighted

6.   Now, **Dropbox** appears in our **Business** group and cannot share data with connectors in the **Non-business** group. Click **Next**:

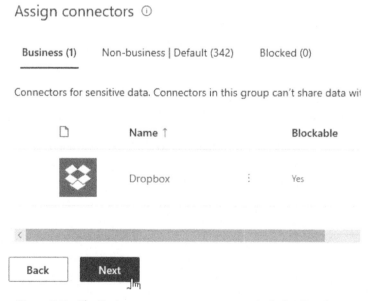

Figure 7.7 – The Business connectors group now includes Dropbox

7. Select the environments to which this policy will apply, then click **Next**:

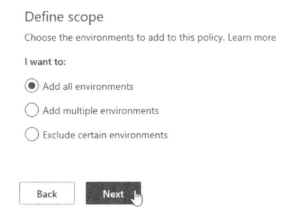

Figure 7.8 – Environment scope definition for connector restriction

8. Review the policy details, then click **Create policy**:

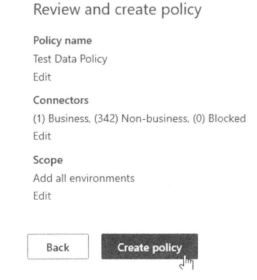

Figure 7.9 – The review screen and the Create policy button for a new policy

How it works...

You've just prevented the users in your organization that are using a data connection to Dropbox in Power Platform apps from transmitting data from Dropbox to any other connector. You can specify connectors as **Business** or **Non-business** in a policy, and data cannot travel between the two groups.

See also

- Learn more about data policies at `https://docs.microsoft.com/en-us/power-automate/prevent-data-loss`.

Installing an on-premises data gateway

On-premises data gateways allow users in your organization to connect Power Platform apps to on-premises data that is otherwise unavailable to the cloud-based apps. In this recipe, we'll install an on-premises data gateway on a server so that users can connect local data to Power Automate, Power BI, and Power Apps.

Getting ready

You'll need local admin access to a server that's always powered on. We'll install the gateway on this server, and the account you use to do so will automatically be made a gateway admin. It's recommended to use a service account if possible, but you can always change the service account used by the gateway later.

How to do it...

1. Log in to the server on which you'll install the gateway.

2. Navigate (and sign in if needed) to `app.powerbi.com` | the download icon | **Data Gateway**:

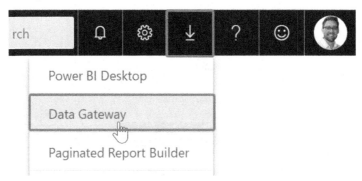

Figure 7.10 – The download Data Gateway option in Power BI

3. Select **Download standard mode**:

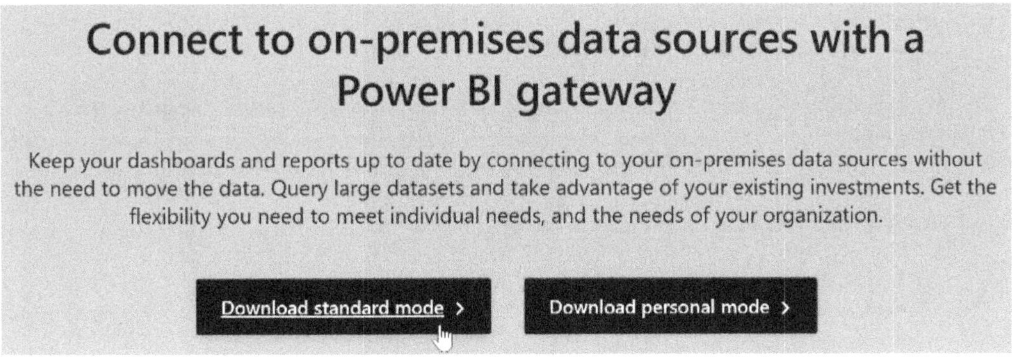

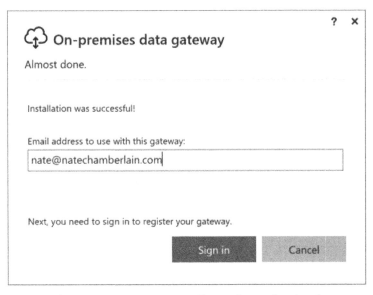

Figure 7.11 – The standard and personal mode options for gateways

4. Run the downloaded installer file, accepting the terms when prompted, and select **Install**.

5. When prompted, enter the admin or service account email to use for signing in and configuring the gateway. This account will automatically be made a gateway admin:

Figure 7.12 – Admin or service account email entry for configuring the new gateway

6.   Leave **Register a new gateway on this computer** selected and choose **Next**:

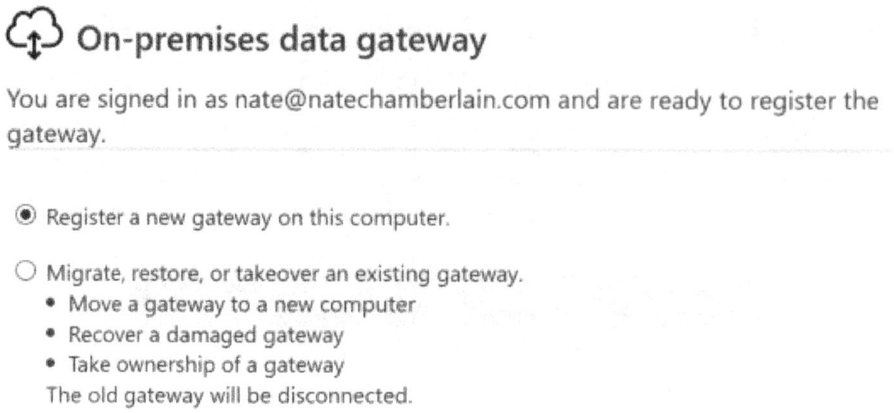

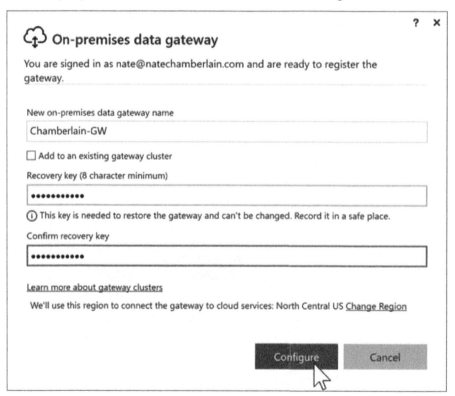

Figure 7.13 – Action options for the new gateway

7.   Name the gateway (this will appear to all the users it's shared with) and choose a recovery key to use for restoration if needed. Click **Configure**:

Figure 7.14 – Gateway name and recovery key configuration

8. When you receive a message that the gateway is online and ready, click **Close**:

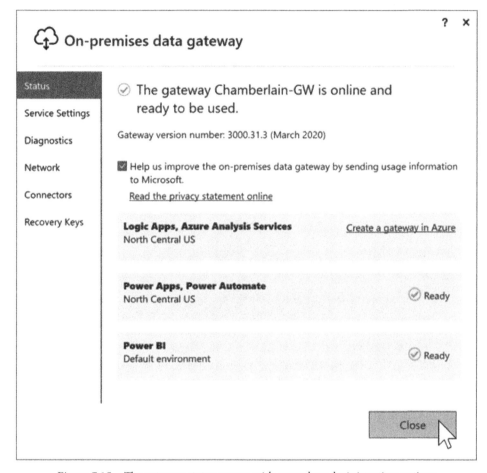

Figure 7.15 – The gateway status screen with everyday administration options

9.   Next, we'll share it with users and other admins so that they can utilize the organizational gateway. Go to the Power Platform admin center at `https://admin.powerplatform.microsoft.com/` and select **Data gateways** from the left-hand navigation menu:

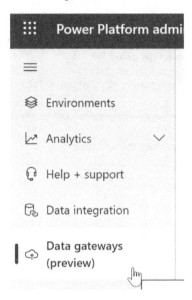

Figure 7.16 – The Data gateways link in the left-hand navigation menu of the
Power Platform admin center

10. Hover over the gateway you're managing, select the ellipsis menu, and click on **Manage users**:

Figure 7.17 – The Manage users link in the ellipsis menu of a gateway cluster

11. Search for and add individual users and/or security groups. For each one you add, you'll need to select it and decide whether the selected person/group can just use the gateway, use and share it, or administer the gateway. When you have finished, select **Share**.

12. You've now installed a gateway and made it available for others to use.

How it works...

You've just installed and shared an on-premises data gateway that can be used for the Power Platform. Since the gateway is installed and configured, you can now manage gateway users and admins via the Power Platform admin center going forward. If a user is granted the ability to use the gateway, it'll appear as an option when they attempt to connect to on-premises data through Power Automate, Power BI, or Power Apps.

There's more

Individual users can also install personal on-premises data gateways on their local machines to use when the machine is on and running a flow, report, or app on demand. Any scheduled runs or refreshes that are triggered when the machine is unavailable will fail.

In some cases, you may wish to restrict users from installing and using their own personal gateways. See the next recipe for instructions on how to accomplish this.

See also

- Always refer to the official documentation for the latest recommendations before initiating any major changes: `https://docs.microsoft.com/en-us/data-integration/gateway/service-gateway-install`.

- Learn how to make a gateway cluster for high availability/load balancing: `https://docs.microsoft.com/en-us/data-integration/gateway/service-gateway-high-availability-clusters`.

Restricting users from installing on-premises data gateways

You may wish to prevent users from installing their own on-premises data gateways from a governance standpoint, perhaps to better monitor and manage the environment, or perhaps it is preferable that users learn to use the shared gateway for better availability and consistency. Whatever your reasoning for wishing to make sure users cannot install their own gateways, this recipe will guide you through the necessary steps.

Getting ready

You must be an Azure **Active Directory (AD)** or **Office 365 (O365)** global admin or a Power BI service administrator to complete this recipe.

How to do it...

1. Go to the Power Platform admin center at `https://admin.powerplatform.microsoft.com/`.

2. Click on **Data gateways**:

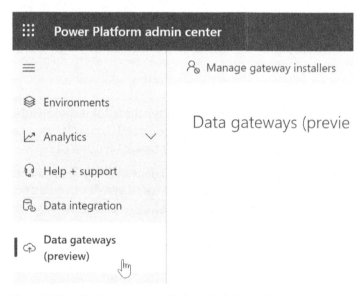

Figure 7.18 – The Data gateways link in the left-hand navigation menu of the Power Platform admin center

3. Click **Manage gateway installers**:

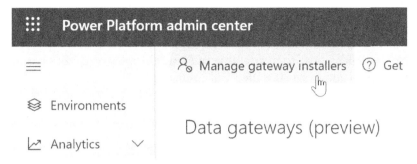

Figure 7.19 – The Manage gateway installers button on the Data gateways screen
of the Power Platform admin center

4. Toggle **Restrict users in your organization from installing gateways** to **On**:

Figure 7.20 – Option to restrict gateway installation to specific users

5. Add authorized users (groups not currently supported) who should be able
to continue installing any type of gateway:

Figure 7.21 – Configuration of users who may install gateways

How it works...

You've now restricted the installation of gateways to specific individuals. Restricting the installation of gateways makes sure individual users attempting to install a gateway won't be able to sign in to your organization through the gateway to access company data. In most cases, you would choose to restrict this and have these users use an organization-wide gateway that an admin has installed and configured.

See also

- Read more about restricting gateway installers in your organization at https://docs.microsoft.com/en-us/power-platform/admin/onpremises-data-gateway-management#manage-installers

Auditing Power BI embed codes created by your organization

Power BI users in your organization may, depending on the license type, be able to generate embed codes that, in some cases, allow anonymous access to data when published or shared outside the organization. As a Power Platform administrator, you should keep an eye on existing embed codes generated/used in your organization to stay familiar with the data potentially being shared and access beyond the security and compliance controls in your organization.

In this recipe, we'll cover the steps for auditing the Power BI embed codes in your organization.

Getting ready

You must be a global admin or Power BI service administrator to complete the steps in this recipe.

How to do it...

1. Go to Power BI at app.powerbi.com.
2. Select the settings wheel | **Admin portal**:

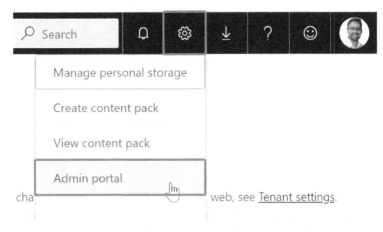

cha[...]web, see <u>Tenant settings</u>.

Figure 7.22 – The Admin portal link in Power BI

3. Select **Embed Codes** from the left-hand menu.

4. Select the ellipsis next to any embed code to either delete it or view the report on the web. You can also view who published it and its current status:

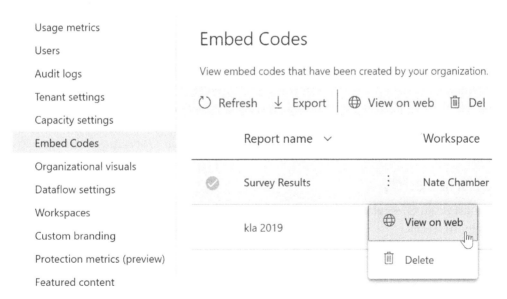

Figure 7.23 – The View on web option for an embed code's ellipsis menu

5. You can also choose **Export** for a CSV file of all report names, their workspace, their publisher, and their status.

How it works...

In this recipe, you learned how to manage embed codes generated by users in your organization. The Power BI admin portal allows Power BI service administrators to view and manage all existing embed codes in the organization. Administrators can delete public embed codes or just view the shared content to ensure it follows best practices and compliance policies. If you notice any private/confidential information in the shared reports, be sure to delete the relevant embed code(s) to end the sharing/publishing of that data immediately.

There's more

You can prevent embed codes from being created by adjusting your Power BI tenant settings, disabling the **Publish to web** setting, at `https://app.powerbi.com/admin-portal/tenantSettings`. See the next recipe, *Restricting Power BI's Publish to Web (anonymous share) ability to specific security group members*, for detailed steps.

Restricting Power BI's Publish to Web (anonymous share) ability to specific security group members

As mentioned in the previous recipe, users can create embed codes using an option called **Publish to Web**. Once this is done, administrators can view the generated codes/shared reports and choose to revoke the embed code. However, administrators can also choose to not allow this ability in the first place, reserving it for specific security group members (perhaps those that are trained in data sensitivity and compliance) instead. In this recipe, we'll cover the steps to restricting the **Publish to Web** option to specific security groups.

Getting ready

You must be an O365 global admin or Power BI service administrator to complete the steps in this recipe.

How to do it...

1. Go to Power BI at `app.powerbi.com`.

2. Select the settings wheel | **Admin portal**:

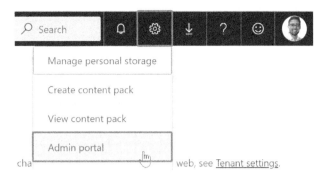

cha   web, see Tenant settings.

Figure 7.24 – The Admin portal link in Power BI

3. Select **Tenant settings** from the left-hand menu.

4. Scroll down to the **Publish to web** section. Change the options to **Allow existing and new codes** and **Specific security groups**, and enter the actual security groups that should be allowed to create new embed codes for public data report sharing:

◢ Publish to web ⓘ
Unapplied changes

People in your org can publish public reports on the web. Publicly published reports don't require authentication to view them.

Go to **Embed Codes** in the admin portal to review and manage public embed codes. If any of the codes contain private or confidential content remove them.

Review embed codes regularly to make sure no confidentail information is live on the web. Learn more about Publish to web

▢ Enabled

Choose how embed codes work
◯ Only allow existing codes
◉ Allow existing and new codes

Apply to:
◯ The entire organization
◉ Specific security groups

| O365 Group Creators ✕   Enter security groups |

▢ Except specific security groups

[Apply] [Cancel]

Figure 7.25 – Security groups allowed to create new embed codes

5. Click **Apply**.

How it works...

These steps make it so that approved security groups are the only ones capable of generating publicly available embed codes and report links. Once you've designated the groups and selected **Apply**, the changes should be near-immediate.

See also

- Learn more about the **Publish to Web** option in Power BI at `https://docs.microsoft.com/en-us/power-bi/service-publish-to-web`.

Restricting the external sharing of Power BI reports

Your users can share dashboards with specific users outside of your organization (as opposed to the open, anonymous access that the **Publish to web** option permits). As in the previous recipe, we could limit this ability to a specific security group (or multiple). However, in this recipe, we'll disable the ability altogether.

Getting ready

You must be an O365 global admin or Power BI service administrator to complete the steps in this recipe.

How to do it...

1. Go to Power BI at `app.powerbi.com`.

2. Select the settings wheel | **Admin portal:**

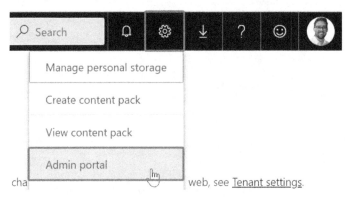

Figure 7.26 – The Admin portal link in Power BI

3. Select **Tenant settings** from the left-hand menu.

4. Scroll down to the **Export and sharing settings** section.

5. Expand **Share content with external users**:

Export and sharing settings

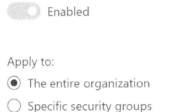
◢ Share content with external users
Enabled for the entire organization

Users in the organization can share dashboards and reports with users outside the
organization.

⬤ Enabled

Apply to:

⦿ The entire organization

◯ Specific security groups

Figure 7.27 – Share content with external users setting enabled with entire organization
scope in Power BI

6. Switch the **Enabled** toggle button to the off (**Disabled**) position and click **Apply**:

Export and sharing settings

◢ Share content with external users
Unapplied changes

Users in the organization can share dashboards and reports with users outside the
organization.

⬤ Disabled

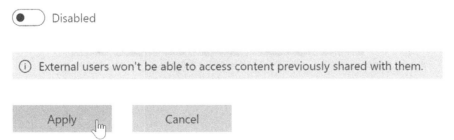
ⓘ External users won't be able to access content previously shared with them.

Apply   Cancel

Figure 7.28 – The export and sharing settings with external share disabled

How it works...

You just used the Power BI admin portal to disable the external sharing of Power BI content for your organization. Disabling external sharing disabled the ability altogether for all users, regardless of their security group membership, admin role, or otherwise. All existing shares, as noted in the warning in the previous screenshot, will be terminated and their content will no longer be accessible to external guests.

See also

- Read more on this setting at `https://docs.microsoft.com/en-us/power-bi/service-admin-portal#export-and-sharing-settings`.

Configuring a default logo, cover image, and theme for Power BI

As a Power BI service administrator, you can configure a logo, cover image, and theme to apply to the Power BI service experience that users see when they log in to `app.powerbi.com`. In this recipe, we'll upload some images and choose a theme color for our organization.

Getting ready

You must be an O365 global admin or Power BI service administrator to complete the steps in this recipe.

How to do it...

1. Go to Power BI at `app.powerbi.com`.
2. Select the settings wheel | **Admin portal**:

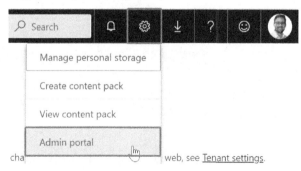

Figure 7.29 – The Admin portal link in Power BI

3. Select **Custom branding** from the left-hand menu.

4. Upload a logo (.png format recommended).

5. Upload a cover image (.jpg or .png).

6. Select or enter a theme color (hex, or selected).

7. Preview your changes first or click **Publish** if you're ready to implement the changes immediately:

Custom branding

Customize the look of Power BI for your whole organization. Learn more

Logo

For best results, upload a logo that's saved as a .png, 10 KB or smaller, and at least 200 x 30 pixels.

↑ Upload   🗑 Delete

Cover image

For best results, upload a cover image that's saved as a .jpg or .png, 1 MB or smaller, and at least 1920 x 160 pixels.

↑ Upload   🗑 Delete

Crop

Theme color

 #050D79

Remove custom branding

Preview   Publish

Figure 7.30 – Custom branding configuration fields and files

How it works...

In this recipe, you customized your branding for the Power BI service in your organization. Once the three components are configured (*steps 4–6*), your users will enjoy a customized online experience with familiar branding elements. Be sure to utilize the **Preview** option before publishing, or you may find that some text (such as the text above the cover image here) becomes unreadable. In this case, darker non-text images may suit the cover image option better:

Figure 7.31 – Example of custom branding in the preview

See also

- Learn more about customized branding for your organization's Power BI reports at `https://powerbi.microsoft.com/en-us/blog/announcing-custom-branding-for-your-organization/`.

Creating a Common Data Service database

In this recipe, you'll create a **Common Data Service** (**CDS**) database from the Power Platform admin center to use as a data store for your apps. Using CDS as opposed to a source such as SharePoint removes the list item limit you may be familiar with, but you'll still be limited by database size. You can also connect to multiple data sources in a single location for your apps and reports.

Getting ready

Before you can create a database, you must have or create a Power Platform environment and be one of its admins. See the first recipe in this chapter, *Creating a new Power Platform environment*, for assistance if you need a new environment.

How to do it...

1. Go to the Power Platform admin center at `https://admin.powerplatform.microsoft.com`.

2. Select **Environments** from the left-hand navigation menu if you are not taken there by default.

3. Select the name of the environment for which you're creating a CDS database:

Figure 7.32 – The Environments screen with the Power Platform environments listed

4. Click on **Add database**:

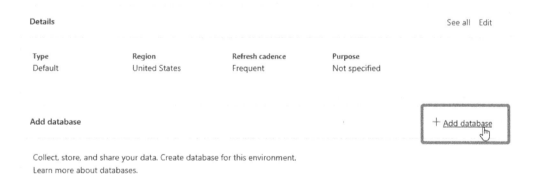

Figure 7.33 – The Add database option for an existing environment

5. Configure the database-specific options available to you (**Language**, **Currency**, and so on):

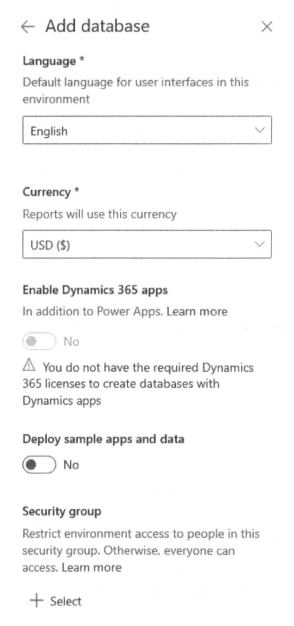

Figure 7.34 – Database configuration fields and options

6. Click **Add**.

7. Your environment will show its state as **PreparingInstance** while the process completes. Refresh it occasionally to check for completion, at which point its state will be **Ready**.

How it works...

In this recipe, you added a CDS database to an existing Power Platform environment by utilizing the Power Platform admin center.

See also

*   Learn more about creating databases at `https://docs.microsoft.com/en-us/power-platform/admin/create-database`.

*   You can integrate data from first- and third-party apps using data integration. This is currently in a steady state of development and growth. Learn more about the data integrator at `https://docs.microsoft.com/en-us/power-platform/admin/data-integrator`.

8
Administering SharePoint Online

SharePoint administration is a significant part of the O365 admin's responsibilities as it, in many ways, serves as one of the core functions and requirements of successful O365 implementation: learning to provision new site collections, managing sharing and site sprawl, and improving the user experience.

Throughout this chapter, you may see site collection or site used interchangeably as Microsoft shifts to a site-based architecture whose language is inclusive of all site template types.

In this chapter, we'll cover the following recipes:

- Creating a new site collection
- Deleting a site collection
- Limiting external sharing abilities
- Setting up stricter external sharing settings for a specific site collection
- Setting up the default share link type
- Configuring site collection storage
- Giving someone access to another user's OneDrive site

- Importing data from network locations using Migration Manager
- Hiding the **Subsite** creation button
- Designating a site collection as a hub site and associating other site collections with it
- Restricting access by **Internet Protocol (IP)** address

Technical requirements

To complete the recipes in this chapter, it's recommended that you're assigned the **Global** or **SharePoint admin** role.

Creating a new site collection

Sites are at the core of SharePoint, providing a designated space for teams to collaborate and be more productive in Office 365. In this recipe, you'll create a new site.

Getting ready

You should be a Global or SharePoint admin to complete this recipe. Depending on organizational settings, licensed SharePoint users may be able to create new site collections as well if allowed.

How to do it...

1. Go to the SharePoint admin center at `https://YOURTENANT-admin.sharepoint.com`, or go to the Microsoft Admin Center and click **SharePoint** from beneath **Admin centers** on the left-hand navigation menu.

2. Click **Sites** > **Active sites**:

Figure 8.1 – Active sites link on the left-hand navigation menu of the SharePoint admin center

3. Click **Create**:

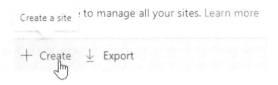

Figure 8.2 – Create option in the Active sites screen of the SharePoint admin center

4. Choose a site type. For this recipe, we'll choose **Communication site**:

Create a site

Choose the type of site you'd like to create.

Team site

Share documents, have conversations with your team, keep track of events, manage tasks, and more with a site connected to an Office 365 group.

Communication site

Publish dynamic, beautiful content to people in your organization to keep them informed and engaged on topics, events, or projects.

Other options

Create a new team site without an Office 365 group, or a Document center, Enterprise wiki, Publishing portal, or Project Web App site.

Figure 8.3 – Site template options when creating a new site in SharePoint

5. Choose a template/design from the left-hand side of the dialog, and then fill in your site's info, including name, **Uniform Resource Locator** (**URL**), site owner, language, time zone, and description:

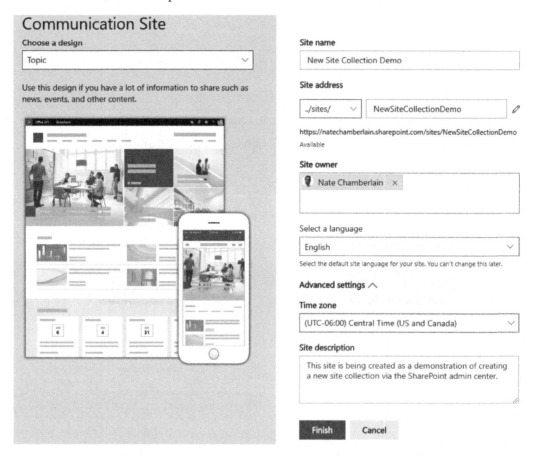

Figure 8.4 – Site design and basic configuration fields for new sites being created in SharePoint

6. Click **Finish**.

How it works...

You've just used the SharePoint admin center to provision a new site collection in your organization. This will appear and be accessible immediately to the site owner, who can further manage access/permissions.

See also

- Read more about creating site collections at `https://docs.microsoft.com/en-us/sharepoint/create-site-collection`.

Deleting a site collection

When a site collection is no longer needed or needs to be deleted for another reason, it's simply done via the SharePoint admin center. In this recipe, we'll go through the steps of deleting a site collection.

Getting ready

You should be a Global or SharePoint admin to complete this recipe. Site owners can also delete their own sites.

How to do it...

1. Go to the SharePoint admin center at `https://YOURTENANT-admin.sharepoint.com`, or go to the Microsoft Admin Center and click **SharePoint** from beneath **Admin Centers** on the left-hand navigation menu.

2. Click **Sites** > **Active sites**:

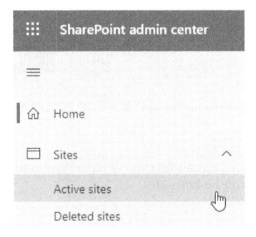

Figure 8.5 – Active sites link on the left-hand navigation menu of the SharePoint admin center

3. Select the site to delete, and then click **Delete**:

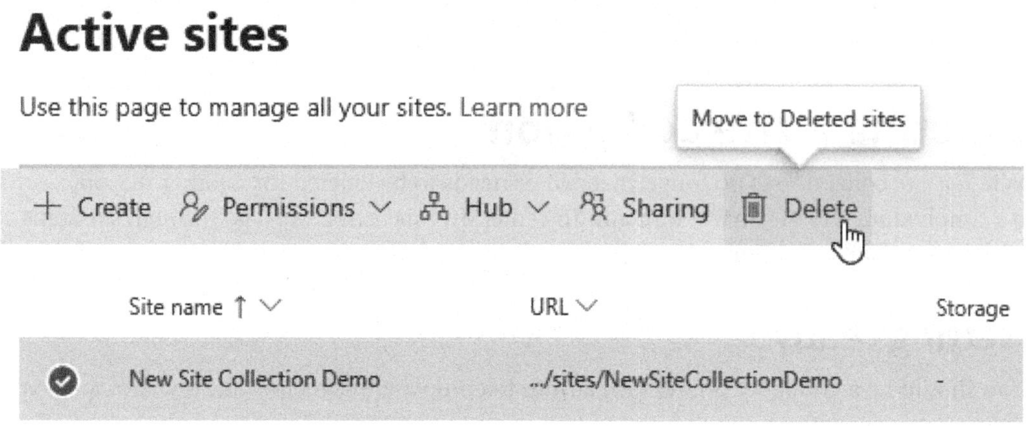

Active sites

Use this page to manage all your sites. Learn more

Move to Deleted sites

+ Create   🗒 Permissions ∨   ⚘ Hub ∨   👥 Sharing   🗑 Delete

Site name ↑ ∨	URL ∨	Storage
✓ New Site Collection Demo	.../sites/NewSiteCollectionDemo	-

Figure 8.6 – Delete option for a selected site in the Active sites screen of the SharePoint admin center

4. When prompted, click **Delete** again to confirm:

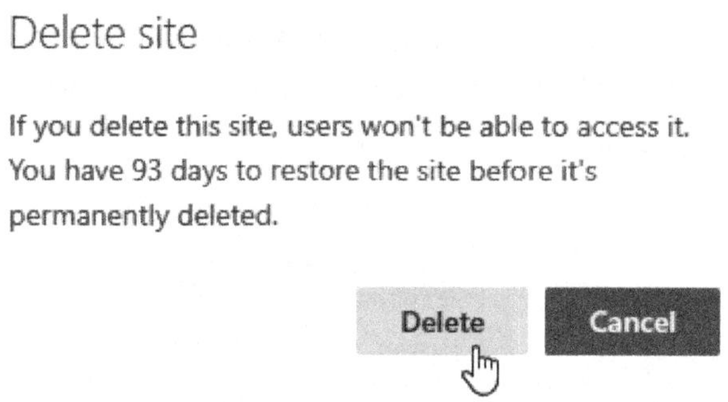

Delete site

If you delete this site, users won't be able to access it.
You have 93 days to restore the site before it's
permanently deleted.

Figure 8.7 – Deletion confirmation for a site with the 93 days' restorability reminder

How it works...

In this recipe, you deleted a site collection via the SharePoint admin center. You can also multi-select if you're deleting multiple sites.

There's more...

Once deleted, the site collection is still available to restore for 93 days from the **Deleted sites** pane on the left-hand navigation menu:

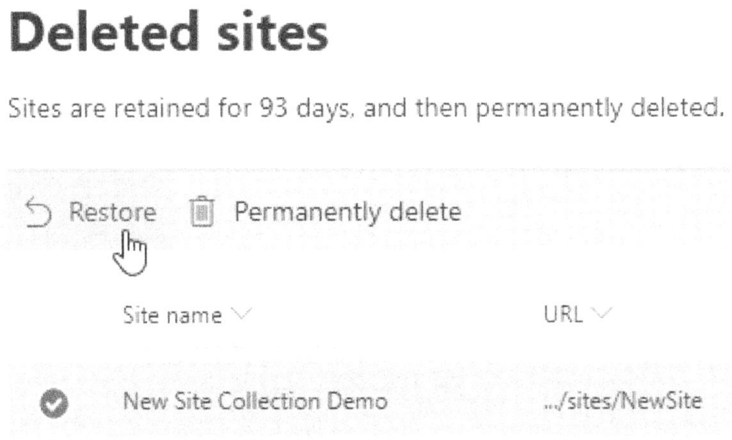

Deleted sites

Sites are retained for 93 days, and then permanently deleted.

↺ Restore   🗑 Permanently delete

Site name ⌄   URL ⌄

✓   New Site Collection Demo   .../sites/NewSite

Figure 8.8 – Restore button in the Deleted sites page of the SharePoint admin center

See also

- Learn more on deleting SharePoint site collections at `https://docs.microsoft.com/en-us/sharepoint/delete-site-collection`.

Limiting external sharing abilities

As a SharePoint (or Global) administrator, you may wish to protect your organization's users from unintentional leakage of sensitive information outside the organization itself. You may also have compliance policies that your administrative setting configurations need to account for. No matter your reasoning for needing to do so, this recipe will guide you through the steps necessary to limit external sharing abilities in your organization's SharePoint environment.

Getting ready

You should be a Global or SharePoint admin to complete this recipe.

How to do it...

1. Go to the SharePoint admin center at `https://YOURTENANT-admin.sharepoint.com`, or go to the Microsoft Admin Center and click **SharePoint** from beneath **Admin Centers** on the left-hand navigation menu.

2. Click on **Policies** > **Sharing** from the left-hand navigation menu:

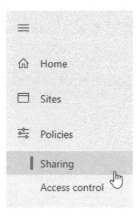

Figure 8.9 – Sharing policies link on the left-hand navigation menu of the SharePoint admin center

3. Scroll down to the **External sharing** section.

4. Slide the SharePoint slider to the desired level of allowed external sharing:

External sharing

Content can be shared with:

SharePoint   **OneDrive**

Most permissive

Anyone
Users can share files and folders using links that don't require sign-in.

New and existing guests
Guests must sign in or provide a verification code.

Existing guests
Only guests already in your organization's directory.

Least permissive

Only people in your organization
No external sharing allowed.

You can further restrict sharing for each individual site and OneDrive. Learn how

Figure 8.10 – SharePoint and OneDrive external sharing settings in the SharePoint admin center

5. Expand **More external sharing settings** and select appropriate options there for additional sharing configuration in your organization:

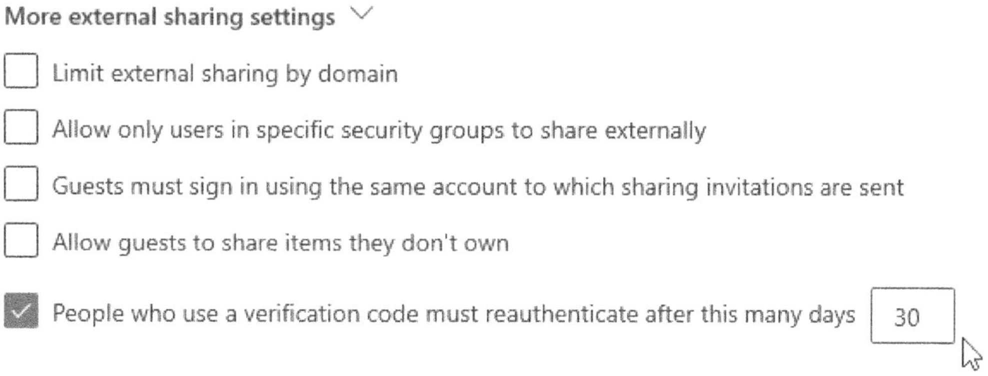

More external sharing settings ∨

☐ Limit external sharing by domain

☐ Allow only users in specific security groups to share externally

☐ Guests must sign in using the same account to which sharing invitations are sent

☐ Allow guests to share items they don't own

☑ People who use a verification code must reauthenticate after this many days   30

Figure 8.11 – Additional configuration options for external sharing in SharePoint

6. Scroll to the bottom of the page and click **Save**.

How it works...

You've just utilized the SharePoint admin center to configure the external sharing settings that will apply to all sites in your SharePoint environment.

Note that any changes made in this way are global throughout your tenant and should be considered the baseline policy. Individual sites can have unique, **stricter** (but not more permissive) settings, which we'll cover in the next recipe, *Setting up stricter external sharing settings for a specific site collection*.

See also

- Learn more about managing external sharing in SharePoint at https://docs. microsoft.com/en-US/sharepoint/turn-external-sharing-on-or-off.

Setting up stricter external sharing settings for a specific site collection

In the previous recipe, *Limiting external sharing abilities*, you set the global baseline policy for external sharing from SharePoint in your organization. In this recipe, we'll further configure a specific site collection to have stricter external sharing settings so that users can only share with other people in the organization.

Getting ready

You should be a Global or SharePoint admin to complete this recipe.

How to do it...

1. Go to the SharePoint admin center at `https://YOURTENANT-admin.sharepoint.com`, or go to the Microsoft Admin Center and click **SharePoint** from beneath **Admin Centers** on the left-hand navigation menu.

2. Select **Sites** > **Active sites** from the left-hand navigation menu:

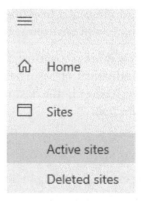

Figure 8.12 – Active sites link on the left-hand navigation menu of the SharePoint admin center

3. Select a site and then **Sharing** from the ribbon menu:

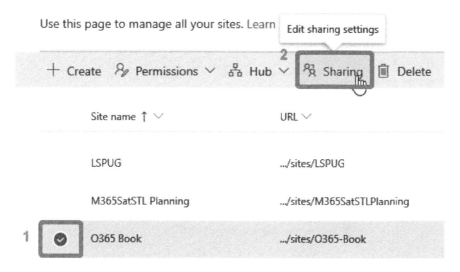

Figure 8.13 – Sharing button available for a selected site in the Active sites screen

4. Choose the specific **External sharing** setting you'd like to enforce for the selected site:

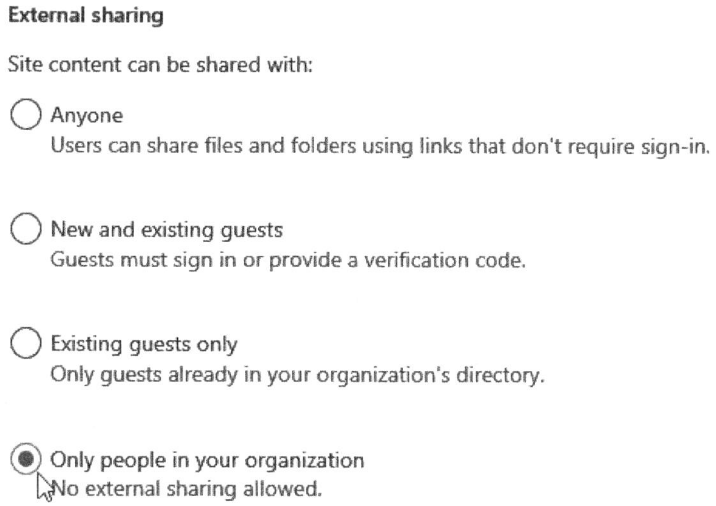

External sharing

Site content can be shared with:

○ Anyone
  Users can share files and folders using links that don't require sign-in.

○ New and existing guests
  Guests must sign in or provide a verification code.

○ Existing guests only
  Only guests already in your organization's directory.

◉ Only people in your organization
  No external sharing allowed.

Figure 8.14 – External sharing choices for the selected site

5. Scroll down and choose whether you'll adjust the **Default sharing link type** or **Default link permission** setting. When finished, click **Save**:

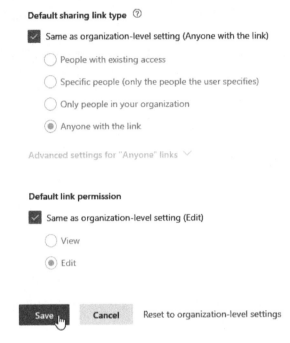

Figure 8.15 – Default sharing link type options for the specific site selected

How it works...

You've just utilized the SharePoint admin center's **Active sites** panel to change external sharing settings for a specific site collection.

There's more...

Notice in the final screenshot that if something should change and you need this site collection to match the global setting again, there's a **Reset to organization-level settings** link that will set the site collection to inherit the global baseline policy for external sharing configured in the previous recipe, *Limiting external sharing abilities*.

See also

- Read more about changing external sharing settings specific to a site collection at https://docs.microsoft.com/en-US/sharepoint/change-external-sharing-site.

Setting up the default share link type

Just as we can in OneDrive, we are able to set the default share link type users are presented with when attempting to share content in SharePoint. This can help reduce accidental permissions sprawl and make it so that additional permissions are only granted if users intentionally change the default type to something that specifically does that. In this recipe, we'll cover the steps needed to adjust the default share link type selection.

Getting ready

You should be a Global or SharePoint admin to complete this recipe.

How to do it...

1. Go to the SharePoint admin center at `https://YOURTENANT-admin.sharepoint.com`, or go to the Microsoft Admin Center and click **SharePoint** from beneath **Admin Centers** on the left-hand navigation menu.

2. Click on **Policies** > **Sharing** from the left-hand navigation menu:

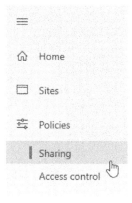

Figure 8.16 – Sharing policies link on the left-hand navigation menu of the SharePoint admin center

3. Scroll down the section entitled **File and folder links** and choose:

--The default link type (specific people, people in the organization with the link, or anyone with the link)

--The permission included with the default link (**View-only** or **Edit**)

--Adjustments specifically for **Anyone** links to set expiration and permissions limits:

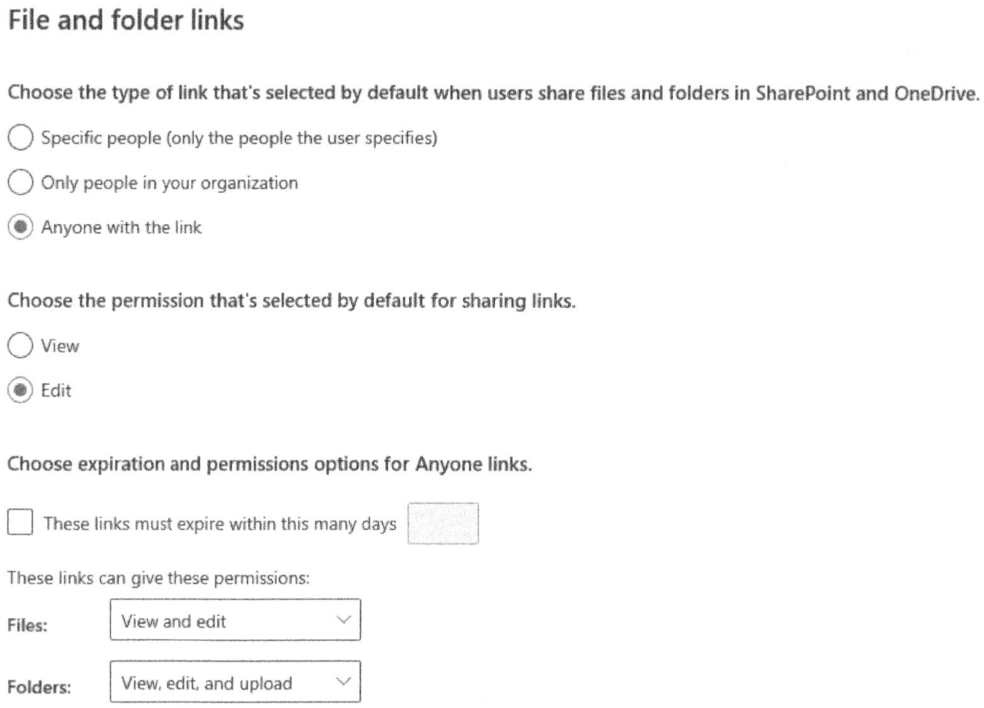

File and folder links

Choose the type of link that's selected by default when users share files and folders in SharePoint and OneDrive.

○ Specific people (only the people the user specifies)

○ Only people in your organization

⦿ Anyone with the link

Choose the permission that's selected by default for sharing links.

○ View

⦿ Edit

Choose expiration and permissions options for Anyone links.

☐ These links must expire within this many days [   ]

These links can give these permissions:

Files: | View and edit ∨ |

Folders: | View, edit, and upload ∨ |

Figure 8.17 – File and folder link types to be created by default

4. Scroll to the bottom and click **Save**.

How it works...

You've just utilized the SharePoint admin center's **Sharing** section to adjust the default share link type and additional options when sharing content in SharePoint. Remember that this isn't limiting their ability to change how they share, but it makes it easier for them to go with your organization's preferred method.

For example, to be safest, you'd likely set the first two settings to **Specific people** and **View**, respectively, and the final setting to include an expiration period and view only by default, as follows:

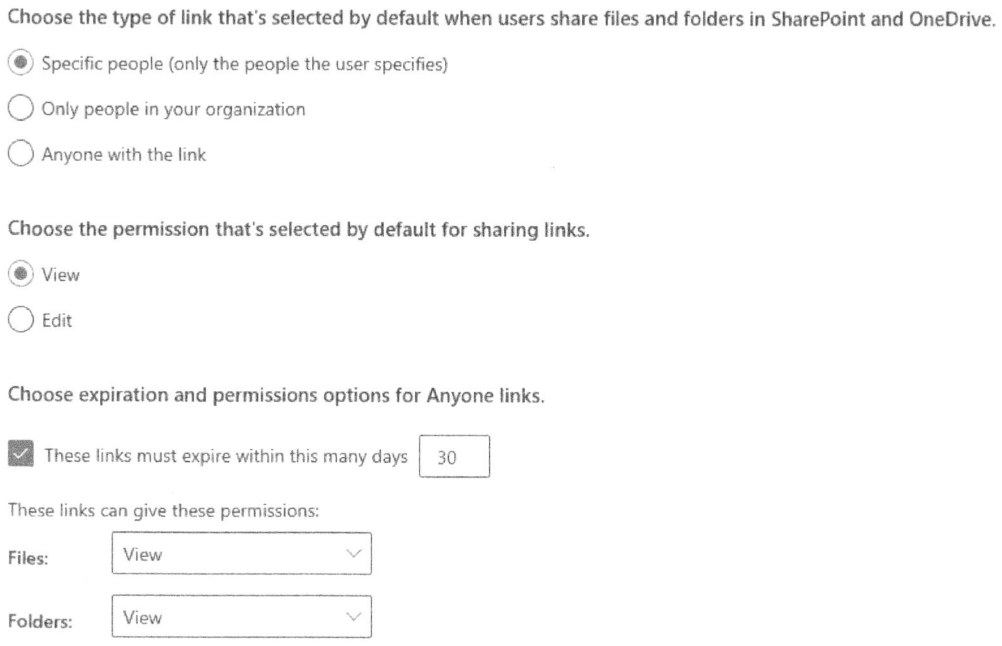

Choose the type of link that's selected by default when users share files and folders in SharePoint and OneDrive.

⦿ Specific people (only the people the user specifies)

◯ Only people in your organization

◯ Anyone with the link

Choose the permission that's selected by default for sharing links.

⦿ View

◯ Edit

Choose expiration and permissions options for Anyone links.

☑ These links must expire within this many days   30

These links can give these permissions:

Files: View ⌄

Folders: View ⌄

Figure 8.18 – Another example of configured default link options

See also

- Learn more about changing these organizational default share link settings at `https://docs.microsoft.com/en-us/sharepoint/turn-external-sharing-on-or-off#file-and-folder-links`.

Configuring site collection storage

Site collection storage quotas are less of a consideration in SharePoint Online than SharePoint Server, but there are still cases in which you may wish to limit how much storage space a site collection has. For example, even in SharePoint Online, your license limits how much storage you have available. Currently, an E1, E3, E5, or SharePoint Plan 1 or 2 license gets you 1 **terabyte (TB)** plus 10 **gigabytes (GB)** per license purchased. Read more on license-specific storage limits at `https://docs.microsoft.com/en-us/office365/servicedescriptions/sharepoint-online-service-description/sharepoint-online-limits`.

Some users who could be considered digital hoarders when subject to a storage limit might be less likely to upload their 100 high-resolution vacation photos. This limit can help encourage better content management and awareness (and hopefully prompt users to reconsider which files are most important to take up space in the site collection). Always pair these sorts of restrictions with education, such as training users to understand appropriate file and content types, implement content life cycles to prevent content sprawl, and prevent nurturing a site collection that only grows and is never reviewed for relevance.

By default, SharePoint Online allows users to have as much space as they need. In this recipe, we'll go over the steps needed to change our organization from automatic storage limits to specific, manual limits, as well as implement a lower storage limit for a specific site collection.

Getting ready

You should be a Global or SharePoint admin to complete this recipe.

How to do it...

1. Go to the SharePoint admin center at `https://YOURTENANT-admin.sharepoint.com`, or go to the Microsoft Admin Center and click **SharePoint** from beneath **Admin Centers** on the left-hand navigation menu.

2. Select **Settings** from the left-hand navigation menu. Then, click **Site storage limits**:

Figure 8.19 – Site storage limits link in the SharePoint admin center

3. Click **Manual**. Then, click **Save**:

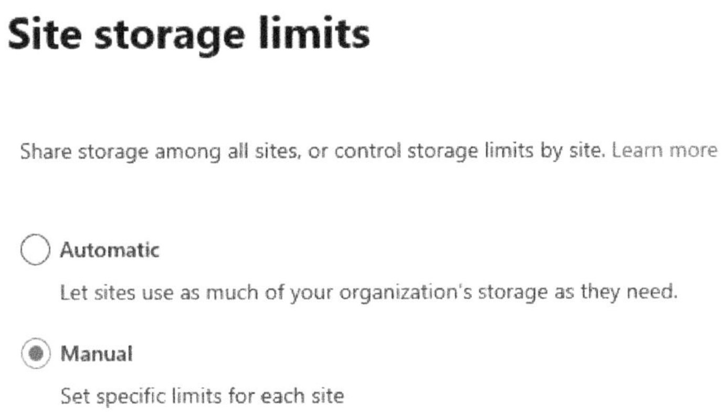

Site storage limits
Share storage among all sites, or control storage limits by site. Learn more
Automatic
Let sites use as much of your organization's storage as they need.
Manual
Set specific limits for each site

Figure 8.20 – Site storage limit set to Manual

4. Select **Sites** > **Active sites** from the left-hand navigation menu:

Home
Sites
Active sites
Deleted sites

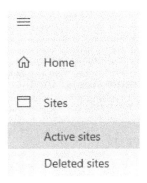

Figure 8.21 – Active sites link on the left-hand navigation menu of the SharePoint admin center

5. Select the name of a site for which you wish to lower (or raise) the storage quota:

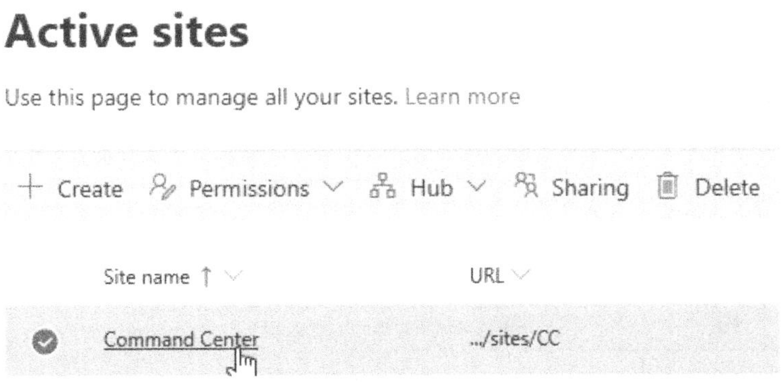

Active sites
Use this page to manage all your sites. Learn more
Create
Permissions
Hub
Sharing
Delete
Site name
URL
Command Center
.../sites/CC

Figure 8.22 – Active sites screen with a site's name being selected for a review of the details

6.   Under **Storage limit**, click **Edit**:

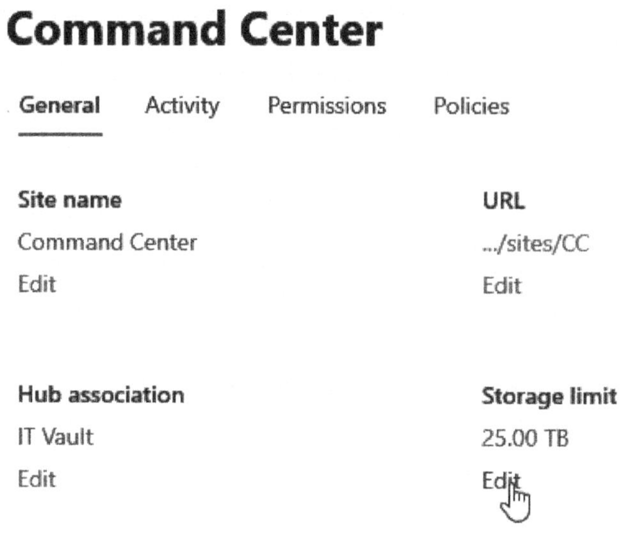

Command Center

General   Activity   Permissions   Policies

Site name   **URL**
Command Center   .../sites/CC
Edit   Edit

Hub association   **Storage limit**
IT Vault   25.00 TB
Edit   Edit

Figure 8.23 – General tab of the site details with the new Edit button under Storage limit

7.   Change the amount in **Maximum storage for this site** (in GB) and the utilization warning threshold, and then click **Save**:

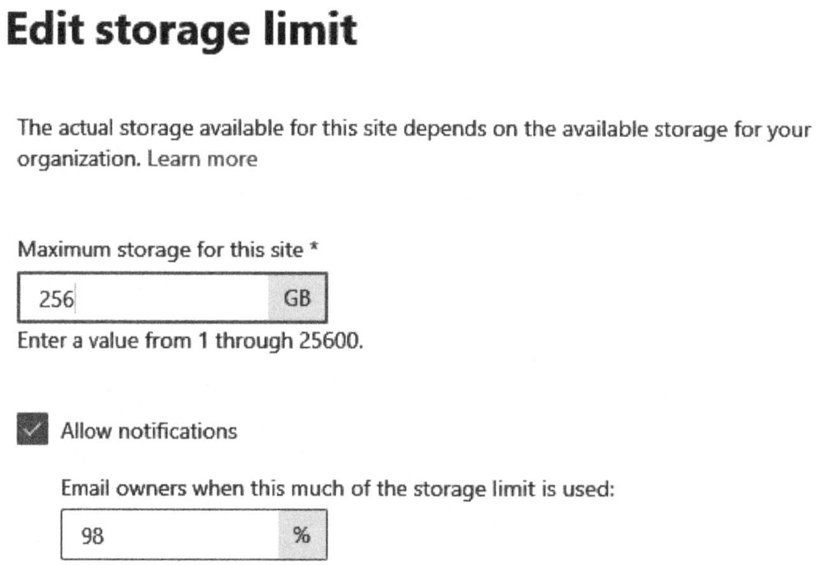

Edit storage limit

The actual storage available for this site depends on the available storage for your organization. Learn more

Maximum storage for this site *

| 256 | GB |

Enter a value from 1 through 25600.

✓ Allow notifications

Email owners when this much of the storage limit is used:

| 98 | % |

Figure 8.24 – Edit the storage limit options

How it works...

In this recipe, we needed to do two things: change our organization's storage limit setting from **Automatic** to **Manual**, and lower the storage limit for a site called **Command Center**.

We accomplished this by using the SharePoint admin center's **Settings** > **Site storage limits** setting, and then **Sites** > **Active sites**.

See also

- Review the steps we took to update our organization from automatic to manual storage limit management at `https://docs.microsoft.com/en-US/ sharepoint/manage-site-collection-storage-limits#set- automatic-or-manual-site-storage-limits`.

- Find more information on managing the storage limit for a specific site collection at `https://docs.microsoft.com/en-US/sharepoint/manage-site- collection-storage-limits#manage-individual-site-storage- limits`.

Giving someone access to another user's OneDrive site

There may be cases where a replacement employee needs access to a former employee's OneDrive site that's still active. Or, perhaps an employee has multiple managers who always need access, or even a colleague on a person's team needs constant access rather than individual shares.

Whatever your purpose, this recipe will demonstrate the implementation concept by generating an access link to Bertha Lestrange's OneDrive site that we'll share with her colleague, Richard Weasley, who will fill in for her while she's on vacation.

We'll do two things for this to work:

1. Grant ourselves access (which adds us as a site collection admin if we're not already).

2. Add Richard as another admin and send him the same access link we generate in *Step 1*.

Getting ready

You should be a Global admin to complete this recipe.

How to do it...

1. Go to the Microsoft 365 Admin Center at `https://admin.microsoft.com`.

2. Select **Users** > **Active users**:

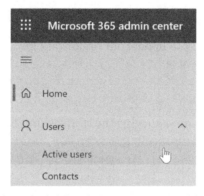

Figure 8.25 – Active users link on the left-hand navigation menu of the Microsoft 365 admin center

3. Find and select the display name of the user whose OneDrive site you're sharing, and then click **OneDrive**. Then, under **Get access to files**, click **Create link to files**:

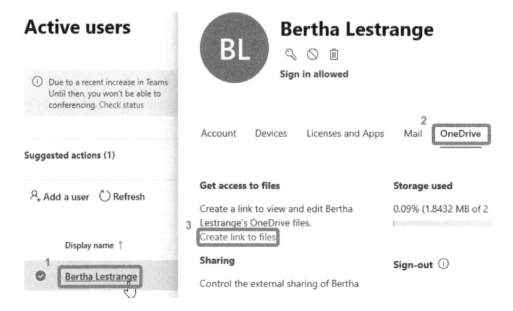

Figure 8.26 – Create link to files option on the details pane of a selected user's OneDrive tab

4. Once the link is generated, you can then copy it to share it with Richard Weasley (or whoever needs access to Bertha's OneDrive site) later. Note that they do not have access, and this link does not grant access to people who have it. We still need to add Richard as a site collection admin of Bertha's OneDrive site:

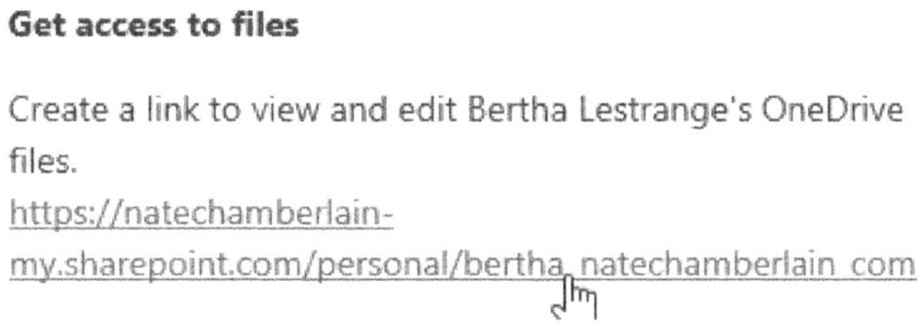

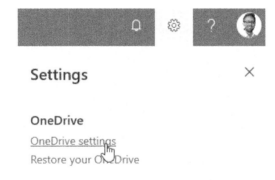

Get access to files

Create a link to view and edit Bertha Lestrange's OneDrive files.
https://natechamberlain-
my.sharepoint.com/personal/bertha_natechamberlain_com

Figure 8.27 – Generated link

5. Click on the link generated in *Step 4*.

6. Go to the settings wheel > **OneDrive settings**:

Settings   ✕

OneDrive

OneDrive settings
Restore your OneDrive

Figure 8.28 – OneDrive settings link

7. Click **More Settings** from the left-hand navigation menu, and then **Site collection administrators**:

Nate Chamberlain   **More Settings**

🔔   Notifications

⚙   **More Settings**   Manage access

                              Site collection administrators

                              Run sharing report

Figure 8.29 – Site collection administrators link in OneDrive settings

8.   Add **Richard Weasley** as an administrator, and then click **OK**.

9.   Now, we can share the link we copied in *Step 4* with Richard to give him one-click access to Bertha's OneDrive site.

How it works...

In this recipe, we made sure we were admins of Bertha's OneDrive site by generating a link from the Microsoft 365 Admin Center. By generating this access link, it makes us a site collection owner, if not already. We then added Richard Weasley as an additional site collection admin, giving him edit access to Bertha's OneDrive site.

Importing data from network locations using Migration Manager

There are at least three tools you can utilize to import data from network locations, and three of them are all conveniently linked from the SharePoint admin center: **Migration Manager**, **SharePoint Migration Tool**, and **Mover**. You utilized the **SharePoint Migration Tool** (**SPMT**) in *Chapter 6, Administering OneDrive*, so we'll look at Migration Manager in this recipe.

Migration Manager is a more complicated and involved tool compared to SPMT because of the agent configuration. However, Migration Manager is also the best pick for larger, more complicated migrations of file-share content. SPMT, on the other hand, is the ideal pick for migrating specifically SharePoint (2010 or 2013) content and small file shares, but perhaps not the best option suited for large file shares.

Getting ready

You should be a Global admin to complete this recipe and will also need admin credentials to machines with access to file shares being migrated.

How to do it...

1.   Go to the SharePoint admin center at `https://YOURTENANT-admin.sharepoint.com`, or go to the Microsoft Admin Center and click **SharePoint** from beneath **Admin Centers** on the left-hand navigation menu.

2.   Go to **Migration** > **Migration manager**:

Figure 8.30 – Migration manager link on the left-hand navigation menu of the SharePoint admin center

3. Download agent setup file(s) to available machines to act as task executors. The more you have, the faster large migrations involving many tasks can go:

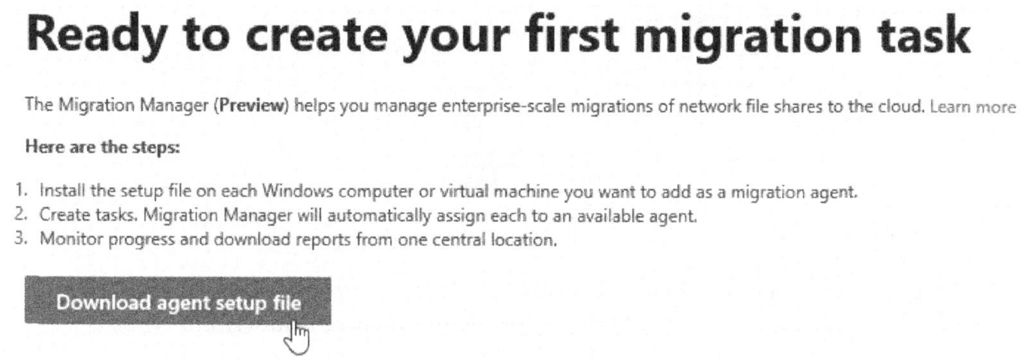

Ready to create your first migration task

The Migration Manager (**Preview**) helps you manage enterprise-scale migrations of network file shares to the cloud. Learn more

Here are the steps:

1. Install the setup file on each Windows computer or virtual machine you want to add as a migration agent.
2. Create tasks. Migration Manager will automatically assign each to an available agent.
3. Monitor progress and download reports from one central location.

Download agent setup file

Figure 8.31 – Download agent setup file option when beginning a migration

4. Run the downloaded setup file if you're installing on your current machine, or else save it and copy it to the machines you intend to have it installed on:

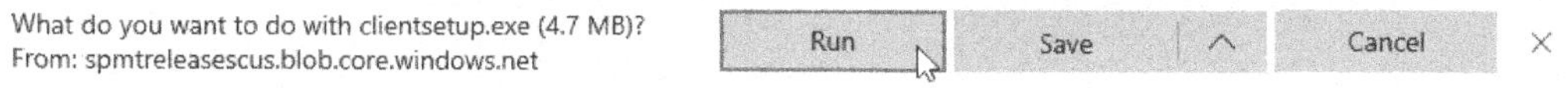

What do you want to do with clientsetup.exe (4.7 MB)?
From: spmtreleasescus.blob.core.windows.net   Run   Save   ∧   Cancel   ✕

Figure 8.32 – Download dialog (differs by browser) with option to run or save the agent setup file

5. You'll be prompted to sign in for each agent you install, probably using your global admin credentials:

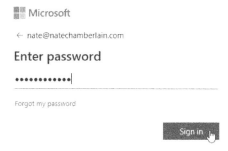

Figure 8.33 – Sign-in prompt for using with the downloaded agent

6. You'll need to provide local Windows credentials to complete installation and guarantee access to file shares:

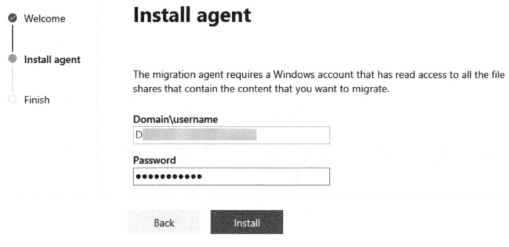

Figure 8.34 – Installation wizard for the agent

7. Once all agents are installed and configured, go back to the SharePoint admin center's **Migration Manager SharePoint library destination. Often, you'll** page and select **Tasks** > **Add task**:

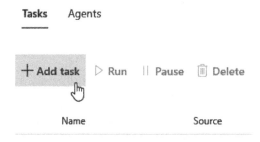

Figure 8.35 – Add task option in the SharePoint admin center's Migration manager page

8. Configure the migration method (one single source, or bulk locations specified via **comma-separated values (CSV)** files, source (file-share path), destination (library path in SharePoint), and migration settings. In this recipe, we've chosen one single source going to a single destination. There are several settings on the **Settings** page you may wish to adjust. When ready, click **Run now**:

Figure 8.36 – Settings fields and options for a migration task

9. Wait for the migration (truly a copy action, as original content is not moved) to complete, or create additional tasks.

How it works...

In this recipe, you were introduced to another free migration tool available to you in the SharePoint admin center. You found it under **Migration** > **Migration manager** and, after installing agents on machines to assist in the migration tasks, created the actual migration task to initiate the move of content.

There's more...

In this recipe, we configured a migration of one single file-share location to one single SharePoint library destination. Often, you'll want to move multiple file-share locations at once. For further details regarding Migration Manager's bulk operation, go to `https://docs.microsoft.com/en-US/sharepointmigration/mm-bulk-upload-format-csv-json`.

See also

- Learn more about Migration Manager at `https://go.microsoft.com/fwlink/?linkid=2105077`.

Hiding the Subsite creation button

Site owners can create subsites (nested within a site) by default. If you're trying to promote a flat architecture, this can become especially problematic. Make it less convenient to create subsites and encourage site owners to request a new site collection or create one themselves if they're able. In this recipe, we'll hide the subsite creation button to promote this practice, seen in the following screenshot:

Figure 8.37 – New subsite menu option in SharePoint

Getting ready

You should be a Global or SharePoint admin to complete this recipe.

How to do it...

1. Go to the SharePoint admin center at `https://YOURTENANT-admin.sharepoint.com`, or go to the Microsoft Admin Center and click **SharePoint** from beneath **Admin Centers** on the left-hand navigation menu.

2. Select **Settings** and then follow the link to the **classic settings page**:

Figure 8.38 – Classic settings page link on the Settings page of the SharePoint admin center

3. Scroll down to **Subsite Creation** and select the **Hide the Subsite command** radio button:

Figure 8.39 – Hide the Subsite command option in the classic settings page

4. Scroll to the bottom and click **OK**.

5. Now, users will no longer see **Subsite** as an option on the **New** menu or the **Site contents** page.

How it works...

In this recipe, we hid the **Subsite** command button via the classic SharePoint settings page of the SharePoint admin center. Hiding the **Subsite** command button makes it easier to enforce and promote a flat site architecture. Users (with permissions) will still be able to create site collections, but those site collections wouldn't as easily get nested subsites (subsites of subsites), creating a messy hierarchy that's difficult to manage and reconfigure.

See also

- Read more about the classic settings page's site creation topics beyond just subsites at `https://docs.microsoft.com/en-us/sharepoint/manage-site-creation#manage-detailed-site-and-subsite-creation-settings-in-the-classic-sharepoint-admin-center`.

- Learn about the modern SharePoint experience and flat architectures achieved by utilizing hub sites at `https://docs.microsoft.com/en-us/sharepoint/information-architecture-modern-experience`. We'll also cover hub site association in the next recipe, *Designating a site collection as a hub site and associating other site collections with it.*

Designating a site collection as a hub site and associating other site collections with it

Hub sites are the connective tissue between related sites. For example, **IT Vault** may be a hub site that connects other site collections such as **Information Security**, **Command Center**, and **End User Support,** as you'll see in this recipe. Site collections that are associated with a hub site inherit that hub site's theme and navigation and can roll content (such as news, events, and documents) up to the hub for simple centralized sharing and communication.

A common example may be Human Resources as a hub site that connects its associated sites – Benefits, Payroll, and Talent. The main hub site may be a landing page that represents all its associated site collections, but also has some unique content of its own. For a deeper dive, users could go to the specific site collections associated with the hub.

One of the major benefits of hub sites is that if your organization goes through a restructuring at some point, you can easily associate site collections with a new hub, and nearly instantly it will inherit the new theme/navigation. It will also then be able to share its content in the hub's web parts that support rolling up content from associated sites (such as news, events, and so on).

In this recipe, we'll designate a site called **IT Vault** as a hub site, and associate three separate site collections with it so that we can benefit from the roll-up and shared theme/navigation.

Getting ready

You should be a Global or SharePoint admin to complete this recipe.

How to do it...

1. Go to the SharePoint admin center at `https://YOURTENANT-admin.sharepoint.com`, or go to the Microsoft Admin Center and click **SharePoint** from beneath **Admin Centers** on the left-hand navigation menu.

2. Click **Sites** > **Active sites**:

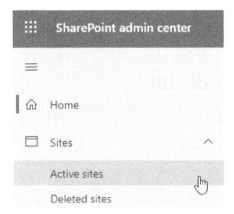

Figure 8.40 – Active sites link on the left-hand navigation menu of the SharePoint admin center

3. Search for and select the site you wish to register as a hub site, and then click
    Hub > Register as hub site:

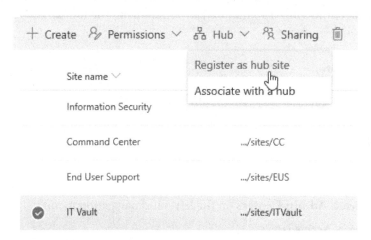

Figure 8.41 – Register as hub site option for a selected active site

4. Add any users who should be able to associate sites with this hub (other than
    global admins):

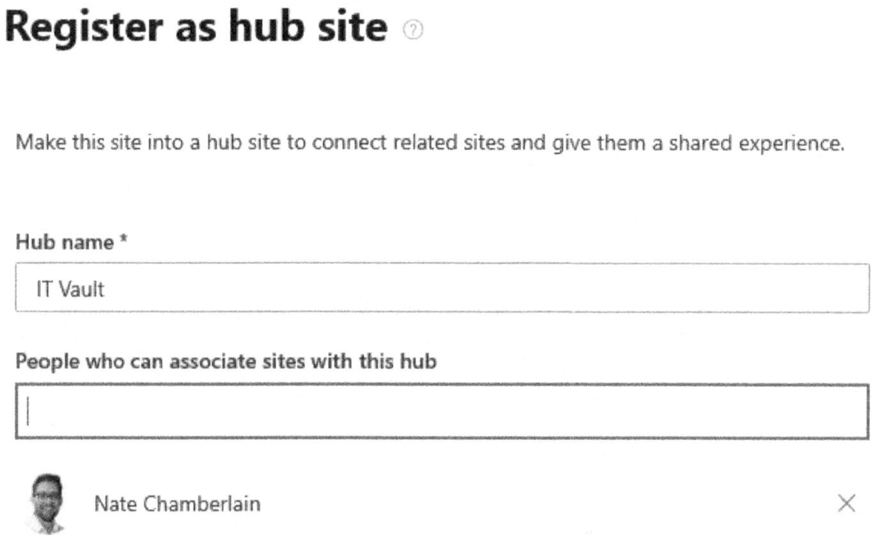

Register as hub site ⓘ

Make this site into a hub site to connect related sites and give them a shared experience.

Hub name *

| IT Vault |

People who can associate sites with this hub

| |

👤 Nate Chamberlain   ✕

Figure 8.42 – Hub name and association permissions for the site being registered

5.   Click **Save**.

6.   Now, select the site(s) that you'd like to associate with the new hub site. Then, click **Bulk edit** (if multiple) or **Hub** (if single), and then **Hub association** or **Associate with a hub**, respectively:

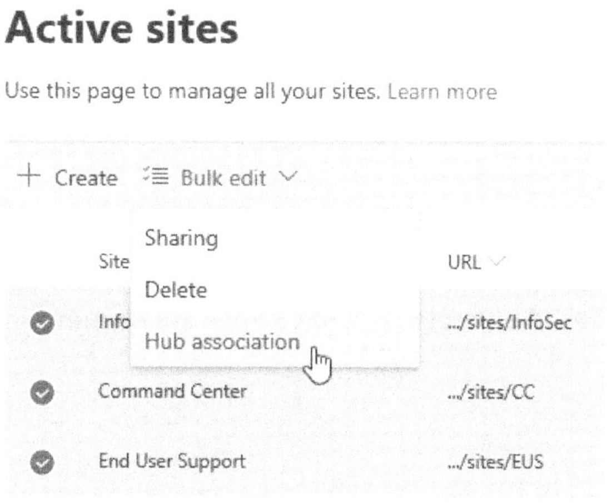

Active sites

Use this page to manage all your sites. Learn more

+ Create   ≔ Bulk edit ∨

	Site	Sharing	URL ∨
		Delete	
✓	Info	Hub association	.../sites/InfoSec
✓	Command Center		.../sites/CC
✓	End User Support		.../sites/EUS

Figure 8.43 – Hub association option for multi-selected sites

7.   Choose the hub site with which you're associating these sites:

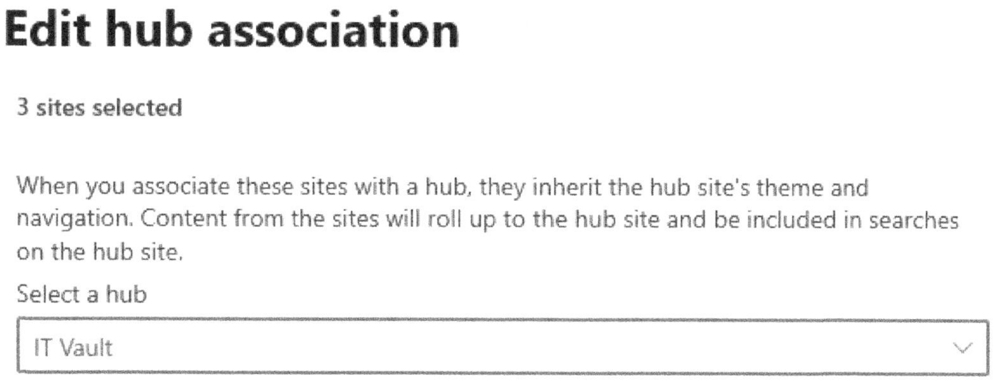

Edit hub association

3 sites selected

When you associate these sites with a hub, they inherit the hub site's theme and navigation. Content from the sites will roll up to the hub site and be included in searches on the hub site.

Select a hub

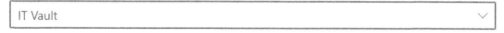

IT Vault   ∨

Figure 8.44 – Hub selection for association

8.   Click **Save**.

How it works...

You've just registered a hub site and associated sites with it via the SharePoint admin center. In just a few steps, you've created a new information architecture that didn't break any URLs in the process or require any migration tools whatsoever. What basically functions as a new hierarchy has zero disruption to the day-to-day functions of users of impacted sites. They may notice visual changes, and any other changes you plan to make to take advantage of hub features, but otherwise, users continue working as they have been.

There's more...

You can follow nearly the same steps to unregister a hub, disassociate sites from a hub, or change their association. The same options you selected in this recipe will now simply read as **Unregister** (instead of **Register**) and **Change association** (instead of **Associate with a hub**).

See also

- If you're unfamiliar with hub sites or just want to dive deeper, check out `https://support.office.com/en-us/article/what-is-a-sharepoint-hub-site-fe26ae84-14b7-45b6-a6d1-948b3966427f`.

Restricting access by IP address

Some organizations choose to restrict employee access to SharePoint Online to only those employees who are accessing it from approved IP addresses specified in the SharePoint admin center. In this recipe, we'll specify which IP addresses can access our SharePoint Online environment.

Getting ready

You should be a Global or SharePoint admin to complete this recipe.

How to do it...

1. Go to the SharePoint admin center at `https://YOURTENANT-admin.sharepoint.com`, or go to the Microsoft Admin Center and click **SharePoint** from beneath **Admin Centers** on the left-hand navigation menu.

2. Choose **Policies** > **Access control** from the left-hand navigation menu. Then, click **Network location**:

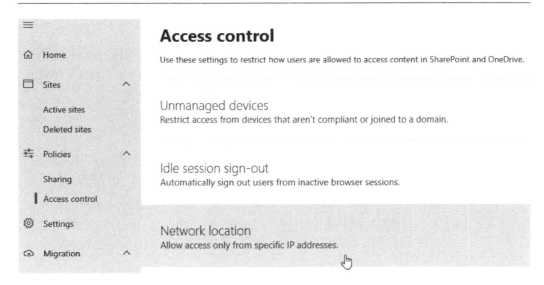

Figure 8.45 – Access control settings in the SharePoint admin center

3. Toggle the **Allow access only from specific IP address ranges** setting to the **On** position, and then specify a comma-delimited list of network IP addresses and ranges that should be able to access your environment (including your own):

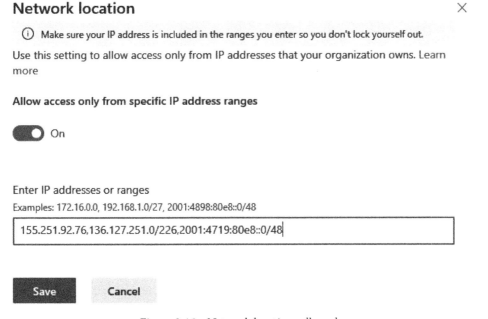

Figure 8.46 – Network locations allowed

4. Click **Save**.

How it works...

You've just limited access to your organization's SharePoint Online environment to only those who are joining from an approved IP address. Users who attempt to access it from a different IP address will receive an *Access Restricted* error message.

See also

- Learn more about controlling access based on IP addresses at `https://docs.microsoft.com/en-US/sharepoint/control-access-based-on-network-location`.

9
Managing Microsoft Teams

Microsoft Teams is a single pane of glass that allows users and their frequent collaborators to access all the resources they need to work, whether they are **Office 365 (O365)**-based or an integrated service. In this chapter, we'll create teams and configure policies and settings for live events, meetings, teams, external access, guests, and messaging.

The Teams recipes included in this chapter are as follows:

- Creating a team
- Creating a Teams policy
- Creating a meeting policy
- Configuring meeting settings
- Creating a live event policy
- Configuring live event settings
- Creating a messaging policy
- Configuring Teams setup policies
- Configuring external access
- Configuring guest access

- Reviewing teams and their owners
- Using PowerShell to export a list of all the teams' owners and members

Technical requirements

Most recipes in this chapter will require you to be either a global or a Teams administrator. You should also have the Microsoft Teams client installed on your machine if not already (it can be downloaded from `https://go.microsoft.com/fwlink/p/?linkid=869426`).

Some of the configurations for the following recipes will take place in the browser (the Teams admin center) and some in the client application. Changes made via either location will be reflected in both the web and desktop versions of Teams, although there can sometimes be a small delay between policy/permissions adjustments and the time they take effect.

Creating a team

One of the most common functions that users and/or admins will utilize is creating new teams within Microsoft Teams. This recipe covers this fundamental process of creating a new team.

Getting ready

Depending on your organizational settings, most users will be able to create new teams without needing any admin roles. If you've restricted O365 group creation (see the *Restricting users from creating new O365 groups* recipe from *Chapter 2, Office 365 Identity and Roles*, only admins and members of the approved security group will be able to create teams.

How to do it...

1. Open the Teams desktop application (or follow the exact same steps in the web app if you are unable to access the desktop app).

2. Choose **Join or create a team** from the lower left-hand portion of the main Teams view:

Figure 9.1 – The Join or create a team option in the Teams client application

3. Click **Create team**:

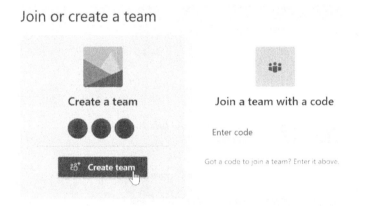

Figure 9.2 – The Create team button in the Teams client application

4. Choose **Build a team from scratch** (this will provision a new O365 group):

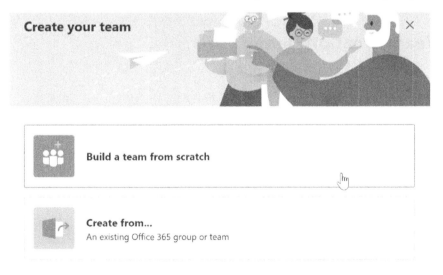

Figure 9.3 – Options to build a Team from scratch or from an existing O365 group or team

5. Select a type of Team – we'll choose **Private** for this recipe:

Figure 9.4 – The permissions options for the new team

6. Name and describe the new Team, then click **Create**:

Figure 9.5 – The Team name and description fields

7. You can add members now or later. If you are adding them now, type a name, distribution list, or security group, then select the correct result. When you have finished adding names, click **Add** and choose a role (**Owner** or **Member**) for each. Note that once you click **Add**, the members added will be notified of having been added to the team:

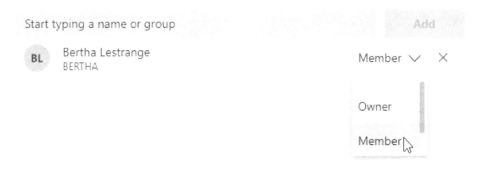

Figure 9.6 – Dialog for adding members and owners to a new team

How it works...

You created a new team from within the Microsoft Teams client in this recipe. Creating a team creates a new O365 group and an associated SharePoint site. Once there's an O365 group, the team can also have a shared Planner plan(s), Stream channel(s), and more. Anyone you designate as an owner (keeping in mind you'll be one by default) will be able to manage team membership and settings such as channel creation.

There's more

You can also create teams directly from the Microsoft Teams admin center (`https://admin.teams.microsoft.com/`), though this can take longer for certain changes (such as making someone an owner) to sync to users' desktop clients:

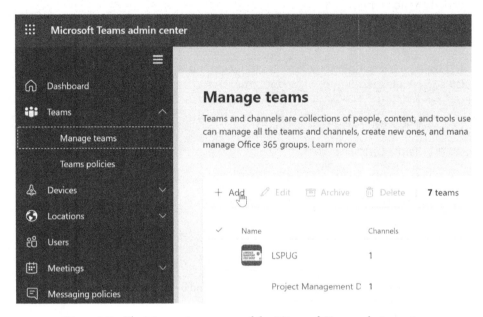

Figure 9.7 – The Manage teams page of the Microsoft Teams admin center

See also

- Learn more about creating teams and channels at `https://docs.microsoft.com/en-us/MicrosoftTeams/get-started-with-teams-create-your-first-teams-and-channels`.

Creating a Teams policy

Teams policies provide the ability to assign certain users a variant of the default/global policy applied to most users. For example, you may adjust the default policy to disallow private channel creation and then create a custom Teams policy to allow only certain members to create private channels. In this recipe, we're going to prevent a certain user (or several) from creating private channels in Teams.

Getting ready

You must be a global or Teams administrator to complete the steps in this recipe.

How to do it...

1. Go to the Microsoft Teams admin center at `https://admin.teams.microsoft.com/`.

2. Select **Teams | Teams policies**:

Figure 9.8 – The Teams policies link in the left-hand navigation menu of the
Microsoft Teams admin center

3. Click **+ Add**.

4. Name and describe the policy and choose whether users to whom this policy applies should be permitted to discover private teams and create private channels:

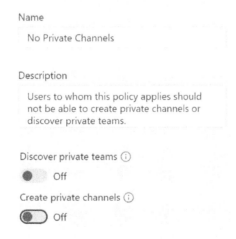

Figure 9.9 – The New teams policy configuration fields

5. Click **Apply**.

6. Now, we need to apply this policy to specific users. Select the new policy, then select **Manage users**:

Figure 9.10 – The Manage users button for a selected policy

7. Add users by display name or username:

Figure 9.11 – Dialog for searching for and selecting users to add

8. Click **Apply**.

How it works...

You've successfully restricted the ability to create private channels in Teams. Any custom Teams policy like this will take precedence over the default global policy. If a user has no policy specifically assigned to them, they'll fall under the global (default) policy. Changes made to the default or custom policies can take up to 24 hours to take effect.

If a user who wasn't previously restricted from creating private channels attempts to do so soon after the new policy is applied, they'll get an error message that says *We're having trouble creating your channel. Please try again later*:

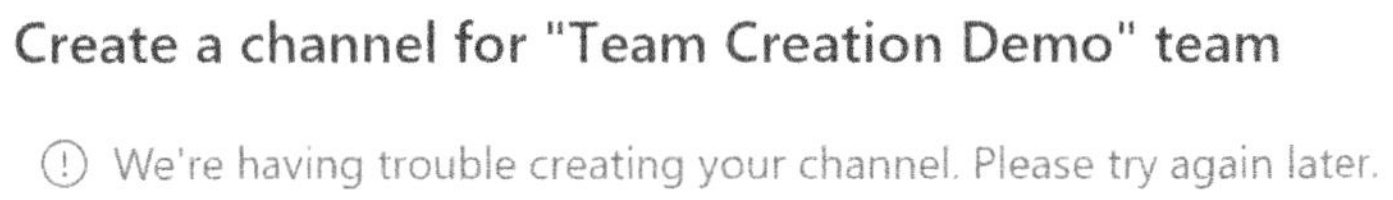

Create a channel for "Team Creation Demo" team

ⓘ We're having trouble creating your channel. Please try again later.

Figure 9.12 – Error presented to users no longer able to create private channels

If you wish to delete a custom Teams policy, you'll need to first reassign all its assigned users to a different policy (such as the default policy).

See also

- Learn more about managing Teams policies at `https://docs.microsoft.com/en-US/microsoftteams/teams-policies`.

Creating a meeting policy

There are six default meeting policies in Teams. You can create additional, custom policies to help control user experiences and abilities when joining Microsoft Teams meetings, such as the ability to schedule channel meetings, share the screen, and bypass the lobby when joining. In this recipe, we'll create a meeting policy in which you can specify your own preferred configurations.

Getting ready

You should be a global or Teams administrator to complete the steps in this recipe.

How to do it...

1. Go to the Microsoft Teams admin center at `https://admin.teams.microsoft.com`.

2. Select **Meetings | Meeting policies**:

Figure 9.13 – The Meeting policies link in the left-hand navigation menu of the
Microsoft Teams admin center

3. Click **+ Add**.

4. Name and describe your new meeting policy:

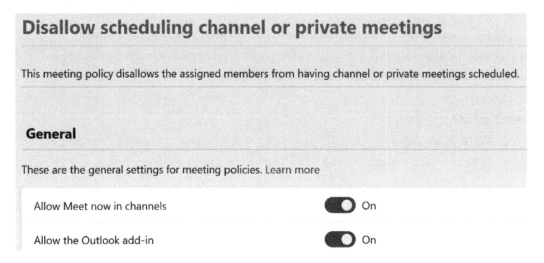

Figure 9.14 – A name and description for the new policy

5. Configure the settings beneath the **General, Audio & video**, **Content sharing**, and **Participants & guests** headers and click **Save**.

6. Select the new policy and then select **Manage users**:

Figure 9.15 – The Manage users option for the selected policy

7. Search for and add members to which you will apply the new policy. When finished, click **Apply**:

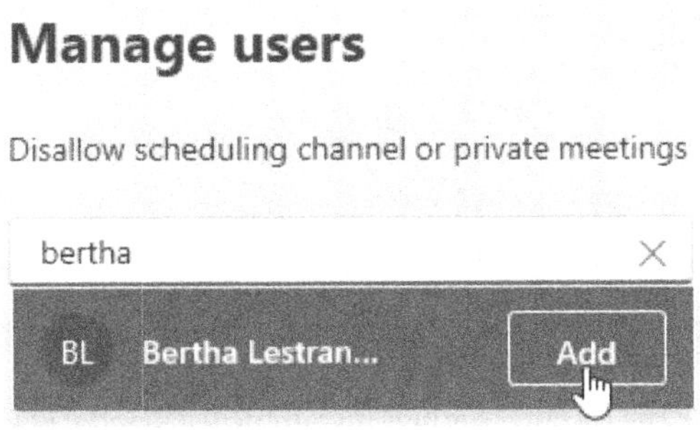

Manage users

Disallow scheduling channel or private meetings

bertha   ✕

BL   Bertha Lestran...   Add

Figure 9.16 – Dialog for searching and selecting users to whom the policy will apply

How it works...

You've created and applied a custom meeting policy to users. Users to whom you apply the policy will have a new Teams meeting experience once the policy takes hold. This may prevent cloud recording, transcription, content sharing, or more. Keep in mind that this isn't a per-team policy, but per-user. The policy settings will apply to the user across all the teams of which they're a member.

See also

- Read more about Microsoft Teams meeting policies at `https://docs.microsoft.com/en-us/microsoftteams/meeting-policies-in-teams`.

Configuring meeting settings

Meeting settings can be configured via the Teams admin center that enable users in your organization to create and run meetings that use your organization's branding, resources, and custom traffic preferences. In this recipe, we'll go over those steps.

Getting ready

You must be a global or Teams administrator to complete the steps in this recipe.

How to do it...

1. Go to the Microsoft Teams admin center at `https://admin.teams.microsoft.com/`.

2. Select **Meetings | Meeting settings** from the left-hand navigation menu:

Figure 9.17 – The Meeting settings link in the left-hand navigation menu
of the Microsoft Teams admin center

3. Choose whether anonymous users should be able to join Teams meetings in your organization:

Figure 9.18 – The Anonymous users can join a meeting toggle option

4. Customize the URLs to your logo and legal and help pages. You can also include a footer message. All of this is included in every meeting invite sent from your organization:

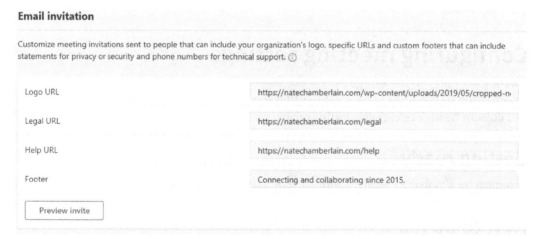

Figure 9.19 – Email invitation customization options

5. Choose whether you want **Quality of Service (QoS)** markers for real-time media traffic and adjust ports for specific media types if you need to:

Network

Set up how you want to handle Teams meetings real-time media traffic (audio, video and screen sharing) that flow across your network. ⓘ

Insert Quality of Service (QoS) markers for real-time media traffic ⓘ	● Off		
Select a port range for each type of real-time media traffic ⓘ	◉ Specify port ranges		
	○ Automatically use any available ports		

Media traffic type	Starting port	Ending port	Total ports
Audio	50000	50019	20
Video	50020	50039	20
Screen sharing	50040	50059	20

Figure 9.20 – Network traffic settings

6. Click **Save**.

How it works...

In this recipe, you chose whether anonymous guests can join Teams meetings hosted by your organization. You also customized the appearance and content of email invitations sent for meetings and adjusted how you wanted to handle Teams traffic and network flow.

See also

- Take a deeper dive into Teams meeting settings at `https://docs.microsoft.com/en-US/microsoftteams/meeting-settings-in-teams`.

Creating a live event policy

Live event policies let you change how certain users can host live events. This includes the ability to restrict who can attend their live events and lets you provide options to the host, such as recording, scheduling, and transcription. In this recipe, we'll create a Teams live event policy to restrict a couple of users' abilities when hosting live events.

Getting ready

You must be a global or Teams administrator to complete the steps in this recipe.

How to do it...

1. Go to the Microsoft Teams admin center at `https://admin.teams.microsoft.com/`.

2. Select **Meetings | Live events policies**:

Figure 9.21 – The Live events policies link in the left-hand navigation menu of the Microsoft Teams admin center

3. Click **Add**:

Figure 9.22 – The Add button on the Live events policies page

4. Configure each of the settings (scheduling, transcription, who can join, and who can record) as you see fit for the specific group of individuals you have in mind. Anyone not assigned to this policy will instead fall under the **Global (Org-wide default)** policy:

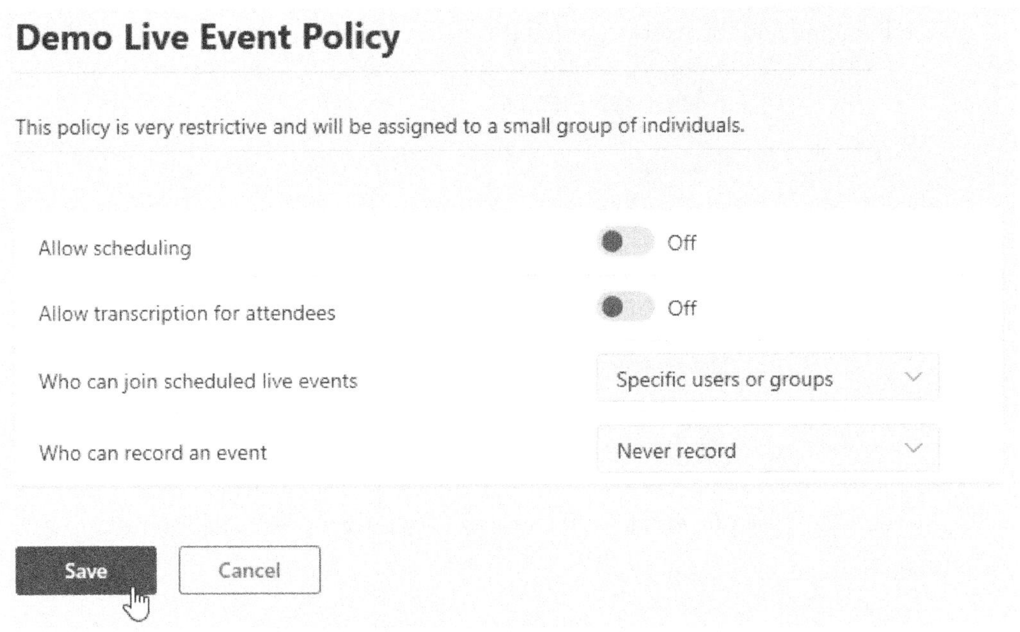

Demo Live Event Policy
This policy is very restrictive and will be assigned to a small group of individuals.
Allow scheduling
Off
Allow transcription for attendees
Off
Who can join scheduled live events
Specific users or groups
Who can record an event
Never record
Save
Cancel

Figure 9.23 – New live event policy configuration fields

5. Click **Save**.
6. Now, select the policy by clicking to the left of its name in the checkmark column. Then, choose **Manage users**:

2
+ Add
Edit
Duplicate
Delete
Reset Global policy
Manage users
2 Items
Name
Custom policy
1
Demo Live Event Policy
Yes
Global (Org-wide default)
No

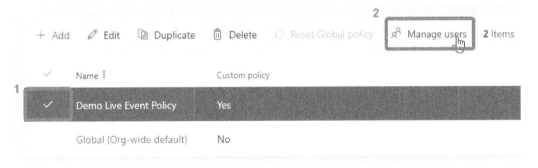

Figure 9.24 – The Manage users options for the selected policy

7.   Search for and add the users to which this policy should apply:

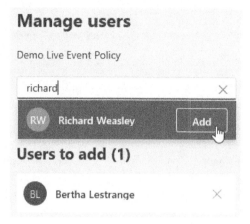

Figure 9.25 – Dialog for searching and selecting users to whom this policy will apply

8.   When finished, click **Apply**.

How it works...

You've just utilized the Microsoft Teams admin center to create a new live event policy and assign it to users. Any users who were not assigned a custom policy will automatically fall under the configuration of the global default policy.

See also

- Learn more about live event policies at `https://docs.microsoft.com/en-US/microsoftteams/teams-live-events/set-up-for-teams-live-events`.

Configuring live event settings

You can configure a couple of settings that will apply to every live event hosted by your organization. In this recipe, we'll look at configuring them.

Getting ready

You must be a global or Teams administrator to complete the steps in this recipe. For the second setting, you need a third-party video service. If you don't have one, just skip that setting.

How to do it...

1. Go to the Microsoft Teams admin center at `https://admin.teams.microsoft.com/`.

2. Select **Meetings | Live events settings**:

Figure 9.26 – The Live events settings link in the left-hand navigation menu of the Microsoft Teams admin center

3. For **Support URL**, type the URL you want users to access if they need support during a live event. For **Third party video distribution providers**, only toggle it to the **On** position if you have a third-party distribution provider. Currently, only Hive and Kollective are supported in this setting and you'll be asked for information provided by them if selected:

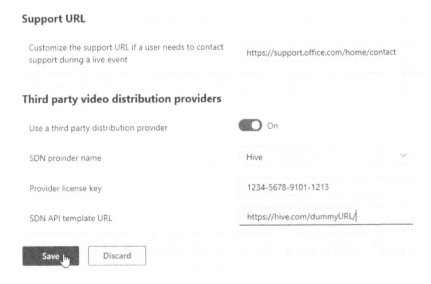

Figure 9.27 – Live events support link and third-party details

4. Click **Save**.

How it works...

This recipe walked you through configuring universal live events policy settings, including a support URL for attendees and third-party video distribution provider information where relevant.

See also

- Learn more about configuring live events settings in Microsoft Teams at `https://docs.microsoft.com/en-US/microsoftteams/teams-live-events/configure-teams-live-events`.

Creating a messaging policy

As with other Teams policies, there's a default/global policy that applies to all users. You can create a custom messaging policy that applies to specific users instead, while still leaving the remaining (unassigned) users to the default policy. In this recipe, we'll create a custom messaging policy to apply to specific users, restricting their abilities when it comes to messaging in channels and in chats.

Getting ready

You must be a global or Teams administrator to complete the steps in this recipe.

How to do it...

1. Go to the Microsoft Teams admin center at `https://admin.teams.microsoft.com/`.

2. Choose **Messaging policies** from the left-hand navigation menu:

Figure 9.28 – The Messaging policies link in the left-hand navigation menu of the Microsoft Teams admin center

3. Click **Add**:

Figure 9.29 – The Add button on the Messaging policies page of the Microsoft Teams admin center

4. Go down through the list of settings, keeping in mind the type of user to which you'll apply this policy, and make selections accordingly. Things you might consider are disallowing deletion of messages, restricting Giphy gifs to strict content ratings (or toggling them to **Off** altogether), and so on:

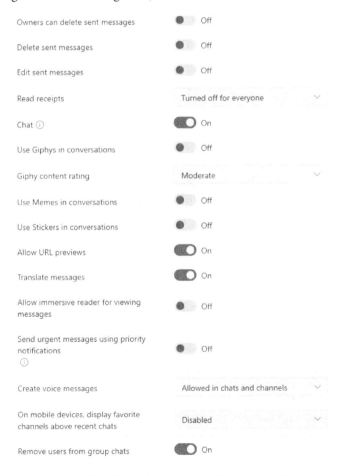

Figure 9.30 – Messaging policy configuration options

5. When you have finished configuring the policy's settings, click **Save**.

6. Now, select the policy by clicking to the left of its name in the checkmark column. Then, choose **Manage users**:

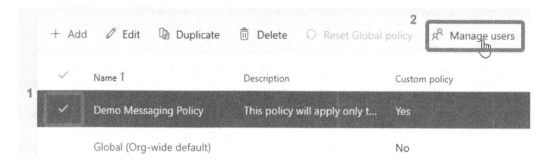

Figure 9.31 – The Manage users option for the selected policy

7. Search for and add the users to which this policy should apply:

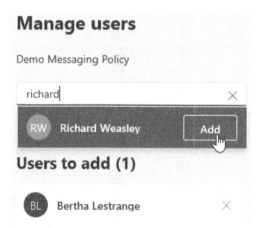

Figure 9.32 – Dialog for searching for and selecting users to whom the policy will apply

8. When finished, click **Apply**.

How it works...

In this recipe, you created a custom messaging policy that would restrict assigned users from utilizing certain features in Teams chat messages and channel conversations. Any user who isn't assigned one of your custom policies will be assigned the global/ default policy.

See also

- Learn more about Teams messaging policies at `https://docs.microsoft.com/en-US/microsoftteams/messaging-policies-in-teams`.

Configuring Teams setup policies

You can have different apps display by default in the left-side navigation menu of Teams for different users. This includes adding additional apps for those users and hiding others. An example of the usefulness of this here would be if only some of your users use the **Shifts** app, you can have it permanently appear for those users without them having to click on the ellipsis first, as seen here:

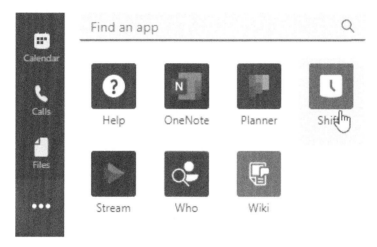

Figure 9.33 – Additional apps available in the Teams client application's left-hand menu's ellipsis menu

In this recipe, we'll create a Teams setup policy that places **Shifts** above **Calls** in the menu for certain users.

Getting ready

You must be a global or Teams administrator to complete the steps in this recipe.

How to do it...

1. Go to the Microsoft Teams admin center at `https://admin.teams.microsoft.com/`.

2. Select **Teams apps | Setup policies** from the left-hand navigation menu:

Figure 9.34 – The Setup policies link in the left-hand navigation menu of the
Microsoft Teams admin center

3. Click **Add**:

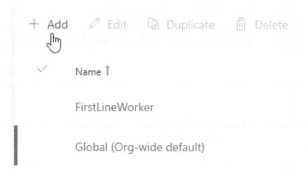

Figure 9.35 – The Add button on the Setup policies page of the Microsoft Teams admin center

4. Configure the first two settings as you wish, allowing/disallowing the upload of custom apps and pinning:

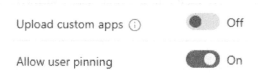

Figure 9.36 – Custom app and user pinning options

5. Under the **Pinned apps** section, click in the checkmark column to the left of the **Shifts** app to select it. Then, click the **Move up** button until it is where you want it, keeping in mind that **Files** is currently the last visible app. By moving an app from beneath **Files** above it, **Files** will be pushed to the section of additional apps that is found when clicking the ellipsis:

Pinned apps

Choose the order that apps are pinned in the Teams app navigation bar.

	Name	App ID	Distributor
	Activity	14d6962d-6eeb-4f48-8890-de55454bb136	Microsoft
	Chat	86fcd49b-61a2-4701-b771-54728cd291fb	Microsoft
	Teams	2a84919f-59d8-4441-a975-2a8c2643b741	Microsoft
	Calendar	ef56c0de-36fc-4ef8-b417-3d82ba9d073c	Microsoft
✓	Shifts	42f6c1da-a241-483a-a3cc-4f5be9185951	Microsoft Corp.
	Calling	20c3440d-c67e-4420-9f80-0e50c39693df	Microsoft

Figure 9.37 – Pinned app order and option to add more

6. Click **Save**.

7. Now, click in the checkmark column to the left of the new policy name to select it.
    Then, click **Manage users**:

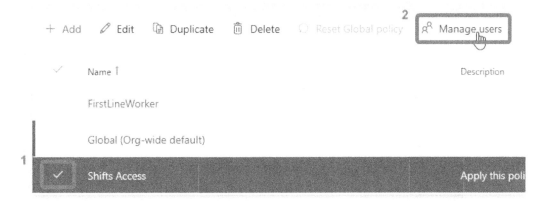

Figure 9.38 – The Manage users option for the selected policy

8. Search for and add the users to which this policy should apply:

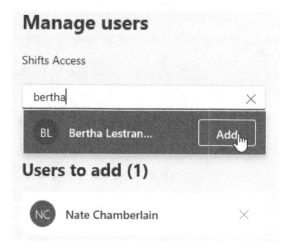

Figure 9.39 – Dialog for searching and selecting users to whom the policy will apply

9. When finished, click **Apply**.

How it works...

You've just created a policy that provides (hopefully) a better, more customized experience for specific users. Specifically, we made the **Shifts** app easier to get to by moving it onto the left-side navigation pane of the Teams client app, reducing a click for users who regularly access it. The following screenshot shows how this policy affects the left-side navigation menu for assigned users:

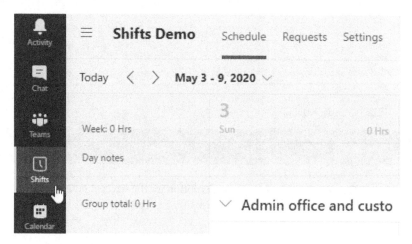

Figure 9.40 – Example of the Shifts app moved up in the navigation menu by the policy

> **Important note**
> Users to whom this policy applies will need to sign out and then back in to the Teams client app for changes to appear.

See also

- Take a deeper dive into the possibilities for customizing the Teams setup for users by reading the information available at `https://docs.microsoft.com/en-US/microsoftteams/teams-app-setup-policies`.

Configuring external access

By default, users in your organization can communicate with people from any domain in or outside your organization. You can choose to add or block domains and change whether your Teams users can communicate with Skype for Business and Skype users by utilizing the **External access** settings in the Microsoft Teams admin center. In this recipe, we'll choose to block specific domains so that our Teams users cannot communicate via Teams with users in those domains.

Getting ready

You must be a global or Teams administrator to configure the settings in this recipe.

How to do it...

1. Go to the Microsoft Teams admin center at `https://admin.teams.microsoft.com`.

2. Select **Org-wide settings | External access**:

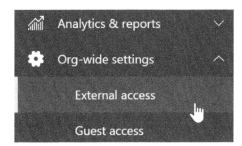

Figure 9.41 – The External access link in the left-hand navigation menu of the Microsoft Teams admin center

3. Click **+ Add a domain**.

4. Type a domain from which you'll block your users from communicating, select **Blocked**, and then select **Done**:

Figure 9.42 – Domain to be added and allowed or blocked

5. Click **Save**.

How it works...

In this recipe, you learned how to allow or block specific domains from interacting with your organization's Teams environment. All domains will be allowed except `sharepointlibrarian.com` in this example. We can add additional domains to block by repeating the steps in this recipe, further limiting the allowed domains with which our users can communicate freely.

There's more

From the **External access** blade of the Microsoft Teams admin center, you can alternatively choose to list domains that are allowed (blocking all that are unlisted).

Also, notice that above the **Domains** section, you can choose to limit users in Teams from communicating with other users in specified domains using Skype for Business, Teams, and Skype (personal):

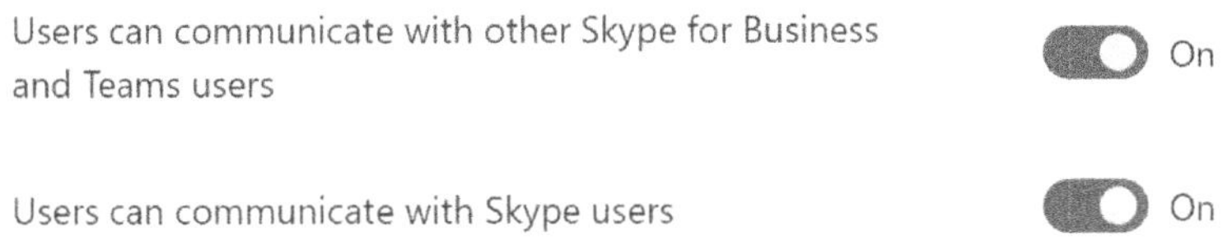

Users can communicate with other Skype for Business and Teams users   On

Users can communicate with Skype users   On

Figure 9.43 – The External access options for allowing Teams users to communicate via specific apps

See also

- Learn more about external access in Teams at `https://docs.microsoft.com/en-US/microsoftteams/manage-external-access`.

Configuring guest access

As a Teams administrator, you can choose whether to allow guests in your organization's Microsoft Teams environment at all, and if so, how those guest users can utilize Teams. For example, you may wish to allow/disallow making private calls or chatting. In this recipe, we'll configure the **Guest access** settings in the Microsoft Teams admin center.

Getting ready

You must be a global or Teams administrator to configure the settings in this recipe.

How to do it...

1. Go to the Microsoft Teams admin center at `https://admin.teams.microsoft.com`.

2. Select **Org-wide settings | Guest access**:

Figure 9.44 – The Guest access link in the left-hand navigation menu of the
Microsoft Teams admin center

3. If you disable **Allow guest access in Teams**, none of the other options on this page will be available. We'll leave it as **On** for this recipe:

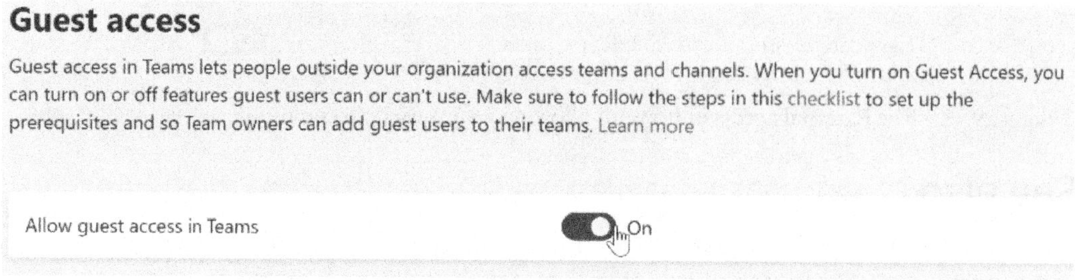

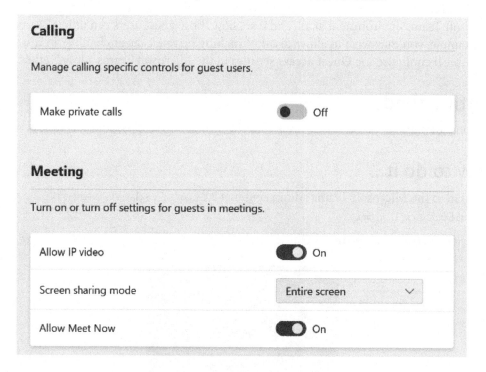

Guest access

Guest access in Teams lets people outside your organization access teams and channels. When you turn on Guest Access, you can turn on or off features guest users can or can't use. Make sure to follow the steps in this checklist to set up the prerequisites and so Team owners can add guest users to their teams. Learn more

Allow guest access in Teams   On

Figure 9.45 – The toggle option for allowing guest access in Teams

4. In the **Calling** and **Meeting** sections, choose whether guests can make private calls, use IP video, share their screen, and use the **Meet Now** function:

Calling

Manage calling specific controls for guest users.

Make private calls   Off

Meeting

Turn on or turn off settings for guests in meetings.

Allow IP video   On

Screen sharing mode   Entire screen

Allow Meet Now   On

Figure 9.46 – Calling and meeting options for guests

5. Scroll down to the last section, **Messaging**. Choose what abilities guest users have relating to editing and chatting with rich features such as stickers and GIFs:

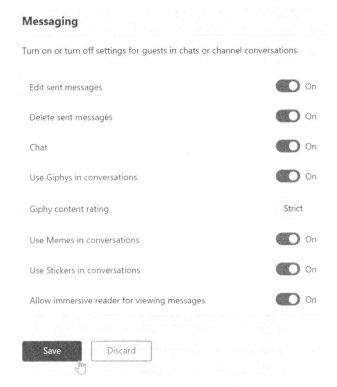

Figure 9.47 – Messaging options for guests

6. Click **Save** when you have finished making changes.

How it works...

In this recipe, you chose what actions guest users are able to perform within your organization's Teams environment. This single settings panel for guest access applies to all guest users in your tenant. Be mindful that if you already have many guest users in your tenant, this may disrupt their experience the next time they join a meeting. Be sure to communicate any effects that your setting alterations may have on your users' interactions with guests.

See also

- Before guests can be added to a team, you'll need to make sure you've gone through the steps at https://docs.microsoft.com/en-US/microsoftteams/guest-access-checklist.

- Learn more about Microsoft Teams guest access at https://docs.microsoft.com/en-US/microsoftteams/guest-access.

Reviewing teams and their owners

Especially as you begin to think about governance and content strategy, you'll want to regularly review all existing teams and perhaps contact their owners. In this recipe, we'll do just that, utilizing the Microsoft Teams admin center.

Getting ready

You must be a global or Teams administrator to complete the steps in this recipe.

How to do it...

1. Go to the Microsoft Teams admin center at `https://admin.teams.microsoft.com`.

2. Select **Teams | Manage teams**:

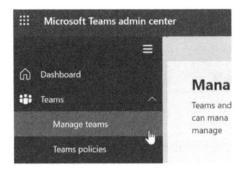

Figure 9.48 – The Manage teams link in the left-hand navigation menu of the
Microsoft Teams admin center

3. At this level, we can see how many channels, team members, owners, and guests each Team has. Search for and/or select a specific team:

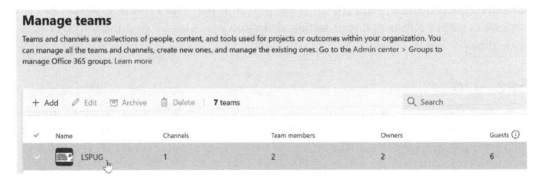

Figure 9.49 – A selected team with counts

4. Once a team is selected, we're able to see more information, including its owners. Select the **Role** column header twice to sort so that owners appear together at the top of the list:

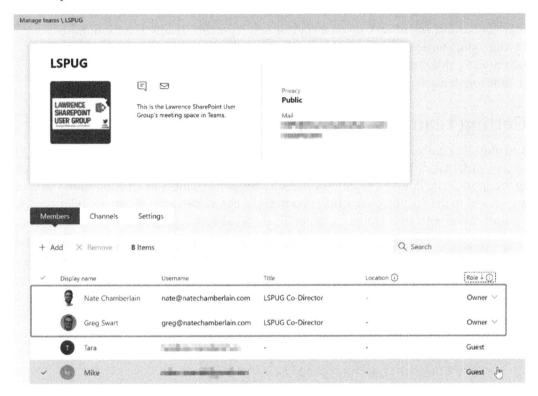

Figure 9.50 – The selected team's details page with specific members, channels, and settings

How it works...

In this recipe, you used the Microsoft Teams admin center to navigate to a listing of all the teams, then clicked on a specific team to view its membership. The Microsoft Teams admin center serves as a command center for designing and deploying setting configurations and policies, but also as a reporting center where we can review things such as all the teams and their owners.

Using PowerShell to export a list of all the teams' owners and members

Sometimes, the click-intensive web experience of reviewing teams, owners, and members may not be ideal when working on analyzing and reporting Teams data for hundreds of teams simultaneously. While the previous recipe is great for looking into a few teams occasionally, this method of exporting all the teams' info is best for creating a snapshot in time for all teams. In this recipe, we'll export a CSV file with all the teams' data.

Getting ready

You must be a global or Teams administrator to complete the steps in this recipe. This script includes code to prompt you for credentials, as well as auto-install and a connection to the appropriate PowerShell modules, so no additional changes or configuration are needed to the script. You'll simply run the script as is, then sign in using modern authentication with your global admin or Teams admin credentials.

Note that this script is from a third-party site, o365reports.com, and should be analyzed and adjusted to your organization's best practices and compliance policies prior to executing.

How to do it...

1. Go to https://o365reports.com/2020/05/28/microsoft-teams-reporting-using-powershell.

2. Click on the link next to **Download Script:** named TeamsReports.ps1.

3. Go to your download location, right-click on the downloaded file, and select **Run with PowerShell**:

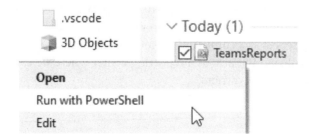

Figure 9.51 – Right-clicking on the downloaded PS file to see the Run with PowerShell option

4. This script includes the option of running several reports:

    1. **All Teams in organization**
    2. **All Teams members and owners report**
    3. **Specific Teams' members and Owners report**
    4. **All Teams' owners report**
    5. **Specific Teams' owners report**
    6. **All channels in organization**
    7. **All channels in specific Team**
    8. **Members and Owners Report of Single Channel**

    For this recipe, we want to export a file of all the teams' members and owners, so we'll type 2 and press *Enter* to select that report:

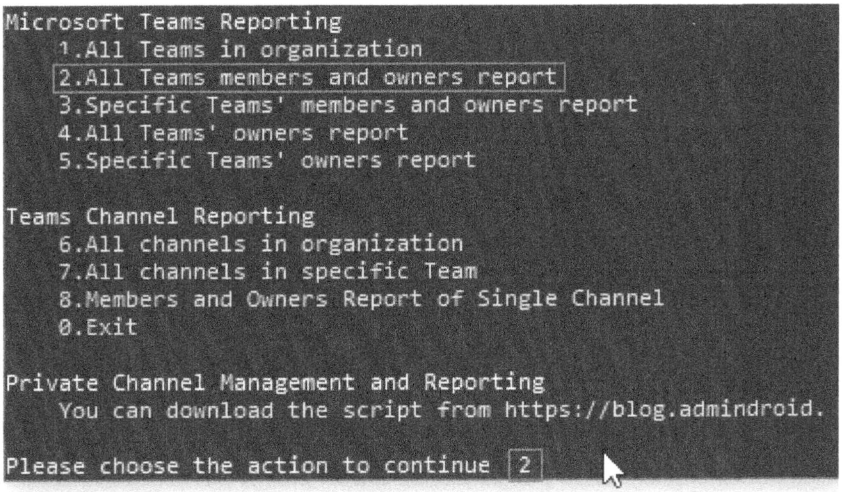

Figure 9.52 – Entering 2 into the PowerShell prompt indicates we'd like to download the All Teams members and owners report

5. Once finished, you'll see a success message with the file location. Open the downloaded file to find your report, resembling the following:

◢	A	B	C	D
1	Teams Name	Member Name	Member Mail	Role
2	LSPUG	Nate Chamberlain	nate@natechambe	owner
3	Project Management Demo	Nate Chamberlain	nate@natechambe	owner
4	Shifts Demo	Nate Chamberlain	nate@natechambe	owner
5	Shifts Demo	Heather Granger	heather@natechan	member
6	Shifts Demo	Herbert Potter	herbert@natechan	member
7	Shifts Demo	Richard Weasley	richard@natecham	member
8	Shifts Demo	Bertha Lestrange	bertha@natechaml	member
9	Shifts Demo	Tyler Riddle	tyler@natechambe	member
10	O365 Group Demo	Nate Chamberlain	nate@natechambe	owner
11	O365 Group Demo	Ronald Hart	nchambe_outlook.	guest
12	O365 Group Demo	Neville Lakemoore	nathanchamberlair	guest

Figure 9.53 – A snippet of an exported report showing all the owners and members of all the teams in our organization

How it works...

In this recipe, you used PowerShell and a script from O365reports.com to gain access to eight different reports that can be run easily when analyzing your organization's Microsoft Teams environment. We specifically chose to export all members and owners of all teams in this recipe, but there are seven other options that you can explore simply by changing the number you entered in *step 4*.

See also

Find more information about this script, read the full write-up on the hosting post at https://o365reports.com/2020/05/28/microsoft-teams-reporting-using-powershell/.

10
Configuring and Managing Users in Azure Active Directory (Azure AD)

Azure Active Directory (**Azure AD** or **AAD**) provides additional functionality and granularity when it comes to managing users, access restrictions, groups, and licensing. It is included by default at the heart of O365 identity and security. We will look at some of the more popular reasons as to why O365 administrators might find themselves in Azure AD.

This chapter includes the following recipes:

- Bulk create users in AAD
- Adding branding to the AAD sign-in page
- Adding a privacy statement to the AAD sign-in page
- Installing and connecting to AAD via PowerShell
- Adding/removing users via PowerShell in AAD
- Creating an access review report in Azure AD
- Allowing/disallowing users from connecting LinkedIn to their account
- Enabling a self-service password reset
- Using SSO to simplify organization-wide sign-in processes

Technical requirements

This chapter will often require that you're a global administrator in your tenant although, in certain cases, a user administrator role will suffice. You'll also need to be able to run PowerShell and may need rights to install software on a machine in order to complete all the recipes.

Bulk create users in AAD

When adding multiple users to Azure AD, it is often more efficient to do so in batches. In this recipe, we'll bulk create users in Azure AD.

Getting ready

You should be a global or user administrator to complete this recipe.

How to do it...

1. Go to https://aad.portal.azure.com/. Sign in if prompted.
2. Click **Users** from the left-hand navigation menu.
3. From **Bulk activities**, select **Bulk create**:

Figure 10.1 – Bulk create option available from the Users blade of Azure Active Directory

4. Click **Download** to download the CSV template to use for properly formatting the soon-to-be-imported users.

5. Open the template and paste or complete rows for each user to be imported, filling in the following column values:

--Name [displayName] *Required*

--User name [userPrincipalName] *Required*

--Initial password [passwordProfile] *Required*

--Block sign in (Yes/No) [accountEnabled] *Required*

--First name [givenName]

--Last name [surname]

--Job title [jobTitle]

--Department [department]

--Usage location [usageLocation]

--Street address [streetAddress]

--State or province [state]

--Country or region [country]

--Office [physicalDeliveryOfficeName]

--City [city]

--ZIP or postal code [postalCode]

--Office phone [telephoneNumber]

--Mobile phone [mobile]

6. Back in Azure AD where you left off, click **Select file** to upload the CSV file you just updated in step 5.,

7. Click **Submit**.

8. Wait for the upload and processing to complete.

How it works...

In this recipe, you used a bulk activity option, **Bulk create**, in Azure AD to import a template-based CSV file of new users for creation.

See also

- Learn more about bulk creating users in Azure AD at `https://docs.microsoft.com/en-us/azure/active-directory/users-groups-roles/users-bulk-add`.

Adding branding to the AAD sign-in page

Adding your own branding to the AAD sign-in page lets your users easily confirm that they're signing into the correct tenant by recognizing familiar graphics. It also gives your organization a more polished, professional appearance, not only to your own users, but also to your guest users signing into your tenant. In this recipe, we'll add branding elements to the AAD sign-in page.

Getting ready

You must be a global administrator to complete the steps in this recipe. You'll also need images ready that match the following specifications (with transparent backgrounds in most cases where appropriate):

- Background: 1920×1080 px | <300 KB | PNG, JPG, or JPEG

- Banner: 280×60 px | 10 KB | PNG, JPG, or JPEG

- Square: 240×240 px | 50 KB | PNG (preferred), JPG, or JPEG

- Square – Dark: 240×240 px | 50 KB | PNG (preferred), JPG, or JPEG

How to do it...

1. Go to the Azure Active Directory Admin Center at `https://aad.portal.azure.com`.

2. Click on **Azure Active Directory** from the left navigation menu and then choose **Company branding**:

Figure 10.2 – Company branding link in Azure AD

3. Select **Configure**:

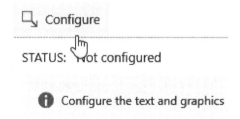

Figure 10.3 – Configure option on the company branding page

4. Upload images for the background of the sign-in page as well as your organization's banner image to customize the sign-in experience:

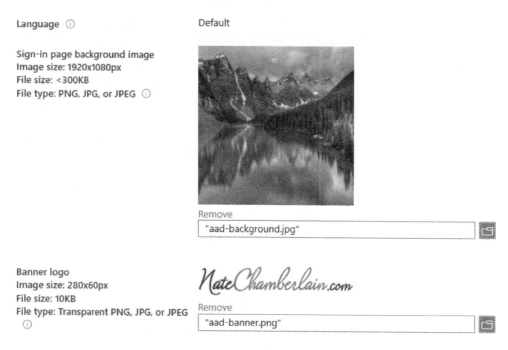

Figure 10.4 – Image/graphic upload options for customizing the AAD sign-in page

---

Important note

Note the instructions to the left of each graphic type. You must create/upload graphics that match the listed requirements, while a best practice for your sign-in page background image would be to choose an image that doesn't have a central focus point, as that's where the sign-in area will appear. Ideal images would have a focal point on the left, right, or top of the screen so that it appears around the sign-in area.

---

5. Choose whether to configure additional instructional text for the username entry box and the footer of the sign-in page. Do not put anything sensitive here and remember that guest users will use the same portal, so some hints may not apply to all users:

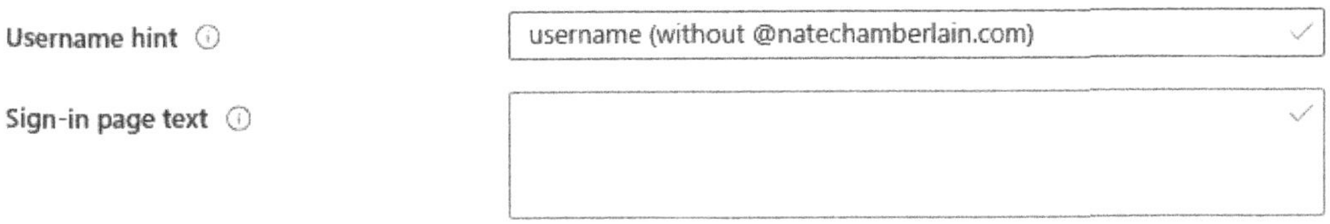

| Username hint ⓘ | username (without @natechamberlain.com) ✓ |
| Sign-in page text ⓘ | ✓ |

Figure 10.5 – Sign-in assistance or information options

6. To ensure that your sign-in page is customized across all experiences, choose a background color and upload square logos for both light and dark experiences. Then, choose whether users should be able to remain signed in:

Advanced settings

Sign-in page background color ⓘ   #00bff8 ✓

Square logo image
Image size: 240x240x (resizable)
Max file size: 50KB
PNG (preferred), JPG, or JPEG ⓘ

Nate Nate

Remove
"aad-sqlogo.png"

Square logo image, dark theme
Image size: 240x240x (resizable)
Max file size: 50KB
PNG (preferred), JPG, or JPEG ⓘ

Nate Nate

Remove
"aad-dark-sqlogo.png"

Show option to remain signed in ⓘ   (Yes   No)

Figure 10.6 – Advanced settings for customizing the AAD sign-in page

7. Click **Save** (at the top):

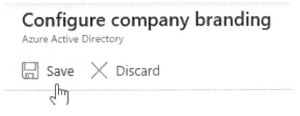

Configure company branding
Azure Active Directory

💾 Save   ✕ Discard

Figure 10.7 – The Save option at the top of the Configure company branding page

How it works...

In this recipe, you configured the branding components that will appear to users signing in to your tenant. This creates a customized/personalized feel for your users and makes it easy for them to recognize a familiar visual when signing in. This can help combat phishing attempts as well, as some O365 phishing attempts commonly resemble the generic (not customized) login screens.

Once you've configured branding, users will be presented with a generic login screen initially until Azure AD knows which tenant they're trying to authenticate to. Once you enter `nate@natechamberlain.com`, for example, it adds our custom banner image to the login screen for password entry:

Figure 10.8 – Sign-in prompt example with custom branding applied

Once the user enters their password correctly, they'll be asked whether they want to remain signed in if you selected `Yes` in *step 6*:

Figure 10.9 – Background image example with custom branding applied

The next time the user signs out and back in, it will remember their email and branding will be visible immediately. This depends on individual computer/browser settings and the individual users' cross-tenant sign-in/out activities, of course:

Figure 10.10 – Remembered account(s) dialog when signing in

See also

- Learn more about customizing the sign-in page user experience when accessing company resources at `https://docs.microsoft.com/en-us/azure/active-directory/fundamentals/customize-branding`.

Adding a privacy statement to the AAD sign-in page

When users view their O365 account (settings wheel > **View account**), there's a link for **Security & privacy** that they can click. There, they'll find a link to **Organization Privacy Statement**, which we'll configure in this recipe:

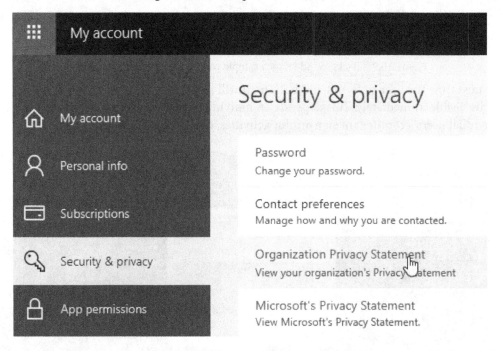

Figure 10.11 – Organization Privacy Statement link in a user's O365 account settings

Getting ready

You must be a global administrator to complete the steps in this recipe.

How to do it...

1. Go to the Azure Active Directory Admin Center at `https://aad.portal.azure.com`.

2. Select **Azure Active Directory** from the left navigation menu.

3. Click **Properties** from under the **Manage** heading.

4. Find the field for your **Privacy statement URL** and add it:

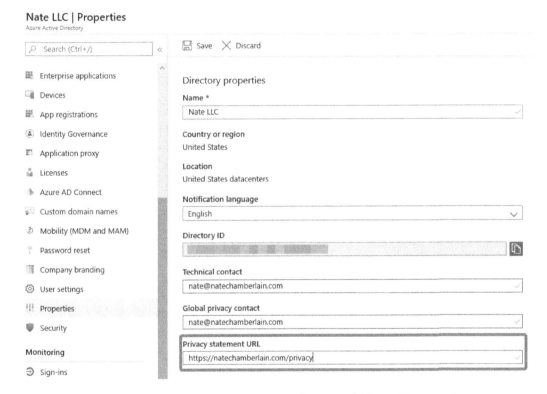

Figure 10.12 – Privacy statement URL configuration field in AAD properties

5. Click **Save** (at the top).

How it works...

In this recipe, you've updated your organization's privacy statement that is made available to users and external guests when accessing your environment. This helps in data usage and visibility transparency.

There's more...

You should always consult your legal department or lawyers when dealing with privacy or legal topics.

See also

- Learn more about updating AAD's properties at `https://docs.microsoft.com/en-us/azure/active-directory/fundamentals/active-directory-properties-area`.

Installing and connecting to AAD via PowerShell

Azure AD can be managed easily using PowerShell cmdlets, in the same way as we've demonstrated with general O365 administration via PowerShell in *Chapter 3, Administering Office 365 with PowerShell*. Remember to run PowerShell as an administrator (right-click, and then choose **Run as administrator**) when running commands to ensure you'll be able to complete actions (assuming your credentials are also valid for the action you're attempting to perform). In this recipe, we'll install and connect to AAD via PowerShell to unlock many more administrative capabilities.

Getting ready

You must be a global administrator to complete the steps in this recipe.

If you haven't done so already (perhaps in *Chapter 3, Administering Office 365 with PowerShell*), download and install the Microsoft Online Services Sign-In Assistant at `http://go.microsoft.com/fwlink/?LinkID=286152`.

How to do it...

1. Install either the `AzureADPreview` module for additional cmdlets in public preview release, or just install the basic `AzureAD` module for the more stable version:

```
Install-Module AzureADPreview
```

2. Run the `Connect-AzureAD` cmdlet, and then provide your Azure AD credentials when prompted. A dialog should appear to accept them:

```
Connect-AzureAD
```

This can be seen in the following screenshot:

Figure 10.13 – Sign-in prompt presented when using Connect-AzureAD in PowerShell

3. If successful, you'll see confirmation of your details resembling this:

Figure 10.14 – Signed-in user details displayed in PowerShell

4. If you'd like to see all the cmdlets you can now use, run `Get-Command` as follows for a listing of new cmdlets:

```
Get-Command -Module AzureADPreview
```

This can be seen in the following screenshot:

```
PS C:\          > Get-Command -Module AzureADPreview

CommandType     Name                                                Version    Source
-----------     ----                                                -------    ------
Cmdlet          Add-AzureADAdministrativeUnitMember                 2.0.2.89   AzureADPreview
Cmdlet          Add-AzureADApplicationOwner                         2.0.2.89   AzureADPreview
Cmdlet          Add-AzureADApplicationPolicy                        2.0.2.89   AzureADPreview
Cmdlet          Add-AzureADDeviceRegisteredOwner                    2.0.2.89   AzureADPreview
Cmdlet          Add-AzureADDeviceRegisteredUser                     2.0.2.89   AzureADPreview
Cmdlet          Add-AzureADDirectoryRoleMember                      2.0.2.89   AzureADPreview
Cmdlet          Add-AzureADGroupMember                              2.0.2.89   AzureADPreview
Cmdlet          Add-AzureADGroupOwner                               2.0.2.89   AzureADPreview
Cmdlet          Add-AzureADMSApplicationOwner                       2.0.2.89   AzureADPreview
Cmdlet          Add-AzureADMSFeatureRolloutPolicyDirectoryObject    2.0.2.89   AzureADPreview
Cmdlet          Add-AzureADMSLifecyclePolicyGroup                   2.0.2.89   AzureADPreview
Cmdlet          Add-AzureADMSPrivilegedResource                     2.0.2.89   AzureADPreview
Cmdlet          Add-AzureADMSServicePrincipalDelegatedPermissio...  2.0.2.89   AzureADPreview
Cmdlet          Add-AzureADScopedRoleMembership                     2.0.2.89   AzureADPreview
Cmdlet          Add-AzureADServicePrincipalOwner                    2.0.2.89   AzureADPreview
Cmdlet          Add-AzureADServicePrincipalPolicy                   2.0.2.89   AzureADPreview
Cmdlet          Close-AzureADMSPrivilegedRoleAssignmentRequest      2.0.2.89   AzureADPreview
Cmdlet          Confirm-AzureADDomain                               2.0.2.89   AzureADPreview
Cmdlet          Connect-AzureAD                                     2.0.2.89   AzureADPreview
Cmdlet          Disconnect-AzureAD                                  2.0.2.89   AzureADPreview
Cmdlet          Enable-AzureADDirectoryRole                         2.0.2.89   AzureADPreview
```

Figure 10.15 – All commands displayed in PowerShell after using Get-Command

How it works...

In this recipe, you added and connected to an Azure AD PowerShell module to expand your cmdlet abilities when administering both O365 apps and services as well as Azure AD specifically. With every PowerShell session, you'll need to connect using credentials, but then you'll be able to utilize cmdlets from both the MSOnline and AzureAD modules, thereby maximizing your efficiency in tenant administration.

There's more...

If you haven't already done so (again, perhaps in *Chapter 3, Administering Office 365 with PowerShell*), you will need to open PowerShell and run the following command to install the MSOnline module for more O365 PowerShell abilities beyond just Azure AD:

```
Install-Module MSOnline
```

See also

- See all cmdlets and functionality in both MSOnline and AzureAD at https://docs.microsoft.com/en-us/powershell/azure/active-directory/overview?view=azureadps-2.0.

Adding/removing users via PowerShell in AAD

This recipe should begin to get you thinking about how you could potentially automate regular processes in your organization by utilizing PowerShell as part of your automated job. While we'll manually add a user to Azure AD in this recipe, you could have the same PowerShell script run based on a trigger from your HR system, by way of an example. For now, we'll start with the basics – running the script itself manually to add a user.

Getting ready

You must be a global administrator to complete the steps in this recipe.

How to do it...

1. Open Windows PowerShell (or your PowerShell client of choice) as the administrator.

2. Connect to Azure AD using `Connect-AzureAD`.

3. Use a script such as the following, replacing the user's specific info where appropriate.

```
$PasswordProfile = New-Object -TypeName Microsoft.Open.
AzureAD.Model.PasswordProfile
```

```
$PasswordProfile.Password = "aBc123!ndc"
```

```
New-AzureADUser -AccountEnabled $True -DisplayName "Andy
Green"
-PasswordProfile $PasswordProfile -MailNickName "AndyG"
-UserPrincipalName "AndyG@natechamberlain.com"
```

This can be seen in the following screenshot:

Figure 10.16 – New user added and confirmed via PowerShell

4. Removing users would simply use the following script requiring the user's email:

```
Remove-AzureADUser -ObjectId "AndyG@natechamberlain.com"
```

How it works...

In this recipe, you created a user by providing the user's details in a PowerShell script.

In the script, we created a `$PasswordProfile` variable to store the required parameter type of `PasswordProfile` for the user's password.

Then, we specified the password itself, updating the variable. You'd likely generate this randomly in whatever script or practice you deploy rather than use an initial static value for all users.

Lastly, we provided the new user's information, including `DisplayName`, `MailNickName`, and `UserPrincipalName` (email).

This recipe also included the single line needed to remove a user.

See also

- Learn more about creating new users via PowerShell at `https://docs.microsoft.com/en-us/powershell/module/azuread/new-azureaduser`.

- More on deleting users via PowerShell can be found at `https://docs.microsoft.com/en-us/powershell/module/azuread/remove-azureaduser`.

Creating an access review report in Azure AD

Access reviews allow you to easily review who has access to which apps and groups on a regular basis. You could recertify memberships routinely, manage guests, and increase governance efficiency by making access privileges more visible to those needing that information. In this recipe, we'll onboard to begin using access reviews and then create a report.

Getting ready

You must be a global or user administrator to complete the steps in this recipe, and need either an *Azure AD Premium P2* subscription or an *Enterprise Mobility + Security E5* subscription to use this feature.

How to do it...

1. Go to the Azure Active Directory Admin Center at `https://aad.portal.azure.com`.

2. Click on **Azure Active Directory** from the left navigation menu and then choose **Identity Governance**.

3. If this is your first time creating an access review, click **Onboard** on the left-hand navigation pane. Otherwise, skip to *step 7*:

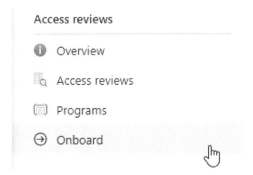

Figure 10.17 – Onboard link for setting up Access reviews initially

4. Review the information and then click **Onboard Now**.

5. Wait for successful onboarding. You'll receive a notification when it's finished:

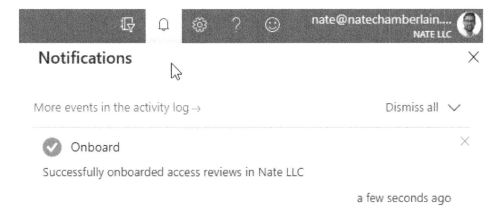

Figure 10.18 – Notifications pane with a successful onboarding message

6. Click on **Azure Active Directory** from the left navigation menu and then choose **Identity Governance**.

7. Select **Access Reviews** from the left navigation menu, followed by **New access review**:

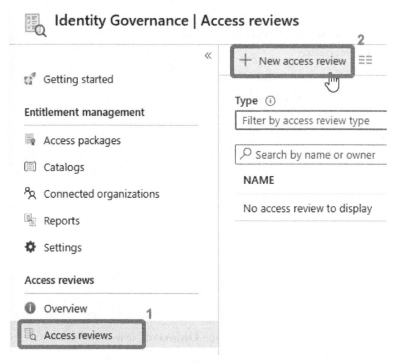

Figure 10.19 – New access review button in the Access reviews section of Identity Governance in AAD

8. Name and describe your access review and choose whether it's a one-time or regular review. If regular, also specify dates and occurrences:

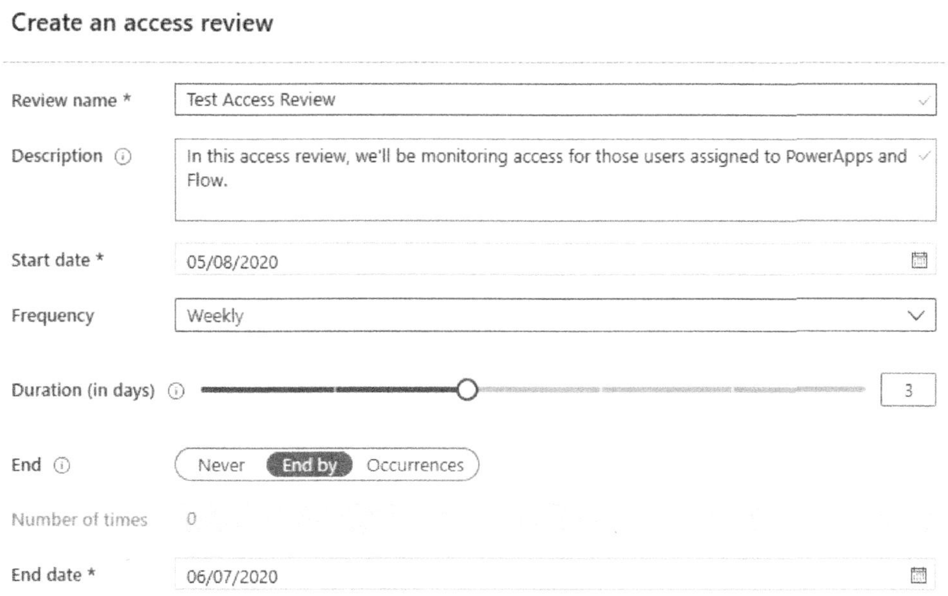

Create an access review

Review name *	Test Access Review
Description ⓘ	In this access review, we'll be monitoring access for those users assigned to PowerApps and Flow.
Start date *	05/08/2020
Frequency	Weekly
Duration (in days) ⓘ	3
End ⓘ	Never **End by** Occurrences
Number of times	0
End date *	06/07/2020

Figure 10.20 – Fields and options for configuration of an access review

9. Choose the parties to whom this access review should apply. You can choose **Guest users only** or **Everyone**. Also specify the **Application**, **Reviewers**, and **Programs** (the default setting is provided):

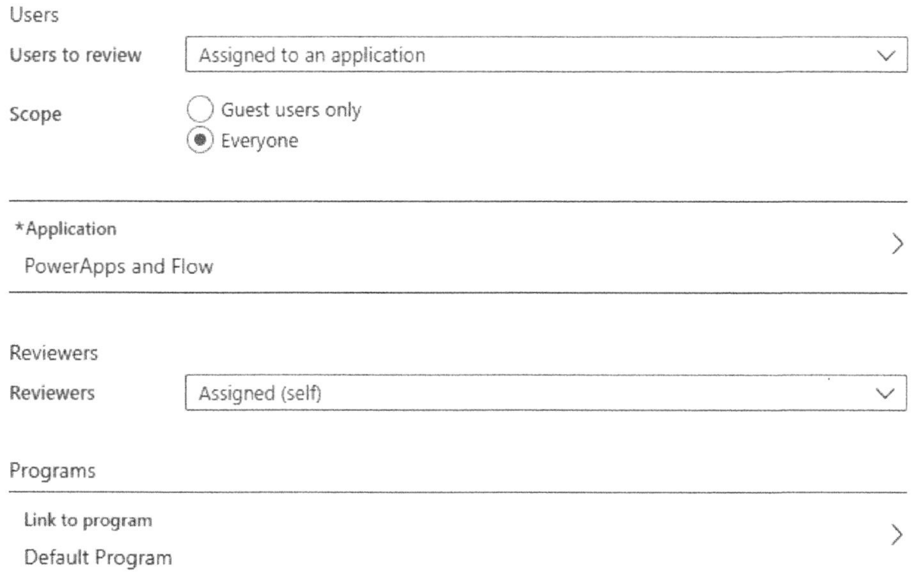

Users

Users to review	Assigned to an application
Scope	◯ Guest users only ◉ Everyone

*Application
PowerApps and Flow   >

Reviewers

Reviewers	Assigned (self)

Programs

Link to program
Default Program   >

Figure 10.21 – Additional fields for access review configuration, including users to review and reviewers

10. You may also specify completion settings and advanced settings by expanding each section and making preference selections. You may, for example, wish to disable **Mail notifications** and **Reminders** in favor of a review process that is less formal:

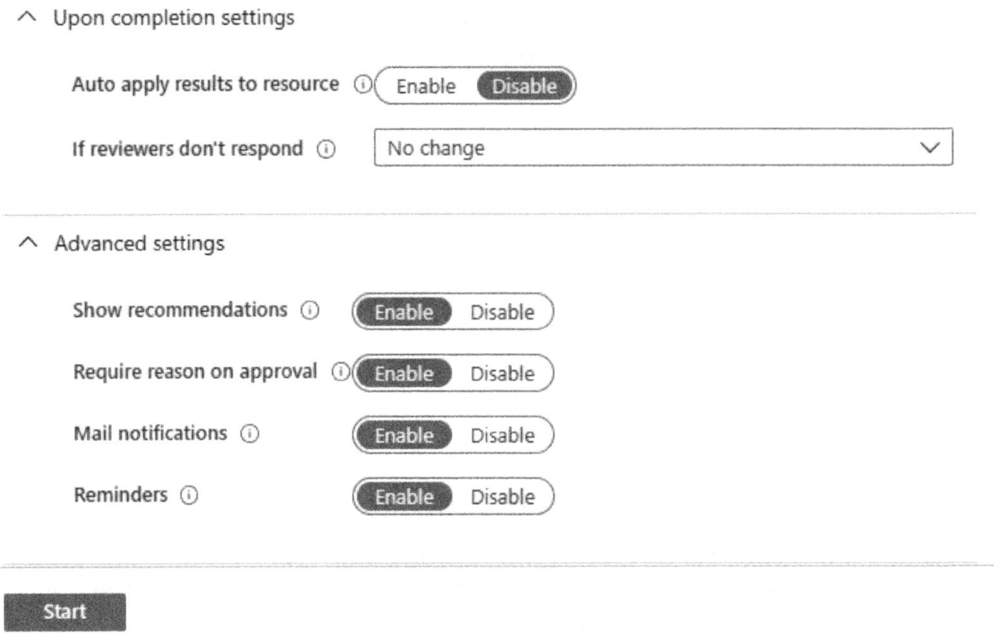

Figure 10.22 – Completion and advanced settings for access reviews

11. Click **Start**.

How it works...

We just created an access review that will let us review access for the PowerApps and Flow application created in our tenant. Whomever you listed as a reviewer will get an email along the lines of the following:

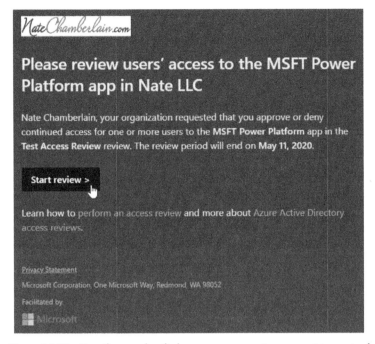

Figure 10.23 – Email example of when an access review request is received

You could also create an access review that has guests review and confirm need of their own access. Check out https://docs.microsoft.com/en-us/azure/active-directory/governance/review-your-access for details regarding that concept, where guests (or your own organization's users) would receive emails like this asking them to confirm their ongoing membership requirement:

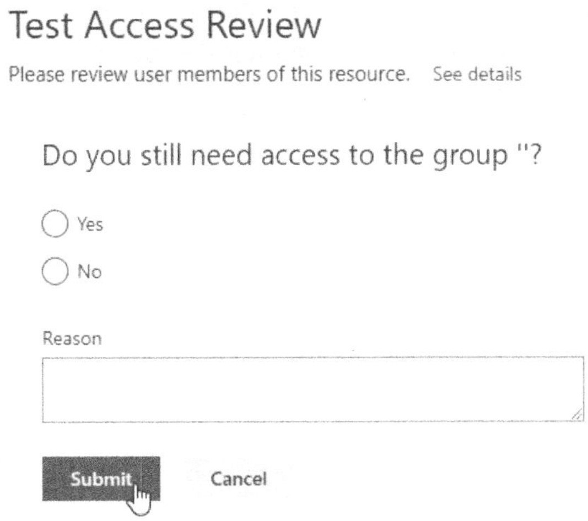

Test Access Review

Please review user members of this resource.   See details

Do you still need access to the group ''?

◯ Yes

◯ No

Reason

Submit   Cancel

Figure 10.24 – Dialog for a user taking action regarding an access review

Or, if you are the reviewer, you'll make decisions for the group and be presented with a recommendation based on user activity:

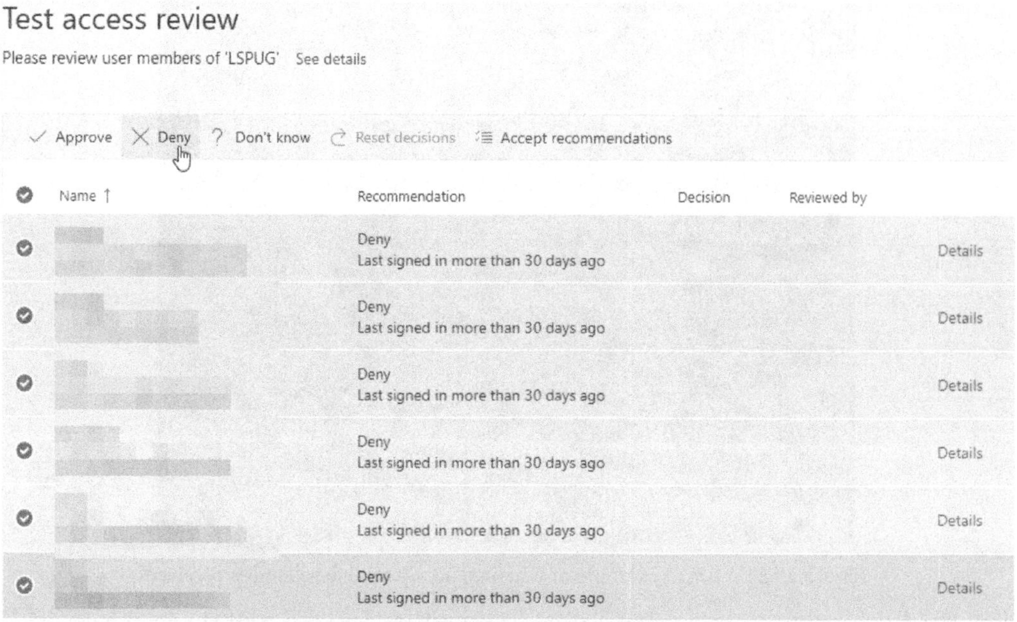

Figure 10.25 – Example of a reviewer with responsibility for many items
who is able to bulk approve and deny

See also

- This is a large topic with many variations in terms of what could be configured in an access review. Check out the documentation at `https://docs.microsoft.com/en-us/azure/active-directory/governance/create-access-review` for more information and depth for different scenarios.

Allowing/disallowing users from connecting LinkedIn to their account

By default, users may be able to connect their LinkedIn accounts to their work or school account in your organization. This allows ease of access to LinkedIn data for their colleagues and provides a pre-built social network for your organization to utilize. You can manage whether this is a possibility via Azure AD. In this recipe, we'll disable the ability to connect to LinkedIn.

Getting ready

You must be a global administrator to complete the steps in this recipe.

How to do it...

1. Go to the Azure Active Directory Admin Center at `https://aad.portal.azure.com`.

2. Click on **Azure Active Directory** from the left navigation menu and then choose **User settings**:

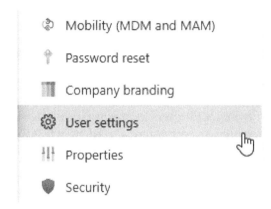

Figure 10.26 – User settings link in the left-hand navigation menu of AAD

3. Change **LinkedIn account connections** to **No**:

LinkedIn account connections

Allow users to connect their work or school account with LinkedIn.
Data sharing between Microsoft and LinkedIn is not enabled until users consent to connect
their Microsoft work or school account with their LinkedIn account.
Learn more about LinkedIn account connections ⓘ

Figure 10.27 – Example showing LinkedIn account connections disabled

4. Click **Save**.

How it works...

In this recipe you disabled the ability for users in your organization to connect their LinkedIn account to their work or school account in your tenant. It's a simple setting that can have a significant impact – be sure to discuss a change like this with your colleagues involved in governance and user adoption.

See also

- Learn more about LinkedIn account connections and the consent users provide when they elect to connect at `https://go.microsoft.com/fwlink/?linkid=2020204`.

Enabling a self-service password reset

Allowing your users to handle their own password resets saves administrative time for IT staff and empowers your users to make better decisions when it comes to their digital identities and security. If it's easier for users to reset their own password, chances are they're more likely to when they suspect potential credential leakage or exposure. It also means that when users are working late, they can reset their own forgotten password at any time instead of waiting for the resolution of a support ticket that might be hours away.

In this recipe, we'll enable self-service password reset via Azure Active Directory.

Getting ready

You must be a global administrator to complete the steps in this recipe.

How to do it...

1. Go to the Azure Active Directory Admin Center at `https://aad.portal.azure.com`.

2. Click on **Azure Active Directory** from the left navigation menu and then choose **Password reset**.

3. Click either **Selected** (to choose which users can reset their own passwords) or **All** (to let all users have the ability). In this recipe, we'll demonstrate the **Selected** option:

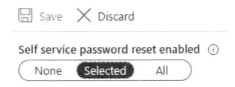

Figure 10.28 – Self service password reset enabled options for None, Selected, or All

4. Click **Select group**.

5. Search for and select the group whose members will be able to reset their own passwords:

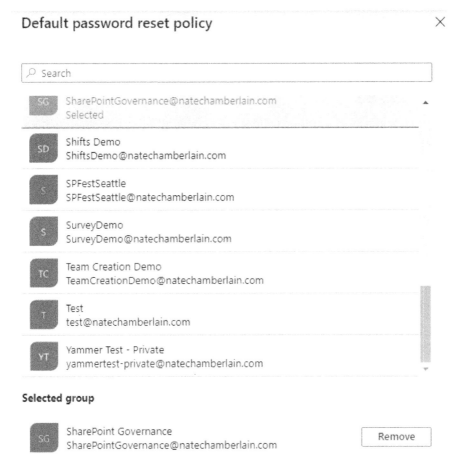

Figure 10.29 – Dialog for selecting the group that will be able to reset their own passwords

6. Click **Select**.

7. Click **Save**.

How it works...

In this recipe, you made it so that members of a specified security group would have the ability to reset their own passwords. This removes some of the administrative burden placed on support staff when users lock themselves out or forget their credentials. It also allows employees who are concerned that their credentials may have been compromised to update their own password, thereby speeding up that risk resolution time significantly.

See also

- Learn more about self-service password reset at `https://docs.microsoft.com/en-us/azure/active-directory/authentication/tutorial-enable-sspr`.

Using SSO to simplify organization-wide sign-in processes

If your organization uses applications and services beyond Microsoft 365, chances are you have multiple sign-in processes. However, you can utilize **single sign-on** (**SSO**) to simplify these multiple sign-in processes by using your O365 credentials to provide authentication vis-à-vis third-party applications.

SSO is a massive topic. In this recipe, we'll share the steps necessary to review the available options and ideas to help you choose the best method to suit your needs.

Getting ready

You must be a global administrator to implement an SSO method, and will need to be an administrator of any third-party apps to which you'll be configuring a connection.

How to do it...

1. Use the flowchart at `https://docs.microsoft.com/en-us/azure/active-directory/manage-apps/what-is-single-sign-on#choosing-a-single-sign-on-method` to help you choose an appropriate single-sign on method.

2. Review integration possibilities for your **software as a service** (**SaaS**) applications, such as Slack and ServiceNow, at `https://docs.microsoft.com/en-us/azure/active-directory/saas-apps/tutorial-list`.

3. Review **Single sign-on tutorials** for many third-party applications such as Adobe Sign at `https://docs.microsoft.com/en-us/azure/active-directory/saas-apps/adobe-echosign-tutorial`. Look along the left-hand navigation menu to view other application tutorials:

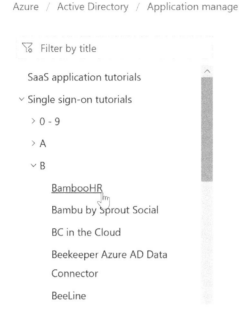

Figure 10.30 – Left-hand navigation when selecting SSO tutorials for third-party apps

4. Review user provisioning tutorials, such as for G Suite, at `https://docs.microsoft.com/en-us/azure/active-directory/saas-apps/google-apps-provisioning-tutorial`. Use the left-hand navigation again to find the relevant apps.

How it works...

In most cases, you'll provide information to the third-party app as well as O365 in order to establish a proper connection for communication and authentication. This then allows users to use their O365 sign-in as authentication in relation to their third-party applications as well.

See also

- Learn more about SSO at `https://docs.microsoft.com/en-us/azure/active-directory/manage-apps/what-is-single-sign-on`.

11
Understanding the Microsoft 365 Security & Compliance Center

This chapter focuses on the many different features and functions of the Microsoft 365 Security & Compliance Center as it relates to Office 365 apps and services. From audit log activities and working with Secure Score to configuring advanced threat protection features, we'll cover the essentials that every admin should know.

This chapter includes the following recipes:

- Viewing a report on all users who have accessed a specific SharePoint file
- Using **Content Search** to find content containing certain keywords
- Creating a retention policy based on the discovery of certain keywords
- Accessing the standard Microsoft BAA
- Accessing and reviewing an organization's secure score

- Complying with Secure Score security configuration recommendations
- Assigning permissions for non-IT users to the Security & Compliance admin center
- Using Communication Compliance to identify potential policy violations in messages

Technical requirements

In this chapter, it would be best to be registered as a **Global Admin**. If you are not, then many recipes in this chapter will still be accessible to you as a **Security Admin**. Check each recipe's *Getting ready* section for its specific requirements.

Viewing a report on all users who have accessed a specific SharePoint file

Sometimes, you will need to know who has accessed specific files and when, whether to verify receipt, investigate a potential data-loss risk, or for another reason. This can be accomplished via the Microsoft 365 Security & Compliance Center. In this recipe, we'll go through the steps of pulling the access report for a file named `FirstDraft.docx`.

Getting ready

You should be a global administrator to complete this recipe. You will also need audit logging turned on for your organization. You can do this from the Office 365 Security & Compliance Center (`https://protection.office.com`) by clicking **Turn on auditing** on the Audit log search page in the Security & Compliance Center. If you don't have that option, then auditing has already been turned on.

How to do it...

1. Go to the Office 365 Security & Compliance Center at `https://protection.office.com`.

2. Click **Search | Audit log search** in the left navigation pane.

3. Expand the **Activities** dropdown and select **Accessed file**:

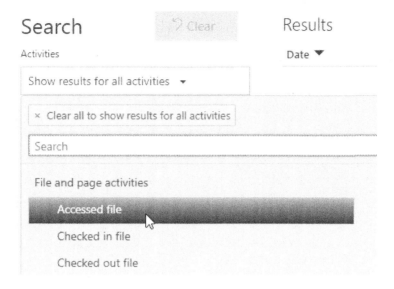

Figure 11.1 – Accessed file option under File and page activities

4. Add the earliest and latest dates of the activities to be included, the specific users to look for, and/or a file, folder, or site name or URL:

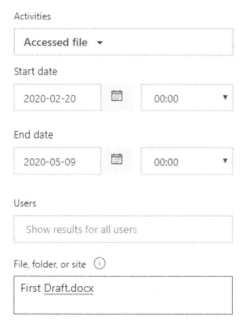

Figure 11.2 – Parameters for the selected activities

5. Click **Search**.

6. You can then filter or search the results to find activities of interest. In this example, I searched to find which users were using anonymous links:

Results   300 results found (More items available, scroll down to see more.)

Date ▼	IP address	User	Activity	Item
		anon ✕		
2020-05-06 03:37:48		urn:spo:anon#6f3ceaa3eb8a8de...	Accessed file	First Draft.docx
2020-05-05 09:51:27		urn:spo:anon#6f3ceaa3eb8a8de...	Accessed file	First Draft.docx
2020-05-04 23:54:04		urn:spo:anon#6f3ceaa3eb8a8de...	Accessed file	First Draft.docx
2020-04-30 23:56:21		urn:spo:anon#6f3ceaa3eb8a8de...	Accessed file	First Draft.docx
2020-04-30 04:00:39		urn:spo:anon#6f3ceaa3eb8a8de...	Accessed file	First Draft.docx

Figure 11.3 – Search results filtered based on the User field

How it works...

In this recipe, you used the audit log in the Office 365 Security & Compliance Center to find out who had accessed a specific file in SharePoint over the last few months. From here, you can save or download results or set an alert based on specific criteria.

There's more...

To set an alert for certain results, select **New alert policy** on the left:

Figure 11.4 – New alert policy button to the left of the search results

See also

- You can learn more about utilizing the audit log at https://docs.microsoft.com/en-us/microsoft-365/compliance/search-the-audit-log-in-security-and-compliance.

Using Content Search to find content containing certain keywords

It can be difficult to track where people copy and save content, or where they're discussing critically sensitive things, such as confidential projects. In this recipe, we'll perform a content search to look through our entire tenant for content containing `DocID-7846`. This would be helpful in ensuring the compliance and confidentiality of specific content.

Getting ready

You should be a global administrator to complete this recipe.

How to do it...

1. Go to the Office 365 Security & Compliance Center at `https://protection.office.com`.

2. Click **Search | Content search** from the left navigation menu:

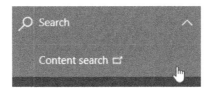

Figure 11.5 – Content search link on the left-hand navigation menu of the
Office 365 Security & Compliance Center

3. Click **New search**.

4. Enter the keyword(s) to search for. In our example, we're entering `DocID-7846`:

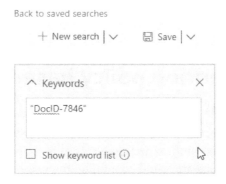

Figure 11.6 – Keyword search terms entry

5. Select **All locations**.

6. Click **Save & run**.

7. Name and describe your search so you can return to its results later, then click **Save**.

8. Wait for it to complete, or close and return to it later (follow *steps 1 to 2* to find it again).

How it works...

You've just performed a content search. This may take some time, as it searches all content in all locations. To find your specific search statistics, you can go to the **Content search** page and select the search you want data for, then choose **Open query** then **Individual results | Search statistics**. Here, you'll be able to view a summary, queries, and top locations.

If there are results matching your query, they'll appear on the same page. You can leave and come back to **Content search** at any time to view its status.

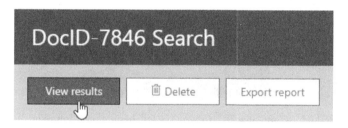

Figure 11.7 – View results button for the saved search

See also

- **Content search** is a large topic and has much more to consider across scenarios. You can check out more details about it at https://docs.microsoft.com/en-us/microsoft-365/compliance/content-search.

Creating a retention policy based on the discovery of certain keywords

Retention policies can be created that are automatically applied to items containing specific keywords when found in the search index. In this recipe, we'll create a retention policy that applies to items that are found containing the word Contoso.

Getting ready

You should be a global administrator to complete this recipe.

How to do it...

1. Go to the Office 365 Security & Compliance Center at `https://protection.office.com`.

2. Click **Information governance | Retention** from the left navigation menu:

Figure 11.8 – Retention link in the left-hand navigation menu of the
Office 365 Security & Compliance Center

3. Click **Create**.

4. Name and describe your retention policy:

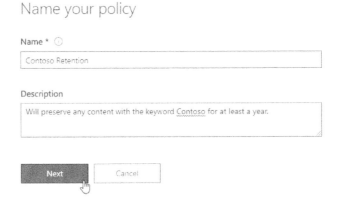

Figure 11.9 – Name and description fields for the new policy

5. Under **Need more options?**, select **Use advanced retention settings** and leave **Detect content that contains specific words or phrases** selected. Click **Next**:

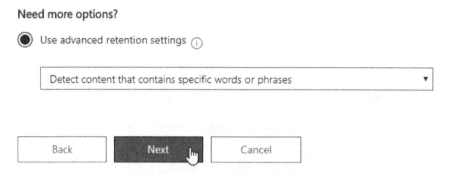

Figure 11.10 – Advanced retention settings available by dropdown

6. Enter Contoso in the keyword query editor.

7. Under **Retention actions**, choose to retain matching content for 1 year, but don't automatically delete it, and base the date on last modified, as shown in the following figure:

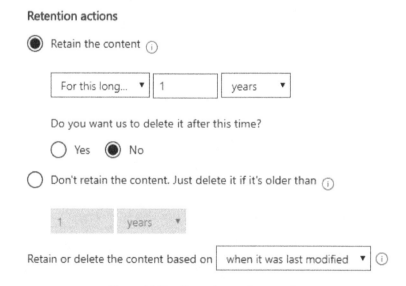

Figure 11.11 – Retention actions to take

8. Click **Next**.

9. Leave **All locations** selected and click **Next**.

10. Review the policy for accuracy, then click **Create this policy**:

Review your settings

⚠ It will take up to 7 days to automatically apply the retention policy on all items that match your conditions.

Policy name   Edit

Contoso Retention

Description   Edit

Will preserve any content with the keyword Contoso for at least
a year.

Applies to content in these locations   Edit

Exchange email

OneDrive accounts

SharePoint sites

Office 365 groups

Settings   Edit

Advanced retention
- Detect content that contains specific words or phrases
  1 year keep

| Back | Save for later | Create this policy | Cancel |

Figure 11.12 – The review screen of the new policy with the option to create or save for later

How it works...

You've just created a retention policy that will look for the word Contoso in content
found throughout Office 365. When it finds matches, it will make sure that the content
is kept for at least a year. At that point, nothing will happen, but users will be able to delete
it if they wish since it has passed its required retention period.

Note the warning that appears when creating this policy that says that it could take up to a week for this to apply.

See also

- Learn more about retention policies on items containing keywords at `https://docs.microsoft.com/en-us/microsoft-365/compliance/ retention-policies?view=o365-worldwide#retain-content- that-contains-specific-keywords`.

Accessing the standard Microsoft BAA

Your subscription agreement included Microsoft's HIPAA **Business Associate Agreement (BAA),** but finding it later for your compliance and audit needs can be tricky. In this recipe, you'll locate the BAA.

Getting ready

Most users can access the BAA. There are no prerequisites.

How to do it...

1. Go to `https://portal.office.com/commerce/supplements.aspx`.
2. Click **Online Services Terms**:

> Optional privacy and security contractual
>
> Data Processing Terms (including the EU Standard Contractual Clauses) and Associate Agreement (BAA) are included in the Online Services Terms, which Microsoft Online Subscription Agreement.

Figure 11.13 – Online Service Terms in the blurb about supplements

3. You can find a lot of valuable documentation and information on this screen. Spend some time checking out all that's available. Then scroll down to **Hot topics** and select **HIPAA-BAA**:

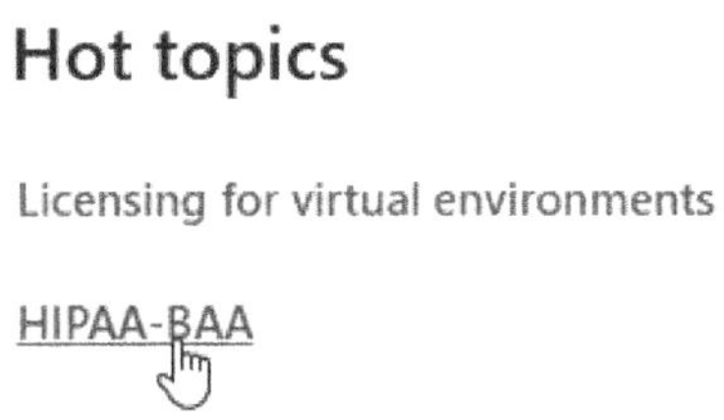

Hot topics

Licensing for virtual environments

HIPAA-BAA

Figure 11.14 – HIPAA-BAA link under Hot topics at the bottom of the page

4. Scroll down to find the available BAA documents. Note the dates for each one:

Title	Language	Sectors	Regions
HIPAABusinessAssociateAgr(WW)(Dec2015)(ENG)(CR)	English	Common Document	WW (World Wide)
HIPAABusinessAssociateAgr(WW)(ENG)(February2018)(CR)	English	Common Document	WW (World Wide)
HIPAABusinessAssociateAgr(WW)(ENG)(May2016)(CR)	English	Common Document	WW (World Wide)

Figure 11.15 – Available HIPAA documents listed in a table

Before you complete step 3, you may also notice other useful documents, such as the following:

- Licensing for virtual environments
- Downgrade rights
- Product activation and keys
- Product lists, terms, and licensing FAQs
- Online services terms
- **Service-level agreements (SLA)**

How it works...

While not straightforward, you found the Microsoft HIPAA-BAA in this recipe. Be sure to save it somewhere for future reference.

There's more...

As long as the URL is active, you can go directly to `http://aka.ms/BAA` as well.

Accessing and reviewing an organization's secure score

Your secure score gives you an idea of how well protected your organization is based on your administrative setting configurations, policies, and activities. In this recipe, you'll learn how to find and analyze your organization's secure score.

Getting ready

You should be a global, security, Exchange, SharePoint, or account administrator to access Secure Score.

How to do it...

1. Go directly to your secure score overview at `https://securescore.microsoft.com/`. You can also go to the Microsoft 365 Security Center (`https://security.microsoft.com/`) and click **Secure Score** from the left navigation menu.

2. Check your secure score breakdown in the leftmost column of the **Overview** tab. You'll notice the categories for each of the following making up your score:

   --**Identity**: Accounts and roles in Azure AD

   --**Data**: Microsoft Information Protection

   --**Device**: Microsoft Defender **Advanced Threat Protection (ATP)**

   --**Apps**: Email and cloud apps (includes Office 365 and Cloud App Security)

   --**Infrastructure**: Azure Security Center score:

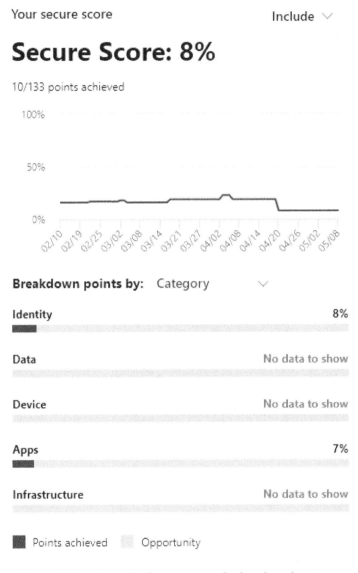

Figure 11.16 – Example of a secure score broken down by category

3. Check the actions to review in the middle column (or scroll down if the screen resolution is small). Click **To address**, or any specific **Top improvement action**, to dive deeper into the suggested actions to improve your score. On this screen, you can also see the percentage by which resolving the action would increase your score:

Actions to review

Regressed ⓘ	To address	Planned	Risk accepted	Recently added ⓘ	Recently updated ⓘ
0	**30**	**0**	**0**	**0**	**0**

Top improvement actions

Improvement action	Score im...	Status	Category
Require MFA for administrative roles	+7.52%	○ To address	Identity
Ensure all users can complete multi-factor authentication for secu...	+6.77%	○ To address	Identity
Enable policy to block legacy authentication	+5.26%	○ To address	Identity
Turn on sign-in risk policy	+5.26%	○ To address	Identity
Turn on user risk policy	+5.26%	○ To address	Identity
Enable Password Hash Sync if hybrid	+3.76%	○ To address	Identity
Stop clear text credentials exposure	+3.76%	○ To address	Identity
Stop legacy protocols communication	+3.76%	○ To address	Identity
Stop weak cipher usage	+3.76%	○ To address	Identity

View all

Figure 11.17 – A list of actions to review for improving your secure score

4. Once an improvement action for you to address has been selected, you can add notes or a plan to resolve it, as well as see the step-by-step instructions needed to resolve it:

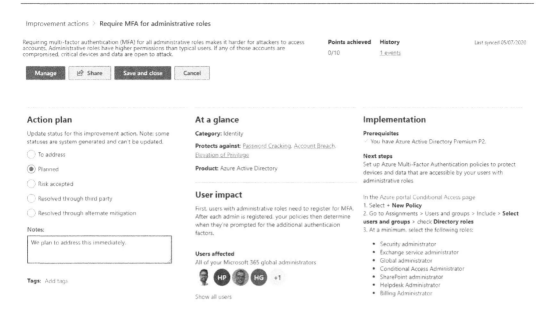

Figure 11.18 – A selected action for review showing all of the details

5. Back on the Secure Score dashboard (**Overview**), you can view your score comparison to see how your organization compares to similar organizations:

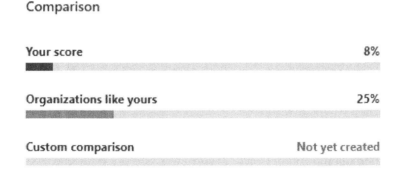

Figure 11.19 – Comparison listing for seeing how your organization compares to similar organizations

6. Under **Metrics & trends**, you can view changes over time in your score:

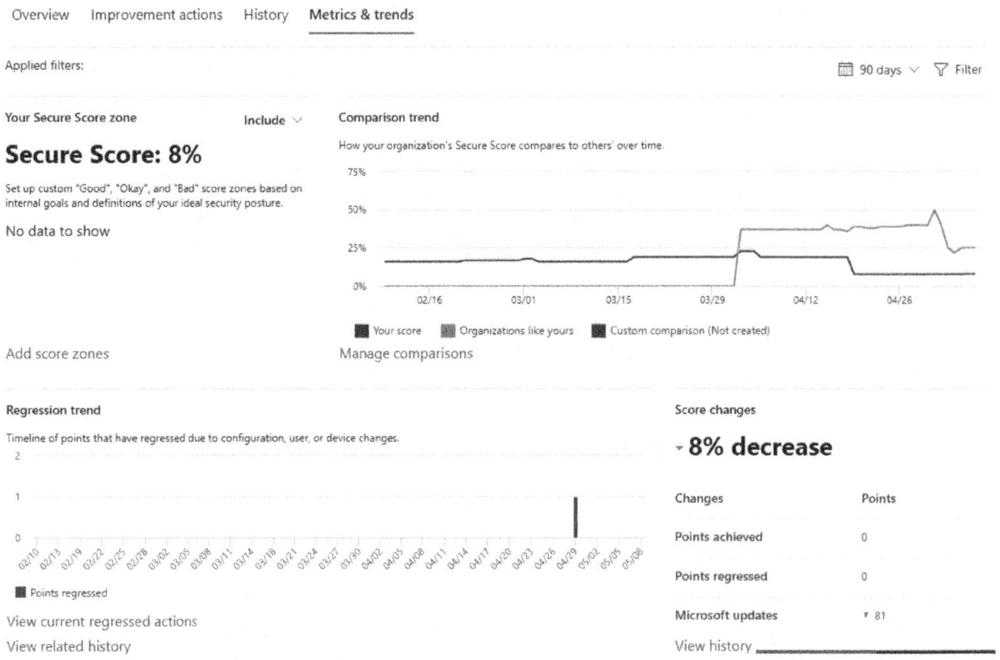

Figure 11.20 – Metrics & trends dashboard with score-over-time visuals

How it works...

In this recipe, you explored the various sections of Secure Score to familiarize yourself with its functions and learn how it can help you enhance your organization's security one action at a time.

See also

- You can find out more about Secure Score at `https://docs.microsoft.com/en-us/microsoft-365/security/mtp/microsoft-secure-score-new`.

Complying with Secure Score security configuration recommendations

In the previous recipe, you accessed and toured Secure Score. In this recipe, we'll dive deeper into improvement actions and resolve one, complying with a recommendation that will boost our secure score.

Getting ready

You should be a global, security, Exchange, SharePoint, or account administrator to access Secure Score.

How to do it...

1. Go directly to your Secure Score overview at `https://securescore.microsoft.com/`. You can also go to the Microsoft 365 Security Center (`https://security.microsoft.com/`) and click **Secure Score** in the left navigation menu.

2. Click **Improvement actions**:

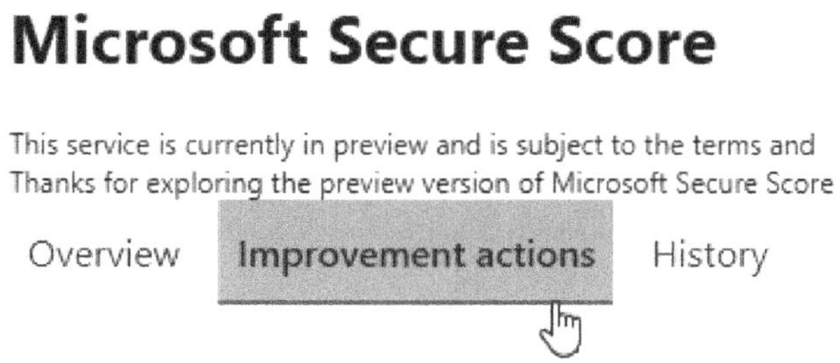

Figure 11.21 – Improvement actions link on the Microsoft Secure Score page

3. Choose an improvement action to complete. For this recipe, we'll click **Enable self-service password reset**:

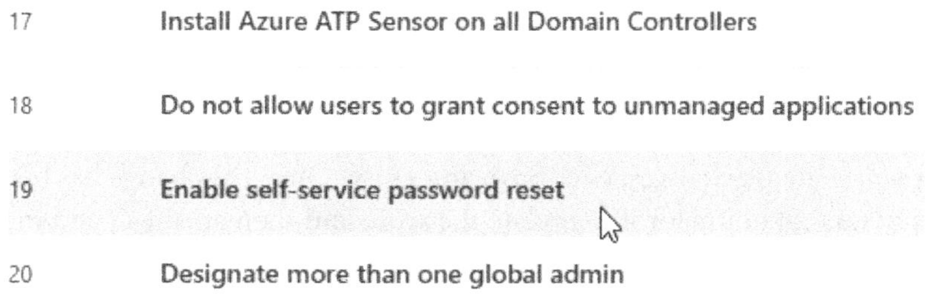

Figure 11.22 – An improvement action being selected

4. See the recipe titled *Enabling self-service password reset* in *Chapter 10, Configuring and Managing Users in Azure Active Directory (Azure AD)* for the steps on how we'll resolve this. Whichever action you choose to resolve, follow the instructions on the right-hand side after selecting it to complete the action. In most cases, the **Manage** button will take you directly to where you need to go to resolve the action:

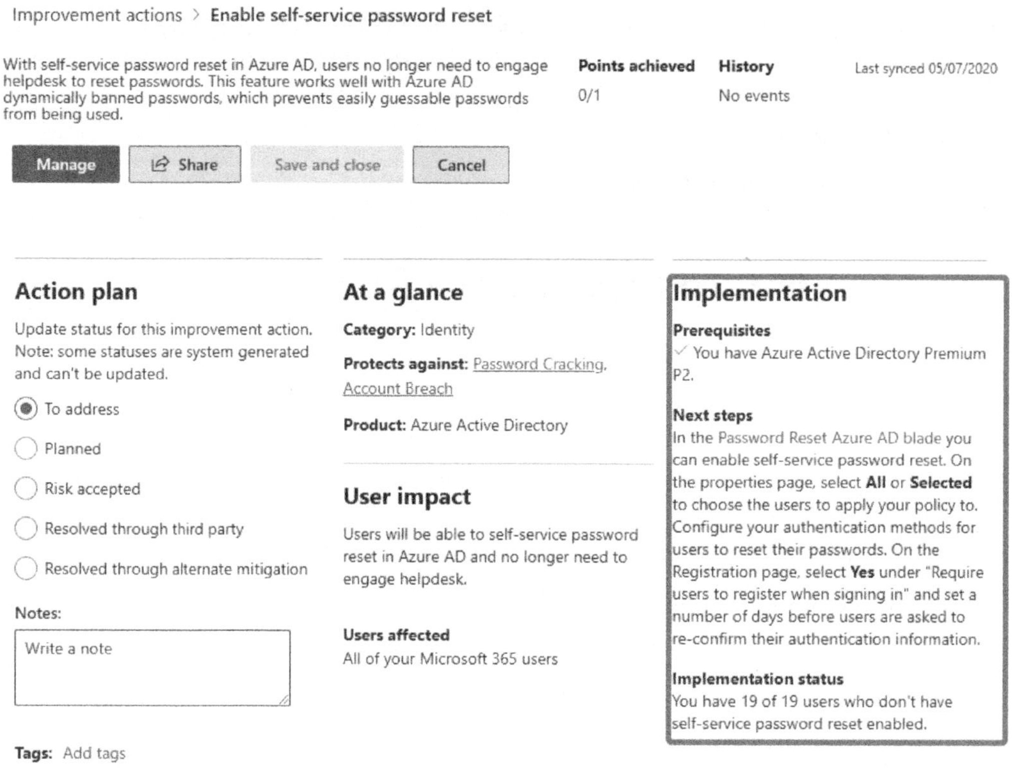

Improvement actions > **Enable self-service password reset**

With self-service password reset in Azure AD, users no longer need to engage helpdesk to reset passwords. This feature works well with Azure AD dynamically banned passwords, which prevents easily guessable passwords from being used.

Points achieved   **History**   Last synced 05/07/2020

0/1   No events

| Manage | ⤶ Share | Save and close | Cancel |

Action plan

Update status for this improvement action. Note: some statuses are system generated and can't be updated.

(●) To address

( ) Planned

( ) Risk accepted

( ) Resolved through third party

( ) Resolved through alternate mitigation

Notes:

Write a note

Tags: Add tags

At a glance

Category: Identity

Protects against: Password Cracking, Account Breach

Product: Azure Active Directory

User impact

Users will be able to self-service password reset in Azure AD and no longer need to engage helpdesk.

Users affected
All of your Microsoft 365 users

Implementation

Prerequisites
✓ You have Azure Active Directory Premium P2.

Next steps
In the Password Reset Azure AD blade you can enable self-service password reset. On the properties page, select **All** or **Selected** to choose the users to apply your policy to. Configure your authentication methods for users to reset their passwords. On the Registration page, select **Yes** under "Require users to register when signing in" and set a number of days before users are asked to re-confirm their authentication information.

Implementation status
You have 19 of 19 users who don't have self-service password reset enabled.

Figure 11.23 – Details for the selected improvement action

5. After you've made changes, click **Save and close**. Once the change has been made, you can wait 24 hours for it to update the score and then go ahead and mark the improvement action as **Planned** with a note on the actions you took:

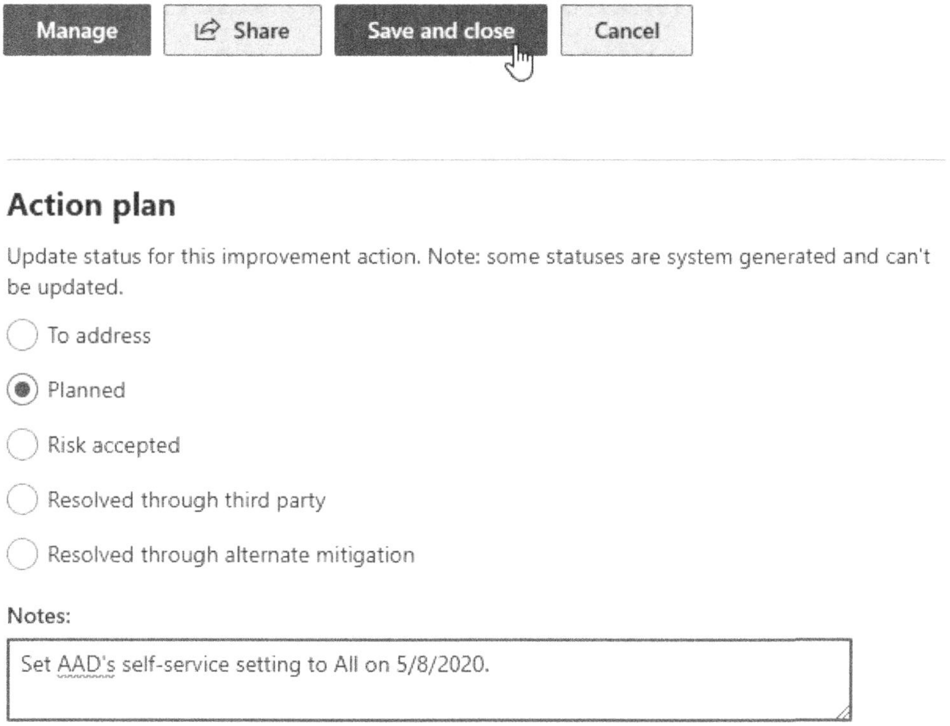
Manage
Share
Save and close
Cancel
Action plan
Update status for this improvement action. Note: some statuses are system generated and can't be updated.
To address
Planned
Risk accepted
Resolved through third party
Resolved through alternate mitigation
Notes:
Set AAD's self-service setting to All on 5/8/2020.

Figure 11.24 – Action plan status and note being saved to the improvement action

How it works...

In this recipe, we looked at an improvement action recommended in our secure score and resolved it by following the provided instructions. Secure Score makes it easy to identify risks in our environment and resolve them.

See also

- You can find out more about Secure Score at `https://docs.microsoft.com/en-us/microsoft-365/security/mtp/microsoft-secure-score-new`.

Assigning permissions for non-IT users to the Security & Compliance admin center

Sometimes, you'll want additional eyes on the Security & Compliance admin center, but they won't usually belong to a global admin. In this recipe, we'll set a non-IT user's role to Security Reader so that they can access, but not administer, the Office 365 Security & Compliance admin center.

Getting ready

You should be a global administrator to complete this recipe (and whenever assigning admin roles).

How to do it...

1. Go to the Office 365 Security & Compliance Center at `https://protection.office.com`.

2. Select **Permissions** from the left navigation menu:

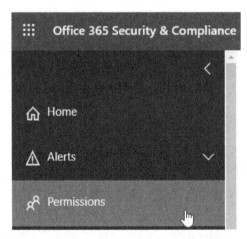

Figure 11.25 – Permissions link in the left-hand navigation menu of the Office 365 Security & Compliance Center

3. Select the role that you're assigning, then click **Edit** in the **Members** section:

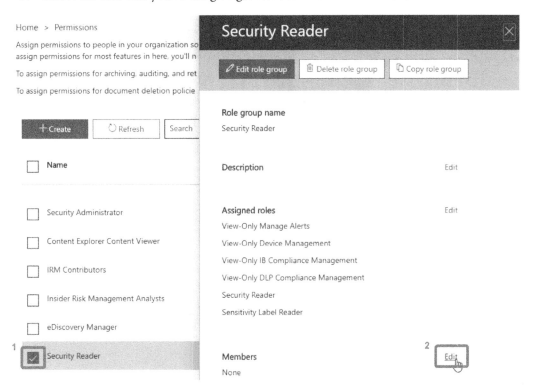

Figure 11.26 – Edit button in the Members section for the selected security role

4. Select **Choose members**.

5. Click **Add**.

6. Select those that you're adding to this role group, then click **Add**:

Figure 11.27 – A selected user to be added to the role group

7. Confirm your changes, then click **Done**:

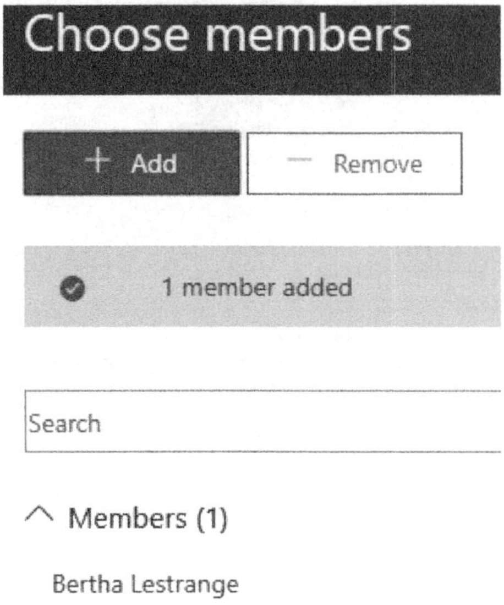

Figure 11.28 – Member(s) added confirmation

8. Click **Save**.
9. Click **Close**.

How it works...

In this recipe, we gave someone permissions for the Office 365 Security & Compliance Center as part of the Security Reader role group. In this group, users have read-only access to much of the Security & Compliance Center, but can't complete tasks or make configuration changes.

See also

- You can learn more about all the roles you could assign users to give a user access to the Security & Compliance admin center at `https://docs.microsoft.com/en-us/microsoft-365/security/office-365-security/permissions-in-the-security-and-compliance-center`.

Using Communication Compliance to identify potential policy violations in messages

With so many different avenues for communication in Office 365, it can be difficult to monitor inappropriate messages or those that could potentially be in violation of organization policies. Communication Compliance allows you to monitor, capture, and alert assigned reviewers of messages in email, Teams, Yammer, and more for predefined or specified risky content.

In this recipe, we'll add the predefined policy from Microsoft that monitors messages for offensive language.

Getting ready

You should be assigned the Supervisory Review Administrator, Case Management, and Review roles from the Office 365 Security & Compliance admin center to access and utilize the Communication Compliance solution. You can do this by creating a new role group from the **Permissions** pane of the Office 365 Security & Compliance admin center with these three roles included.

How to do it...

1. Go to the Microsoft 365 Compliance Center at `https://compliance.microsoft.com`.

2. Click **Show all** in the left navigation menu.

3. Select **Communication compliance**:

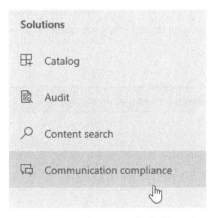

Figure 11.29 – Communication compliance in the left-hand navigation menu of the Microsoft 365 Compliance Center

4. Under **Monitor for offensive language**, click **Get started**:

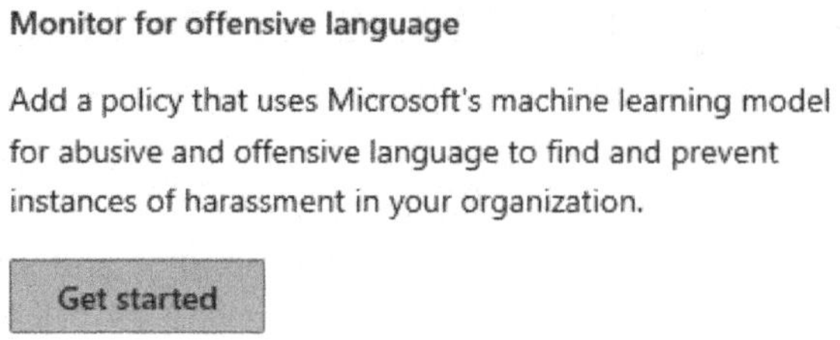

Monitor for offensive language

Add a policy that uses Microsoft's machine learning model for abusive and offensive language to find and prevent instances of harassment in your organization.

Get started

Figure 11.30 – Get started button for the Monitor for offensive language policy

5. Name the policy and choose which groups of users to monitor and who should review any violations:

Monitor communications for offensive language

Let us know whose communication to supervise and who should review them, and we'll create a communication compliance policy that uses an abusive language machine learning model to detect content that might be considered harassment.

Settings we'll fill out for you

✓ **Policy name**

Offensive or threatening language

✓ **Communications to monitor**

Internal communications in Exchange mail, Teams chat, Skype for Business conversations, Yammer, Inbound, Outbound, Internal,

✓ **Conditions**

Review 100% of communications containing offensive language or bad words.

Settings we need from you

Users or groups to supervise *

BA Book Authors   ✕   Start typing to find users or groups

Reviewers *

Choose users to review the communications that are returned by this policy.

NC Nate Chamberlain   ✕   Start typing to find users

Figure 11.31 – Policy name and associated people and groups

6. Click **Create policy**.

How it works...

You've just created the offensive language policy in your tenant via the Communication Compliance solution from the Microsoft 365 Compliance Center. Within an hour it will be active, and it could take up to 24 hours before violating communications are captured and reported as alerts to the assigned reviewer(s).

See also

- Check out the video at `https://youtu.be/z33ji7a7Zho/` on detecting workplace harassment using Communication Compliance.

- You can learn more about Communication Compliance at `https://docs.microsoft.com/en-us/microsoft-365/compliance/communication-compliance`.

12
Deploying Data Loss Prevention and eDiscovery

In this chapter, we'll discover recipes involving both **Data Loss Prevention** (**DLP**) and eDiscovery in Office 365. With the right data loss prevention settings in place, your organization's sensitive data will be protected from creation through its entire content lifecycle. eDiscovery adds to your organization's ability to perform investigations involving placing legal holds on content, creating cases for in-depth analysis of content across several apps and services and more.

We'll cover these specific recipes related to DLP and eDiscovery:

- Creating a DLP policy to protect content with HIPAA-protected data detected
- Using DLP to automatically report HIPAA incidents
- Creating a DLP policy for content with custom keywords in the name or subject
- Tuning a sensitive information type's confidence level
- Creating an eDiscovery case
- Managing eDiscovery cases
- Creating an advanced eDiscovery case
- Changing who has access to an advanced eDiscovery case

Technical requirements

You should be a global or compliance administrator to complete most recipes in this chapter.

Creating a DLP policy to protect content with HIPAA-protected data detected

In this chapter, we'll be utilizing the Microsoft 365 compliance admin center to create a **DLP** policy that detects HIPAA-protected content, warns users about sharing the protected content, and blocks people from outside the organization from accessing it. It will also provide users with the opportunity to override for false positives (HIPAA-protected content detected but not actually present) or with business justification.

Getting ready

You should be a global or compliance administrator to complete this recipe.

How to do it...

1. Go to the Microsoft 365 compliance center at `https://compliance.microsoft.com`.

2. Click **Show all** from the left navigation menu.

3. Select **Data loss prevention**:

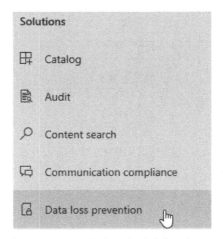

Figure 12.1 – Data loss prevention link in the left-hand navigation menu of the
Microsoft 365 compliance center

4. Click **Create policy**:

Data loss prevention

Use data loss prevention (DLP) policies to

$+$ **Create policy** $\downarrow$ Export $\circlearrowright$ Refr

Figure 12.2 – The Create policy button on the Data loss prevention page

5.   Select **Medical and health** > **U.S. Health Insurance Act (HIPAA)** > **Next**:

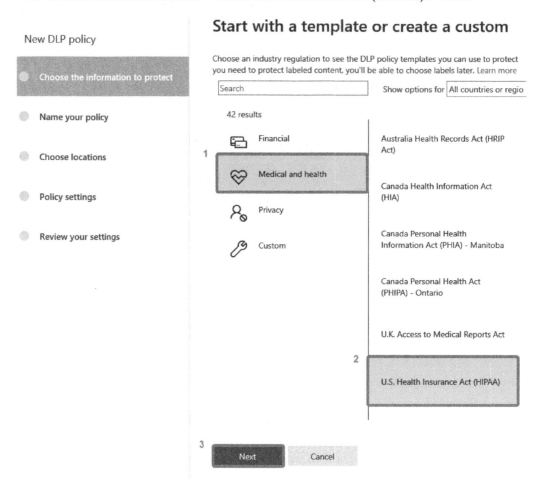

Figure 12.3 – Selecting HIPAA in the New DLP policy configuration wizard

6. Rename and describe the policy if you wish, then click **Next**:

Name *

U.S. Health Insurance Act (HIPAA)

Description

Enter a friendly description for your policy

Back   Next   Cancel

Figure 12.4 – Policy name and description configuration

7. Click **Next** to continue with all default locations selected:

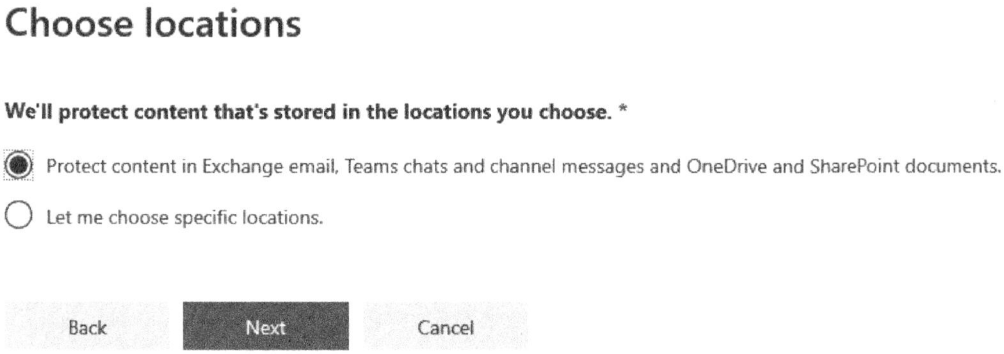

Choose locations

We'll protect content that's stored in the locations you choose. *

◉ Protect content in Exchange email, Teams chats and channel messages and OneDrive and SharePoint documents.

◯ Let me choose specific locations.

Back   Next   Cancel

Figure 12.5 – DLP policy location scope configuration

8. Leave the default settings to set the policy to detect when HIPAA-protected content is shared outside your organization. Click **Next**:

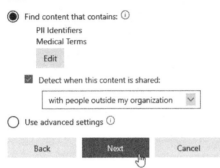

Customize the type of content you want to protect

Select 'Find content that contains' if you want to quickly set up a policy that protects only sensitive info or labeled content. Use advanced settings for more options, such as protecting content in email messages sent to specific domains, attachments with specific file extensions, and more.

● Find content that contains: ⓘ

    PII Identifiers
    Medical Terms

    Edit

    ☑ Detect when this content is shared:

        with people outside my organization ⌄

○ Use advanced settings ⓘ

    Back   Next   Cancel

Figure 12.6 – DLP policy content scope configuration

9. Check all boxes and configure settings for each to your liking. This will help to warn users when sensitive content is detected and inform the appropriate people when it's been shared anyway, and it can block people from sharing and restrict access automatically. Click **Next** when ready:

What do you want to do if we detect sensitive info?

We'll automatically create detailed activity reports so you can review the content that matches this policy. What else do you want to do?

Notify users when content matches the policy settings

☑   Show policy tips to users and send them an email notification.
    Tips appear to users in their apps (Outlook, OneDrive, SharePoint, and Teams) and help them learn how to use sensitive info responsibly. You can use the default tip or customize it to your liking. Learn more about notifications and tips

    Customize the tip and email

☑   Send incident reports in email
    By default, you and your global admin will automatically receive the email.

    Choose what to include in the report and who receives it

☑ Restrict access or encrypt the content

    ● Block people from sharing and restrict access to shared content

    ○ Encrypt email messages (applies only to content in Exchange)

    Back   Next   Cancel

Figure 12.7 – Actions to take as part of the DLP policy

10. Because we chose to block people from sharing, we need to configure a few additional settings. Leave **Only people outside your organization** selected, but toggle **on** the, **Let people who see the tip override the policy option**. Then, click the checkboxes to require business justification on overrides and reports of false positives. Click **Next**:

Customize access and override permissions

By default, users are blocked from sending email and Teams chats and channel messages that contain the type of content you're protecting. But you can choose who has access to shared SharePoint and OneDrive files. You can also decide if you want to let people override the policy's restrictions.

Block these people from accessing SharePoint, OneDrive, and Teams content

○ Everyone ⓘ

◉ Only people outside your organization ⓘ

Let people who see the tip override the policy

🔘 On

☑ Require a business justification to override
☑ Override the rule automatically if they report it as a false positive

| Back | Next | Cancel |

Figure 12.8 – Access and override permissions configuration

11. Choose whether you'd like to test the policy or turn it on immediately (keeping in mind it will take up to an hour to take effect), then click **Next**:

Do you want to turn on the policy or test things out first?

Do you want to turn on the policy right away or test things out first?

Keep in mind that after you turn it on, it'll take up to an hour for the policy to take effect.

◉ Yes, turn it on right away

○ I'd like to test it out first

☐ Show policy tips while in test mode

○ No, keep it off. I'll turn it on later.

| Back | Next | Cancel |

Figure 12.9 – Choice to turn on the policy immediately or test it

12. Review the policy details and, when satisfied, click **Create**:

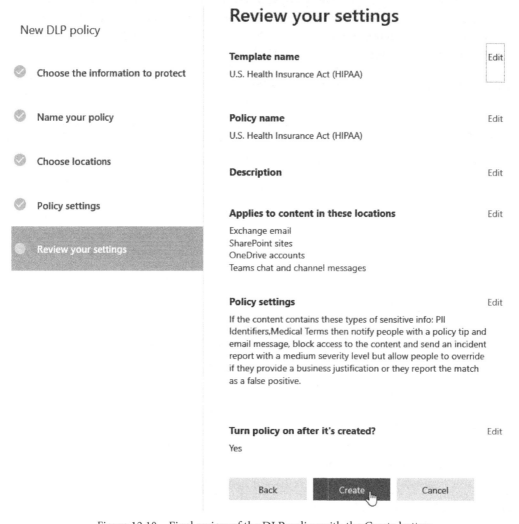

Review your settings

New DLP policy

✓ Choose the information to protect

✓ Name your policy

✓ Choose locations

✓ Policy settings

Review your settings

Template name   Edit
U.S. Health Insurance Act (HIPAA)

Policy name   Edit
U.S. Health Insurance Act (HIPAA)

Description   Edit

Applies to content in these locations   Edit
Exchange email
SharePoint sites
OneDrive accounts
Teams chat and channel messages

Policy settings   Edit
If the content contains these types of sensitive info: PII
Identifiers,Medical Terms then notify people with a policy tip and
email message, block access to the content and send an incident
report with a medium severity level but allow people to override
if they provide a business justification or they report the match
as a false positive.

Turn policy on after it's created?   Edit
Yes

Back   Create   Cancel

Figure 12.10 – Final review of the DLP policy with the Create button

How it works...

In this recipe, we created a DLP policy from the Microsoft 365 compliance center.
This involved many steps guided by a wizard in which we were able to select
pre-defined sensitive information types such as HIPAA. Within an hour, this policy
will take effect on our organization, helping to prevent potential data loss involving
HIPAA-protected content.

> **Important note**
> In step 9, you need an Azure Information Protection subscription to encrypt sent messages containing HIPAA-protected content. See `https://docs.microsoft.com/en-us/azure/information-protection/requirements` for subscription information and requirements.

See also

- Learn more about data loss prevention in Microsoft 365 at `https://docs.microsoft.com/en-us/microsoft-365/compliance/data-loss-prevention-policies`.

Using DLP to automatically report HIPAA incidents

In the previous recipe, we created a DLP policy that detected HIPAA-protected content and sent an incident report as part of its handling. In this recipe, we'll edit an existing DLP policy and add an incident report as part of its response.

Getting ready

You should be a global or compliance administrator to complete this recipe.

How to do it...

1. Go to your DLP policies directly at `https://compliance.microsoft.com/datalossprevention`. You could also go to the Microsoft 365 compliance center and select **Show all** > **Data loss prevention** from the left navigation menu.

2. Select the policy for which you're configuring an incident report, then click **Edit policy**:

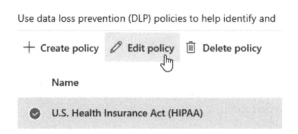

Figure 12.11 – The Edit policy button available for a selected DLP policy

3. Select **Policy settings** > expand the content specifications > **Edit rule**:

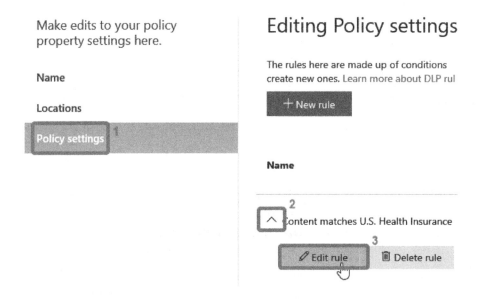

Figure 12.12 – Edit rule button available for a specific rule in the selected policy

4. Select **Incident reports**:

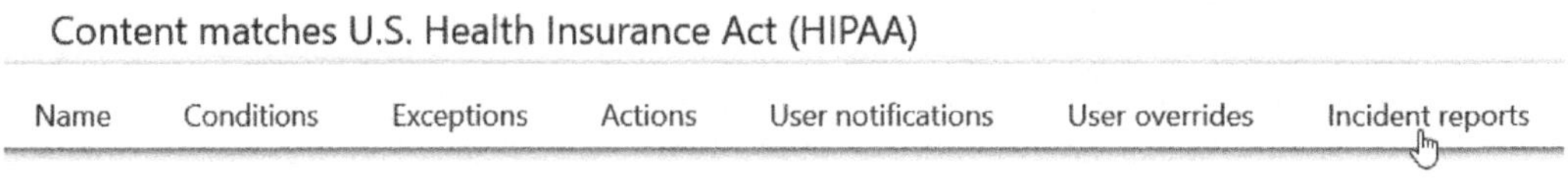

Content matches U.S. Health Insurance Act (HIPAA)

Name	Conditions	Exceptions	Actions	User notifications	User overrides	Incident reports

Figure 12.13 – Incident reports link in the DLP policy configuration screens

5. Choose whether to notify admins or specific users. Then, choose which additional information other than where the match occurred and which rules/policies were triggered should be included:

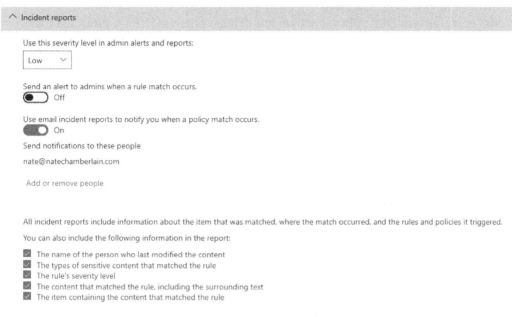

Figure 12.14 – Incident report details and contents options

6. When finished, click **Save**.

7. Click **Save** again.

How it works...

In this recipe, we modified an existing DLP policy so that it will also email specific individuals when the policy is triggered. We also customized the content of the message, choosing to include as much information as available.

See also

*   Learn more about DLP in Microsoft 365 at https://docs.microsoft.com/en-us/microsoft-365/compliance/data-loss-prevention-policies.

Creating a DLP policy for content with custom keywords in the name or subject

Earlier in this chapter in the *Using DLP to automatically report HIPAA Incident Reports* recipe, you created a DLP policy based on pre-defined criteria (HIPAA-protected data types). In this recipe, we'll create another DLP policy, but this one will look for content that includes custom keywords we specify. Specifically, we'll be looking for content that contains any reference to our top-secret, fictional Project `Wildebeest`.

Getting ready

You should be a global or compliance administrator to complete this recipe.

How to do it...

1. Go to the Microsoft 365 compliance center at `https://compliance.microsoft.com`.

2. Choose **Data classification** from the left-hand navigation menu.

3. Choose **Sensitive info types**:

Figure 12.15 – The Sensitive info types button on the top navigation menu of the Data classification page

4. Click **Create info type**.

5. Name and describe the sensitive info type then click **Next**:

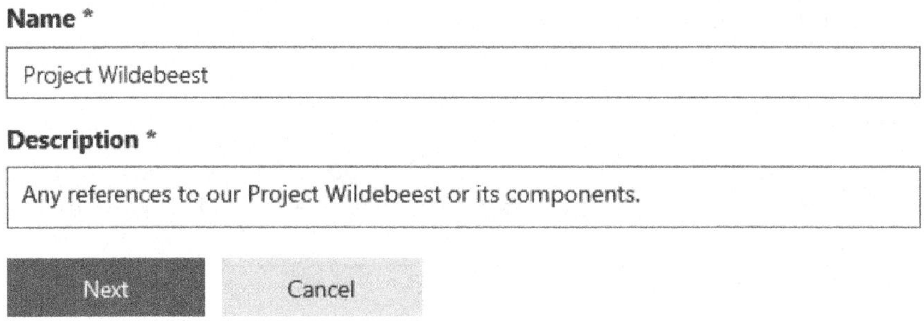

Name *

Project Wildebeest

Description *

Any references to our Project Wildebeest or its components.

Next   Cancel

Figure 12.16 – Information type name and description fields

6. Click **Add an element**.

7. Change the **Detect content containing** drop-down menu to **Keywords**. Then, enter
    `"Project Wildebeest"`, `PRJWDBST`, `WDBST` to catch content containing any
    of the three comma-separated values:

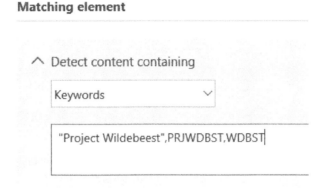

Figure 12.17 – Info type matching elements configuration

8. Click **Next**, then **Finish**.

9. On the testing prompt, you can choose **Yes** if you'd like but for this demo, we'll
    choose **No**:

compliance

Sensitive type is successfully saved. It is recommended to test the sensitive type before
use. Do you want to test created sensitive type?

Figure 12.18 – Recommendation to test prior to saving

10. Click **Show all** from the left navigation menu.

11. Select **Data loss prevention**:

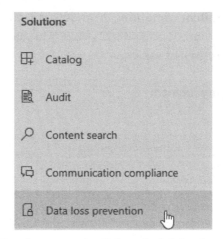

Figure 12.19 – The Data loss prevention link on the left-hand navigation menu of the Microsoft 365 compliance center

12. Click **Create policy**:

Data loss preventio

Use data loss prevention (DLP) policies to

Figure 12.20 – The Create policy button on the Data loss prevention page

13. Leave the default selections as **Custom** > **Custom policy**. Click **Next**:

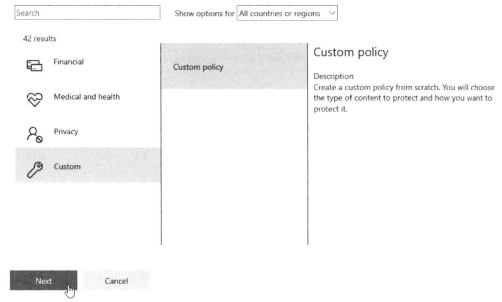

Figure 12.21 – The DLP policy wizard on the Custom policy screen

14. Name and describe the policy, then click **Next**:

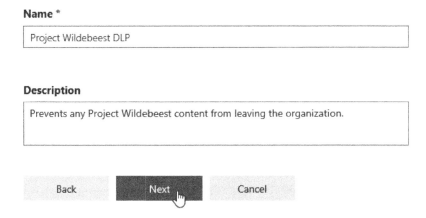

Figure 12.22 – Name and description fields

15. Click **Next** to stick with the default locations:

Choose locations

We'll protect content that's stored in the locations you choose. *

⦿ Protect content in Exchange email, Teams chats and channel messages and OneDrive and SharePoint documents.

◯ Let me choose specific locations.

Figure 12.23 – Location scope configuration

16. Under **Find content that contains**, click **Edit**:

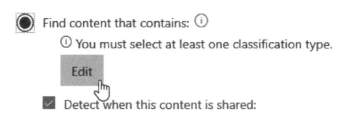

Figure 12.24 – Content scope configuration

17. Click **Add** > **Sensitive info types**:

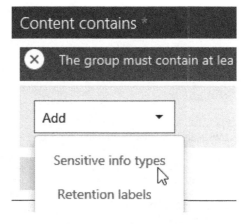

Figure 12.25 – Required sensitive info type or retention label selection

18. Click **Add**.

19. Find and select your custom sensitive information type created in steps 1-9:

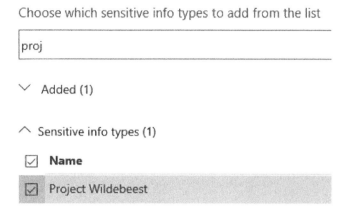

Figure 12.26 – Selected info type for the DLP policy

20. Click **Add**. Then, click **Done** and **Save**.

21. Click **Next**:

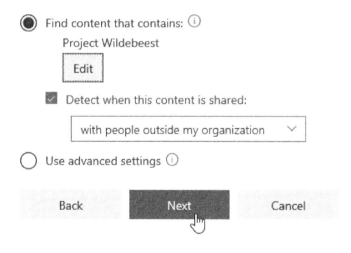

Figure 12.27 – Confirmation of the selected info type with behavior specification

22. Choose which actions you want to take if `Project Wildebeest` content is detected. When finished, click **Next**:

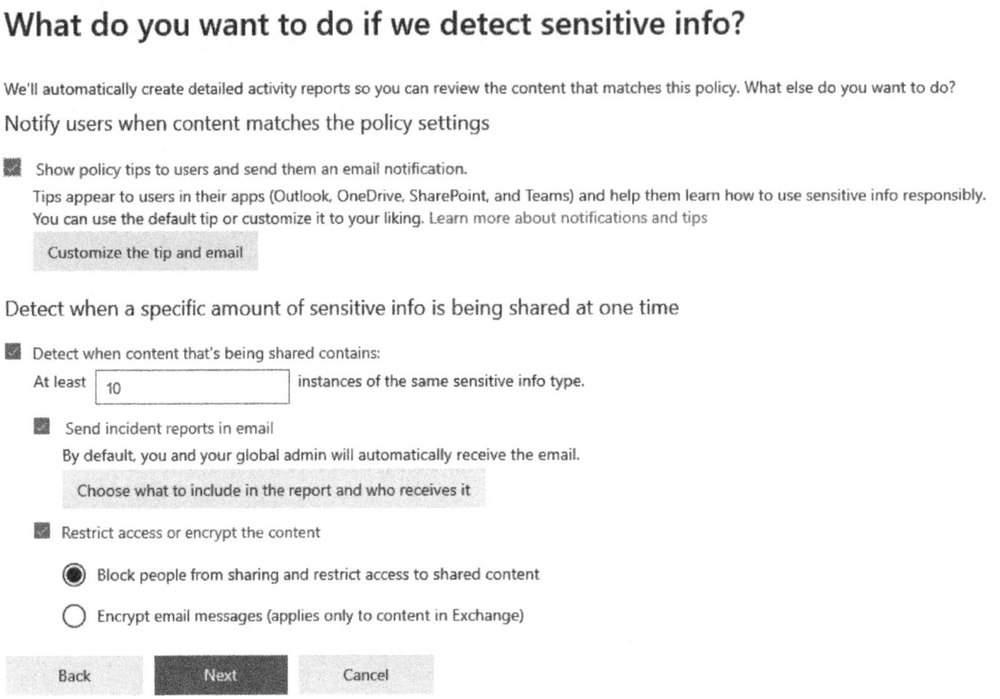

What do you want to do if we detect sensitive info?

We'll automatically create detailed activity reports so you can review the content that matches this policy. What else do you want to do?

Notify users when content matches the policy settings

☑ Show policy tips to users and send them an email notification.
Tips appear to users in their apps (Outlook, OneDrive, SharePoint, and Teams) and help them learn how to use sensitive info responsibly. You can use the default tip or customize it to your liking. Learn more about notifications and tips

Customize the tip and email

Detect when a specific amount of sensitive info is being shared at one time

☑ Detect when content that's being shared contains:
At least [10]   instances of the same sensitive info type.

☑ Send incident reports in email
By default, you and your global admin will automatically receive the email.

Choose what to include in the report and who receives it

☑ Restrict access or encrypt the content

🔘 Block people from sharing and restrict access to shared content

⚪ Encrypt email messages (applies only to content in Exchange)

Back   Next   Cancel

Figure 12.28 – Actions to take upon detection of sensitive info

23. If you chose to restrict access to the content when shared externally, you'll also need to configure the following settings. For this example, let's check both boxes under **Let people who see the tip override the policy**. Then, click **Next**:

Customize access and override permissions

By default, users are blocked from sending email and Teams chats and channel messages that contain the type of content you're protecting. But you can choose who has access to shared SharePoint and OneDrive files. You can also decide if you want to let people override the policy's restrictions.

Block these people from accessing SharePoint, OneDrive, and Teams content

◯ Everyone ⓘ

◉ Only people outside your organization ⓘ

Let people who see the tip override the policy

🔘 On

☑ Require a business justification to override
☑ Override the rule automatically if they report it as a false positive

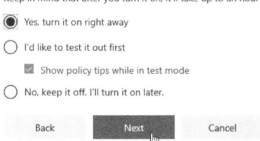

Back	Next	Cancel

Figure 12.29 – Configuration of access and override permissions

24. Choose to turn your policy on right away, then click **Next**:

Do you want to turn on the policy or test things out first?

Do you want to turn on the policy right away or test things out first?

Keep in mind that after you turn it on, it'll take up to an hour for the policy to take effect.

◉ Yes, turn it on right away

◯ I'd like to test it out first

☑ Show policy tips while in test mode

◯ No, keep it off. I'll turn it on later.

Back	Next	Cancel

Figure 12.30 – Option to turn on the policy immediately or test it

25. Review the policy and, when satisfied, click **Create**:

Review your settings

Policy name   Edit

Project Wildebeest DLP

Description   Edit

Prevents any Project Wildebeest content from leaving the
organization.

Applies to content in these locations   Edit

Exchange email
SharePoint sites
OneDrive accounts
Teams chat and channel messages

Policy settings   Edit

If the content contains these types of sensitive info: Project
Wildebeest then notify people with a policy tip and email
message.

If there are at least 10 instances of the same type of sensitive
info, block access to the content and send an incident report
with a high severity level but allow people to override if they
provide a business justification or they report the match as a
false positive.

Turn policy on after it's created?   Edit

Yes

| Back | Create | Cancel |

Figure 12.31 – Final review of the policy with the Create button

How it works...

In this recipe, we created a sensitive information type associated with any content
including keyword matches for Project Wildebeest or its official acronyms in our
organization. We then configured a DLP policy to search for that custom sensitive info
type and block it from being shared outside the organization. If it was shared, we provided
a way for users to override the block with business justification or false positive reporting.

See also

- Learn more about data loss prevention in Microsoft 365 at `https://docs.microsoft.com/en-us/microsoft-365/compliance/data-loss-prevention-policies`.

- Learn more about creating custom sensitive information types at `https://docs.microsoft.com/en-us/microsoft-365/compliance/create-a-custom-sensitive-information-type`.

Tuning a sensitive information type's confidence level

When you're creating a DLP policy, you can use sensitive information types (such as `Project Wildebeest` in the previous recipe). Matches are based on specific patterns and confidence level. The higher the confidence level, the more certain the match must be whereas a lower confidence level will catch more similar matches (though these will include false positives).

You may wish for a higher confidence level when you're more absolutely certain data that should be caught follows a specific pattern each time, such as a routing number within a certain proximity of an account number or SSN. Lower confidence levels will be more inclusive of potential matches and may be helpful for more loosely structured data where, perhaps, a confidential project may be discussed or referenced in numerous ways and structures.

In this recipe, we'll adjust a sensitive information type from the previous recipe (`Project Wildebeest`) to require less confidence when matching.

Getting ready

You should be a global or compliance administrator to complete this recipe.

How to do it...

1. Go to the Microsoft 365 compliance center at `https://compliance.microsoft.com`.

2. Choose **Data classification** from the left-hand navigation menu.

3. Choose **Sensitive info types**:

Figure 12.32 – The Sensitive info types link on the top navigation menu of the Data classification page

4. Search for and select the name of the sensitive information type for which you'll be adjusting the sensitivity.

5. Click **Edit**:

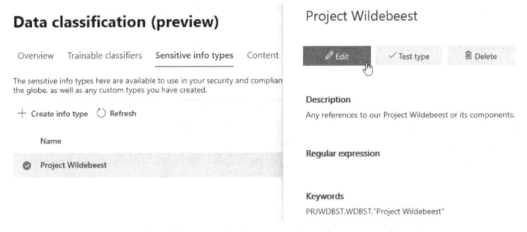

Figure 12.33 – The Edit button on an existing, selected sensitive information type

6. Click **Requirements for matching**:

Make edits to your sensitive
type property settings here.

Name and description

Requirements for matching

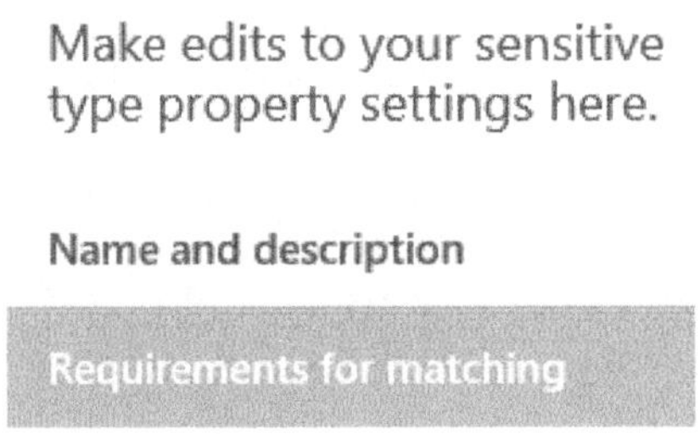

Figure 12.34 – Requirements for matching selected

7. Adjust the **Confidence level** to a lower percentage to increase its sensitivity and catch more potential matches:

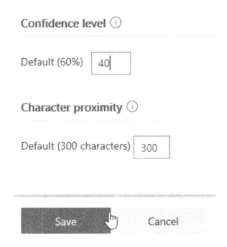

Figure 12.35 – Confidence level configuration

8. Click **Save**.

How it works...

In this recipe, you adjusted a sensitive information type's confidence level so that any DLP policy utilizing it might find more potential matches.

There's more...

You can additionally configure a DLP policy's sensitivity when adding the sensitive information type to the policy. This allows you to customize sensitivity per policy, rather than universally for all uses of the sensitive information type:

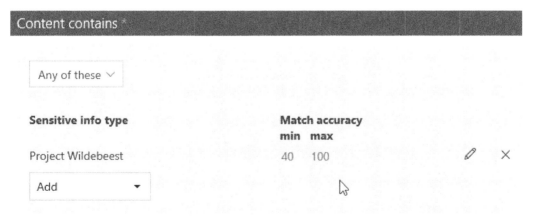

Figure 12.36 – Policy-specific sensitive information type accuracy configuration

See also

- Learn about pre-defined sensitive information types and what is being looked for in matches at `https://docs.microsoft.com/en-us/microsoft-365/compliance/what-the-sensitive-information-types-look-for`.

- Learn more about tuning a DLP policy specifically at `https://docs.microsoft.com/en-us/microsoft-365/compliance/create-test-tune-dlp-policy#tune-a-dlp-policy`.

Creating an eDiscovery case

Think of an eDiscovery case as a container for an investigation or search for content related to a specific inquiry. Perhaps the legal team requires access to search all content in the environment related to a user—an eDiscovery case would be a way to containerize the scope of their search and provide them access. You may also be asked to investigate a user's inbox or a specific site, placing a hold on it first with an eDiscovery case. In this recipe, we'll create an eDiscovery case to provide specific people access to review specific content related to a fictional investigation.

Getting ready

You should be a global, compliance, or eDiscovery administrator or an eDiscovery manager to complete this recipe.

How to do it...

1. Go to the Microsoft 365 compliance center at `https://compliance.microsoft.com`.

2. Select **Show all** > **eDiscovery** > **Core** from the left-hand navigation menu:

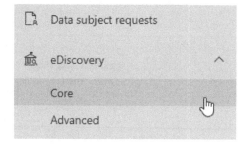

Figure 12.37 – The Core eDiscovery link in the left-hand navigation menu of the Microsoft 365 compliance center

3. Click **Create a case**.

4. Name and describe the eDiscovery case so that you can find it again later easily. Click **Save**:

Figure 12.38 – Name and description for the eDiscovery case

5. Select the *Open* icon next to the new case's name:

Figure 12.39 – Open icon next to the newly created case's name

6. Click **Searches**:

Figure 12.40 – The Searches link along the top navigation of the selected case

7. Click **New search** (or **Guided search** if you prefer).

8. Click **Add conditions**.

9. Select all fields that are people properties. Then, click **Add**:

Figure 12.41 – Conditions to be configured as part of the case

10. For each added condition, add `nate@natechamberlain.com` since we're looking at all of Nate Chamberlain's activities in this case:

Figure 12.42 – An example of one of the selected conditions and its configurable fields

11. Remove **Keywords** since this case won't involve that filter:

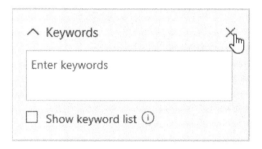

Figure 12.43 – The Keywords list appears by default, but is being removed here

12. Choose **All locations**, then **Save & run**:

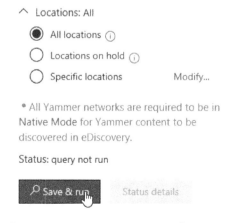

Figure 12.44 – Location scope configuration

13. Name and describe your search. Click **Save**:

Figure 12.45 – Name and description for the search within the case

14. Go back to eDiscovery Core (steps *1-2*).

15. Select the name of the case then add members and role groups who should have access to the case:

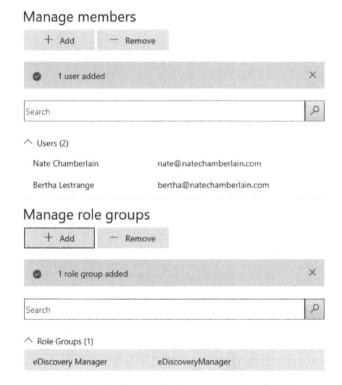

Figure 12.46 – Members and role groups assigned to the case

16. Click **Save**.

How it works...

In this recipe, we created a simple eDiscovery case that includes a search for content throughout Office 365. We then added members and role groups who should have access to the case.

There's more...

You may have noticed you can also create holds for eDiscovery cases to essentially freeze content as is if need be. This is common in legal matters.

See also

- Learn more about creating eDiscovery cases at `https://docs.microsoft.com/en-us/microsoft-365/compliance/get-started-core-ediscovery`.

Managing eDiscovery cases

In the previous recipe, you created an eDiscovery core case and shared it with members for review. In this recipe, we'll cover a couple more things you can do when managing eDiscovery cases.

Getting ready

You should be a global, compliance, or eDiscovery administrator to complete this recipe. You could also be an eDiscovery manager if only managing cases you created or were assigned to.

How to do it...

1. Go to the Microsoft 365 compliance center at `https://compliance.microsoft.com`.

2. Select **Show all** > **eDiscovery** > **Core** from the left-hand navigation menu:

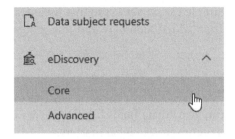

Figure 12.47 – The Core eDiscovery link on the left-hand navigation menu of the Microsoft 365 compliance center

3. Click **Export** to get a CSV file of all cases and their top-level details:

	A	B	C	D	E
1	Name	Status	Created date	Last modified	Last modified by
2	Chamberlain Investigation December 2019	Closing	2020-05-10T15:25:59.813Z	2020-05-10T15:26:08.770Z	Nate Chamberlain
3	Chamberlain Investigation May 2020	Active	2020-05-10T01:51:25.077Z	2020-05-10T01:51:25.077Z	Nate Chamberlain
4	Demo eDiscovery Case	Active	2020-05-10T15:25:20.957Z	2020-05-10T15:25:20.957Z	Nate Chamberlain
5	Project Wildebeest	Active	2020-05-10T15:25:34.780Z	2020-05-10T15:25:46.337Z	Nate Chamberlain
6	Test	Active	2020-02-24T02:57:40.480Z	2020-02-24T02:57:40.480Z	Nate Chamberlain

Figure 12.48 – Example CSV file of exported case details

4. Use the **Group by**, **Search**, and **Filter** buttons to quickly find and organize your cases. You might, for example, use **Group by** to filter cases by their current status instead of all together:

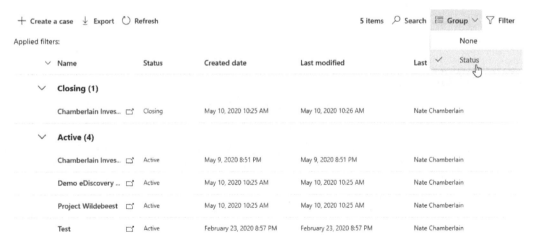

Figure 12.49 – Cases viewed by status groups in the admin center

5. If you need to close (end) or delete (remove) a case, select its name then scroll down to the bottom of its details pane to find options for both:

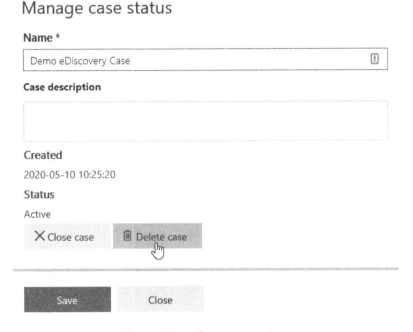

Figure 12.50 – Case status options

How it works...

In this recipe, you explored the eDiscovery core case management options available to you as an administrator. You learned to navigate to, search, filter, and export the case list as well as how to close and delete cases from the list of active cases.

See also

- For more information on closing, deleting, and restoring cases, see `https://docs.microsoft.com/en-us/microsoft-365/compliance/close-reopen-delete-core-ediscovery-cases`.

Creating an advanced eDiscovery case

In the *Creating an eDiscovery case* recipe earlier in this chapter, you created a basic eDiscovery case. In this recipe, you'll create an advanced eDiscovery case that has a few more options and abilities.

Getting ready

You should be a global or compliance administrator to complete this recipe. eDiscovery also requires an Office 365 or Microsoft 365 E5 subscription.

How to do it...

1. Go to the Microsoft 365 compliance center at `https://compliance.microsoft.com`.
2. Select **Show all** > **eDiscovery** > **Advanced** from the left-hand navigation menu:

eDiscovery
Core
Advanced

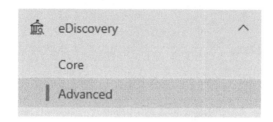

Figure 12.51 – The Advanced eDiscovery link on the left-hand navigation menu of the Microsoft 365 compliance center

3. Click **Cases**.
4. Click **Create a case**.
5. Enter a **Case name, Case number** (optional), and **Case description** for the case:

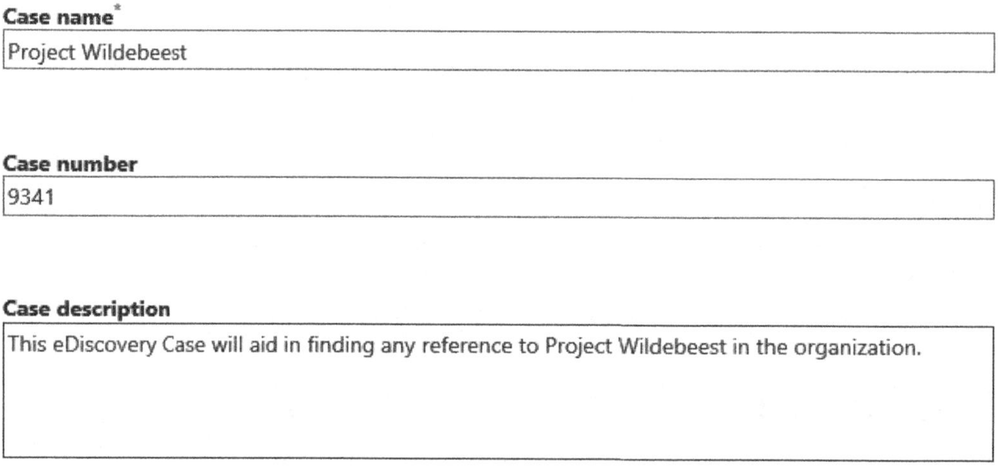

Case name*
Project Wildebeest
Case number
9341
Case description
This eDiscovery Case will aid in finding any reference to Project Wildebeest in the organization.

Figure 12.52 – Case basic details configuration

6. Change **Do you want to configure additional settings after creating this case?** to **No**. The next recipe will cover adding members via the **Settings** page for the case to which this would redirect you if left as **Yes**.

7. Click **Save**.

8. You've created your advanced eDiscovery case. Now, like core eDiscovery, you can create **Holds** and **Searches**. You can also monitor processing errors, create review sets, and monitor jobs:

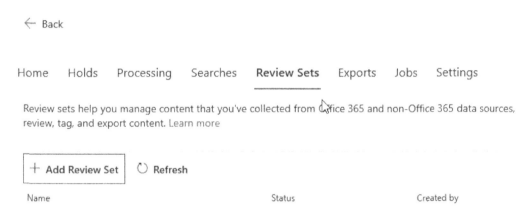

Figure 12.53 – The Review Sets page of a specific advanced eDiscovery case

How it works...

In this recipe, you created an advanced eDiscovery case that gives a few more options in eDiscovery such as Review Sets and improved monitoring.

See also

- Learn more about advanced eDiscovery at `https://docs.microsoft.com/en-us/microsoft-365/compliance/overview-ediscovery-20`.

Changing who has access to an advanced eDiscovery case

In the last recipe, you created an advanced eDiscovery case. In this recipe, we'll modify an existing case to add members and role groups to have access.

Getting ready

You should be a global, compliance, or eDiscovery administrator or an eDiscovery manager to complete this recipe.

How to do it...

1. Go to the Microsoft 365 compliance center at `https://compliance.microsoft.com`.
2. Select **Show all** > **eDiscovery** > **Advanced** from the left-hand navigation menu:

eDiscovery
Core
Advanced

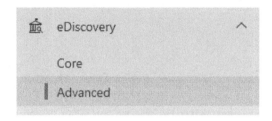

Figure 12.54 – The Advanced eDiscovery link on the left-hand navigation menu of the Microsoft 365 compliance center

3. Click **Cases**.
4. Select the name of the case for which you're adding members or role groups to permissions.
5. Select **Settings**:

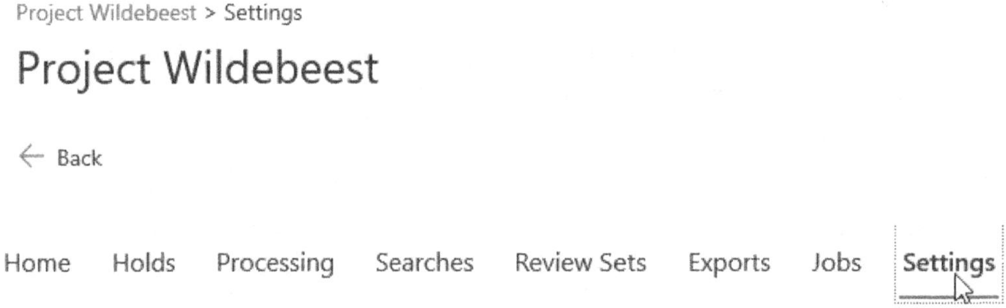

Project Wildebeest > Settings
Project Wildebeest
Back
Home
Holds
Processing
Searches
Review Sets
Exports
Jobs
Settings

Figure 12.55 – The Settings link along the top navigation of a specific eDiscovery case

6. Under **Access & permissions**, click **Select**:

Figure 12.56 – The Select button under Access & permissions

7. Click **Update**.

8. Add members and/or role groups to the advanced eDiscovery case then click **Save**:

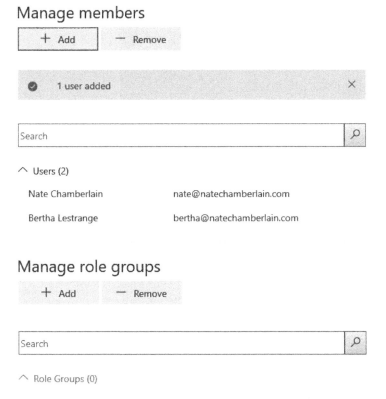

Figure 12.57 – Members and role groups configuration

How it works...

In this recipe, you added members and role groups to an existing advanced eDiscovery case. The process varies slightly from doing the same for a core eDiscovery case but it's functionally the same.

See also

- Learn more about advanced eDiscovery at `https://docs.microsoft.com/en-us/microsoft-365/compliance/overview-ediscovery-20`.

13
Monitoring Office 365 Apps and Services

There's no shortage of reporting and analysis abilities in Office 365. In each admin center, you'll find unique reports and information about your users, their activities and behaviors, your content's protection, and so much more. This chapter covers how to procure reports on important and helpful topics that will enable you, as an administrator, to respond to risks and plan for growth in Office 365.

We'll be covering the following recipes in this chapter:

- Finding at-risk users
- Creating alerts for specific activities performed by users in OneDrive
- Reviewing mail handling to see spam and malware history
- Identifying your least active SharePoint sites
- Reviewing search activity across SharePoint site collections

- Checking the service health status and known issues
- Checking general usage data for Office 365 apps and services
- Checking Teams usage and user activity
- Monitoring Power Apps and Power Automate usage

Let's get started!

Technical requirements

The only requirement to complete the recipes in this chapter is to be either a global administrator or another administrator with read permissions for the reports for specific apps and services being monitored. For example, if you're looking for Teams usage and user activity, a Teams administrator role would be sufficient. Global admins will have sufficient privileges for all recipes.

Finding at-risk users

At-risk users are users in your organization that have been flagged for behavior that seems out of the ordinary, mostly when signing in. It could be that the user's credentials have been compromised (showing suspicious activity consistent with such events), or perhaps just a false positive when a user is signing in when traveling. In this recipe, you'll learn how to find users that have been identified as at-risk and learn how to address them.

Getting ready

You need to be a global or security administrator or reader to complete this recipe.

How to do it...

1. Go to the Microsoft 365 Security admin center at `https://security.microsoft.com`.

2. Select **Reports** from the left-hand navigation menu and click **Users at risk**:

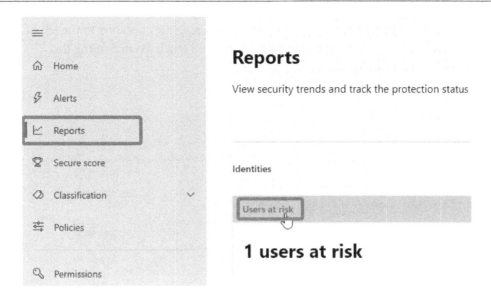

Figure 13.1 – Users at risk link on the Reports page of the Microsoft 365 Security admin center

3.   Select an at-risk user to view more details:

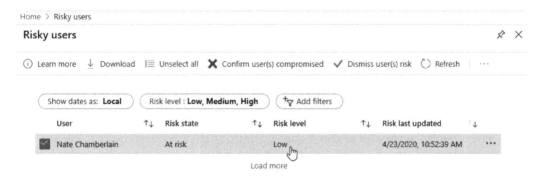

Figure 13.2 – A selected at-risk user

4.   A **Details** panel will appear at the bottom of the screen with information and available actions for that user:

Figure 13.3 – The selected at-risk user details

5. To act on multiple users, you can select them (using the checkbox to the left of each) and then choose a bulk action to take on them all (such as confirming the compromised user or dismissing the risk):

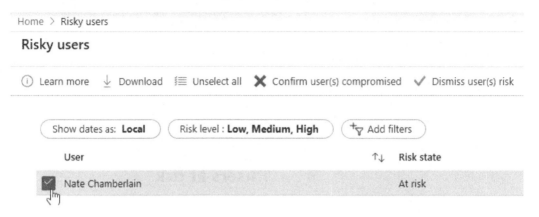

Figure 13.4 – Checkboxes for multi-select appear to the left of user's names for bulk actions

How it works...

In this recipe, you discovered users in your organization who are deemed at-risk, meaning they may have had risky sign-ins (unusual behavior), unfamiliar sign-in properties, or other risk detections.

See also

*   You can learn more about at-risk users at https://docs.microsoft.com/en-us/azure/active-directory/reports-monitoring/concept-user-at-risk.

Creating alerts for specific activities performed by users in OneDrive

As an administrator, you can create alerts to be notified when users perform certain actions in OneDrive for Business (or any other app). In this recipe, we'll focus on creating an alert for when users share OneDrive files externally.

Getting ready

You need to be a global administrator to complete this recipe.

How to do it...

1. Go to the Office 365 Security & Compliance Center at `https://protection.office.com`.

2. Select **Alerts** > **Dashboard** from the left navigation pane.

3. Select **New alert policy** from under **Alert policies**.

4. Define the **Name**, **Description**, **Severity**, and **Category** details of the alert:

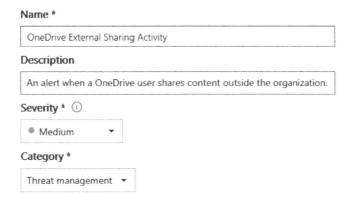

Figure 13.5 – Alert policy basic details configuration

5. Set the **Activity is** dropdown to **Shared file externally** and the **Site collection URL is** text box so that it includes your root OneDrive site collection followed by an asterisk, similar to `https://natechamberlain-my.sharepoint.com*`:

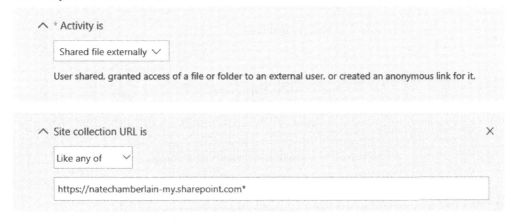

Figure 13.6 – Activity and URL scope for the alert policy

6. Leave the alert frequency to **Every time an activity matches the rule** and click **Next**:

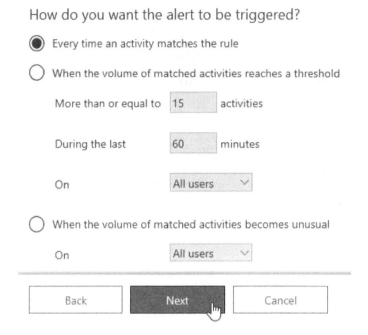

Figure 13.7 – Alert trigger configuration

7. Choose who should receive the alert and how frequently to set the max notification limit:

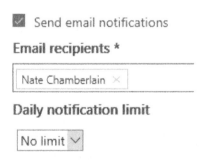

Figure 13.8 – Email notification configuration

8. Click **Next**.

9. Review your new alert's settings and, when satisfied, click **Finish**:

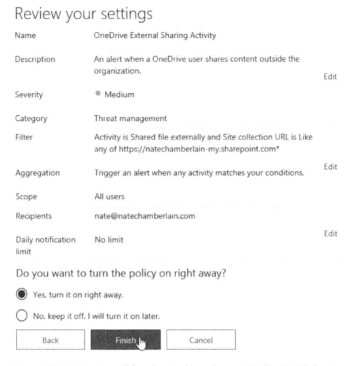

Figure 13.9 – Review of the alert policy, along with the Finish button

How it works...

In this recipe, you created a new alert policy in the Office 365 Security & Compliance admin center that notifies a specified user when someone in your organization shares a OneDrive file externally. These kind of notifications help prevent data loss and ensure compliance by providing convenient monitoring and data management abilities.

See also

- You can learn more about alert policies at `https://docs.microsoft.com/ en-us/microsoft-365/compliance/alert-policies`.

Reviewing mail handling to see spam and malware history

Several of the reports available in the Office 365 Security & Compliance Center are related to mail handling. In this recipe, we'll explore how to analyze mail activity, specifically when looking for spam and malware history.

Getting ready

You need to be a global administrator, global reader, or reports reader to complete this recipe.

How to do it...

1. Go to the Office 365 Security & Compliance Center at `https://protection.office.com`.

2. Select **Reports** > **Dashboard** from the left-hand navigation menu:

Figure 13.10 – Dashboard link on the left-hand navigation menu of the
O365 Security & Compliance center

3. Scroll down and find **Malware detected in email**:

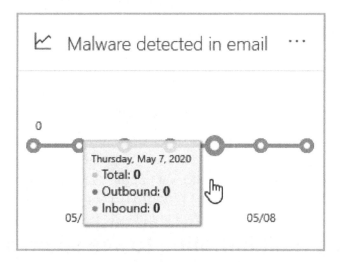

Figure 13.11 – Malware detected in email card

4. Click the center of the report tile to maximize the report and see it in greater detail:

Figure 13.12 – Selected card enlarged in detail

5. Go back to the dashboard and find the **Spam detections** report:

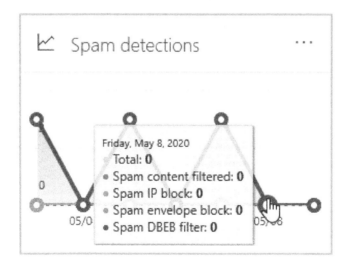

Figure 13.13 – Spam detections card

6. As you did previously, click the center of the **Spam detections** report tile to maximize the report and see it in greater detail:

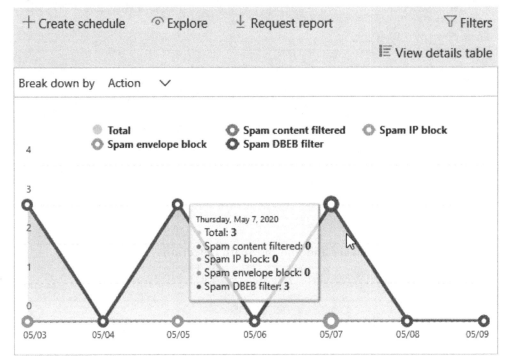

Figure 13.14 – Selected card expanded in greater detail

7. Notice how, on all the reports, you can create a schedule and request a report or view it as a table (non-graphically).

How it works...

In this recipe, you found email-related security reports in the Office 365 Security & Compliance admin center. These are just two of several default reports available for reporting on activity and security topics in all of O365's apps and services.

See also

-   You can read more about email security reports at https://docs.microsoft.com/en-us/microsoft-365/security/office-365-security/view-email-security-reports.

Identifying your least active SharePoint sites

It can be helpful to know which of your organization's SharePoint site collections are inactive or rarely used when reviewing sites for cleanup. A good governance strategy includes routinely reviewing existing site collections. In this recipe, we'll go through the steps to identify the least active SharePoint site collections in your tenant.

Getting ready

You need to be a global or SharePoint administrator, global reader, or reports reader to complete this recipe.

How to do it...

1. Go to the SharePoint Admin Center at `https://YOURTENANT-admin.sharepoint.com`.

2. Above the SharePoint site usage report, click **Details**:

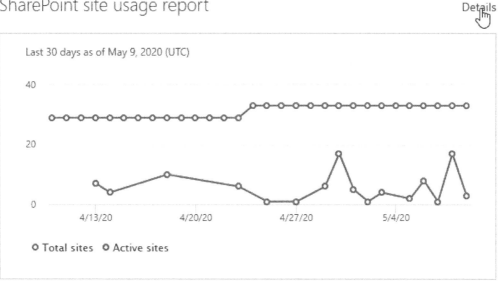

Figure 13.15 – SharePoint site usage report visual

3. Select the column header for **Last activity date** and choose **Sort ascending**:

Details

Site URL		Site owner principal ...	Last activity date (UT...	Files	
https://natechamberlain.sh...		ProjectManagementDemo...	Friday, May 08, 2020	Sort ascending	
https://natechamberlain.sh...		KWOneNoteinTeamsDemo...	Friday, May 08, 2020		
https://natechamberlain.sh...		LSPUG@natechamberlain....	Friday, May 08, 2020	Sort descending	
https://natechamberlain.sh...		test@natechamberlain.com			

Figure 13.16 – Details for specific sites and last activity dates

4. The sites that are now listed at the top of the table are your least active sites. Click **Export** to get a CSV file of this data you can manipulate more easily and share:

↓ Export

Storage used (MB)		Page views	
1			
1			
1			
28			
2			

Figure 13.17 – Export option for the CSV file of active sites

How it works...

In this recipe, you found the SharePoint site collections in your organization that are least used. You also learned how to export this for additional manipulation and sharing.

There's more...

You can also find this report from the Office 365 Security & Compliance Center's **Reports** dashboard.

See also

- You can learn more about SharePoint site usage at `https://docs.microsoft.com/en-US/microsoft-365/admin/activity-reports/sharepoint-site-usage`.

Reviewing search activity across SharePoint site collections

Search activity reports from SharePoint site collections will help you and your governance team improve the search experience by taking actual user search behaviors into account when creating search enhancements such as bookmarks, promoted results, Q&A results, location results, and so on. In this recipe, we'll find the search activity reports in the SharePoint admin center.

Getting ready

You need to be a global or SharePoint administrator to complete this recipe.

How to do it...

1. Go to the SharePoint Admin Center at `https://YOURTENANT-admin.sharepoint.com`.

2. Select **More features** from the left-hand navigation menu:

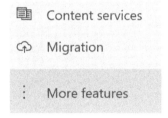

Figure 13.18 – More features link on the left-hand navigation menu of the SharePoint admin center

3. Under **Search**, click **Open**:

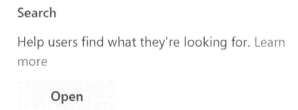

Figure 13.19 – Open button for the Search settings

4. Click **View Usage Reports**.

5. From here, you can utilize several different search reports by day and month. Check out the following:

    --**Top Queries** (most searched)

    --**Abandoned Queries** (searched but selected none of the results)

    --**No Result Queries** (searched but no results were found):

Top Queries by Day

This report shows the most popular search queries. Use this report to understand what types of information visitors are seeking.

Top Queries by Month

This report shows the most popular search queries. Use this report to understand what types of information visitors are seeking.

Abandoned Queries by Day

This report shows popular search queries that received low click-through. Use this report to identify search queries that might create user dissatisfaction and to improve the discoverability of content. Then, consider using query rules to improve the query's results.

Abandoned Queries by Month

This report shows popular search queries that received low click-through. Use this report to identify search queries that might create user dissatisfaction and to improve the discoverability of content. Then, consider using query rules to improve the query's results.

No Result Queries by Day

This report shows popular search queries that returned no results. Use this report to identify search queries that might create user dissatisfaction and to improve the discoverability of content. Then, consider using query rules to improve the query's results.

No Result Queries by Month

This report shows popular search queries that returned no results. Use this report to identify search queries that might create user dissatisfaction and to improve the discoverability of content. Then, consider using query rules to improve the query's results.

Query Rule Usage by Day

This report shows how often query rules fire, how many dictionary terms they use, and how often users click their promoted results. Use this report to see how useful your query rules and promoted results are to users.

Query Rule Usage by Month

This report shows how often query rules fire, how many dictionary terms they use, and how often users click their promoted results. Use this report to see how useful your query rules and promoted results are to users.

Figure 13.20 – Available usage reports as downloadable Excel files

How it works...

In this recipe, you found the SharePoint search usage reports. By utilizing the data found in these, you can find out what your users are looking for most often, and what they're looking for but not finding. This could help you adjust content metadata; search for configuration, including bookmarks to promote results; or create new content or Q&A results to answer common queries.

See also

- You can read more about the SharePoint search usage reports at `https://docs.microsoft.com/en-us/sharepoint/view-search-usage-reports`.

Checking the service health status and known issues

Service health lets you know about any current advisories or known incidents involving the apps and services included in your subscription. You're also able to report issues you've noticed from the Service health page. In this recipe, we'll locate **Service health**.

Getting ready

You need to be a global or service administrator or reader to complete this recipe.

How to do it...

1. Go to the Microsoft 365 admin center at `https://admin.microsoft.com`.

2. Select **Show all** from the left-hand navigation menu.

3. Click **Health** > **Service health**:

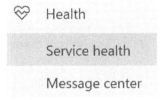

Figure 13-21 – Service health link on the left-hand navigation menu of the Microsoft 365 admin center

4. The main table of the page shows each service, with those known to have incidents or advisories at the top. You'll also notice the **Report an issue** option here:

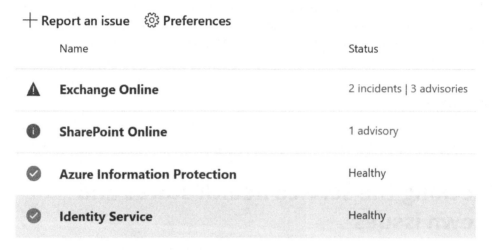

Figure 13.22 – Service health statuses and known issues

5. Across the top, you'll notice navigation that allows you to view different components of Service health, such as specific status details or historical data:

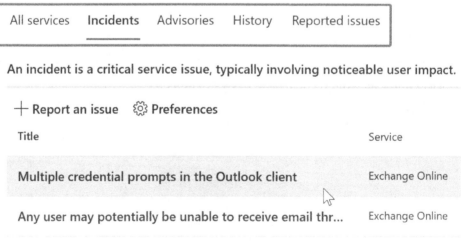

Figure 13.23 – Incidents tab of the Service health page

How it works...

In this recipe, you located and became familiar with Service health in the Microsoft 365 admin center. Being able to monitor Service health helps you understand potential issues your users may experience and aids in communicating to users about problems or downtime.

See also

- You can read more about Service health at `https://docs.microsoft.com/en-us/office365/enterprise/view-service-health`.

Checking general usage data for Office 365 apps and services

Office 365 has a single page that you can us to monitor usage for all Office 365 apps and services. These reports offer a glimpse into the usage and adoption of Office 365 throughout the organization and may help guide governance, training, and administration decisions. In this recipe, we'll navigate to and explore these reports.

Getting ready

You need to be a global administrator or reader to complete this recipe.

How to do it...

1. Go to the Microsoft 365 admin center at `https://admin.microsoft.com`.
2. Select **Show all** from the left-hand navigation menu.
3. Click **Reports** > **Usage**:

Figure 13.24 – Usage link on the left-hand navigation menu of the Microsoft 365 admin center

4.   Here, you can find a graphic representation of usage data for Microsoft 365 apps and services. By clicking on any one of the data cards, you will be taken to a larger version to dive into more detail where you will see the accompanying data rows. Also, notice the ability to change the time span represented on the usage dashboard from 7 days to 180 days:

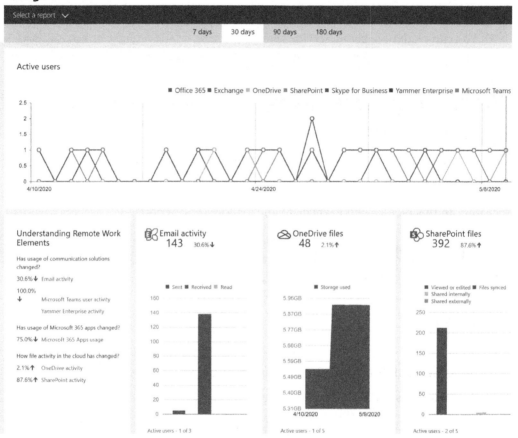

Figure 13.25 – Usage data for all O365 apps

How it works...

In this recipe, you found the Microsoft 365 admin center's **Usage data** dashboard. This dashboard gives you easy access to usage data across all your apps and services in one convenient location. From this single place, you're able to get an idea of trends, potential issues, and general activity in your organization.

See also

- You can read more about the usage data available in the Microsoft 365 admin center at `https://docs.microsoft.com/en-US/microsoft-365/admin/activity-reports/activity-reports`.

Checking Teams usage and user activity

As you deploy and administer Teams in your organization, it's helpful to know how to track usage and general user activity data. This insight allows you to gauge adoption and opportunities. In this recipe, we'll locate Teams usage and user activity from the Teams admin center.

Getting ready

You need to be a global or Teams administrator to complete this recipe.

How to do it...

1. Go to the Teams admin center at `https://admin.teams.microsoft.com`.

2. Select **Analytics & reports** > **Usage reports** from the left-hand navigation menu:

Figure 13.26 – Usage reports link on the left-hand navigation menu of the
Microsoft Teams admin center

3. Select **Teams usage** or **Teams user activity** from the **Report** dropdown and choose a time span the report should cover (the last 7, 30, or 90 days). Then, click **Run report**:

Figure 13.27 – Teams usage report options

4.   The **Teams usage** report shows you specific Teams and activity over time:

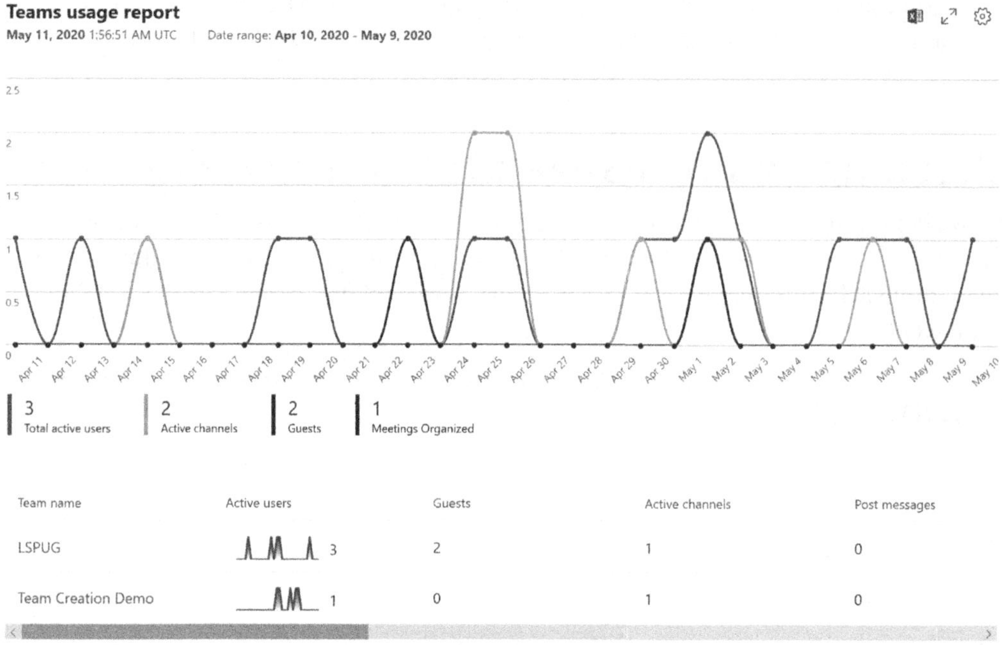

Teams usage report
May 11, 2020 1:56:51 AM UTC   Date range: **Apr 10, 2020 - May 9, 2020**

3	**2**	**2**	**1**
Total active users	Active channels	Guests	Meetings Organized

Team name	Active users	Guests	Active channels	Post messages
LSPUG	3	2	1	0
Team Creation Demo	1	0	1	0

Figure 13.28 – Teams usage report example

5.   The **Teams user activity** report shows you meetings you have organized and participated in, as well as messages in various areas of Teams by individual users.

How it works...

In this recipe, you learned how to access usage data for Microsoft Teams via the Microsoft Teams admin center. This data can be helpful in identifying active (or inactive) Teams, as well as users who may be great candidates as Champions in your organization to help promote the usage, understanding, and adoption of Teams to their peers.

There's more...

Each report has an Excel icon that can be used to export the data to Excel:

Figure 13.29 – Excel icon for exporting Teams usage reports

See also

- You can find more information about the Microsoft Teams usage report at `https://docs.microsoft.com/en-us/microsoftteams/teams-analytics-and-reports/teams-usage-report`.

Monitoring Power Apps and Power Automate usage

In this recipe, you'll locate information on Power Apps and Power Automate active users and flow runs. This can be helpful to gauge adoption, but also look at the usage of limited subscription allowances.

Getting ready

You need to be a global or Power Platform service administrator to complete this recipe.

How to do it...

1. Go to the Power Platform admin center at `https://admin.powerplatform.microsoft.com`.

2. Select **Analytics** > **Power Automate** from the left-hand navigation menu:

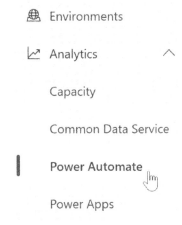

Figure 13.30 – Power Automate analytics link on the left-hand navigation menu of the Power Platform admin center

3. **Power Automate analytics** shows you flow runs, usage, flows created, errors, flows shared, and connector usage stats over time. Click through each of the tabs along the top:

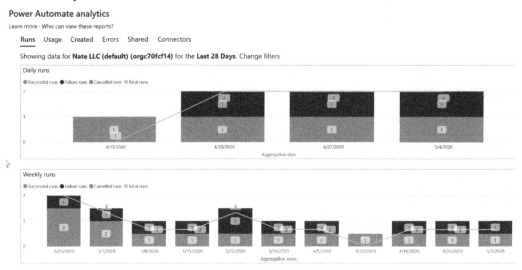

Figure 13.31 – Power Automate runs visuals

4. Select **Analytics** > **Power Apps** from the left-hand navigation menu:

Figure 13.32 – Power Apps analytics link on the left-hand navigation menu of the Power Platform admin center

5. **Power Apps analytics** shows you **Usage**, launches by **Location**, **Toast errors**, **Service Performance**, and **Connectors** usage data:

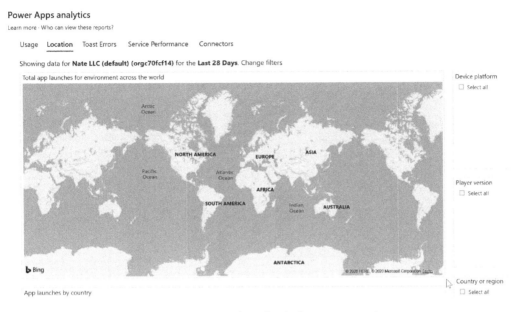

Figure 13.33 – Power Apps launches by location example report

How it works...

In this recipe, you found the usage reports for Power Automate and Power Apps. This lets you find your active users, usage over time, and much more data about the implementation of Power Apps and Power Automate in your organization.

See also

- You can read more about Power Automate analytics at `https://docs.microsoft.com/en-us/power-platform/admin/analytics-flow`.

- You can read more about Power Apps analytics at `https://docs.microsoft.com/en-us/power-platform/admin/analytics-powerapps`.

14
Appendix – Office 365 Subscriptions and Licenses

Because subscriptions and licenses evolve and change frequently, the best place to find information is directly from Microsoft. To learn more about subscriptions and licenses, I recommend reviewing the following resources:

- Compare Microsoft 365 Enterprise Plans: `https://www.microsoft.com/en-us/microsoft-365/compare-microsoft-365-enterprise-plans`.

- Aaron Dinnage's licensing diagrams will help you understand what services and packages fall into which subscriptions and are frequently updated. I particularly benefited from the Venn diagram model: `https://github.com/AaronDinnage/Licensing`.

- Matt Wade has created the Periodic Table of Office 365, an excellent visualization of the O365 platform and all its apps and service. This can be found at `https://www.jumpto365.com/tables/en`.

- Staying current can be a challenge but `https://msft365admincenter.com/` has gathered many resources that'll help you keep up and find relevant, timely information you need to make administrative decisions:

  -- M365 podcasts and blogs: Excellent resources for research, community, and news.

  -- Twitter account links: These are a great way to stay current regarding feature releases and news directly from each product group, conveniently collected in this central space.

- `CleanShelf.com` has two guides that are helpful for when you're trying to make sense of license types and maximizing usage of available features within each. They provide a good place to start for your analysis and decision-making:

  -- Easy-to-Read Guide to Microsoft 365 and Office 365 License Types: `https://www.cleanshelf.com/resources/guide-to-microsoft-office-365-license-types/`.

  -- 5-Step Guide to Microsoft Office 365 License Optimization: `https://www.cleanshelf.com/resources/5-step-guide-to-microsoft-office-365-license-optimization/`.

Other Books You May Enjoy

If you enjoyed this book, you may be interested in these other books by Packt:

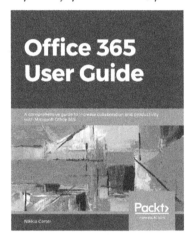

Office 365 User Guide

Nikkia Carter

ISBN: 978-1-78980-931-2

- Understand the UI of Office 365
- Perform a variety of email functions through Exchange
- Communicate using Skype for Business and Microsoft Teams
- Explore file management using OneDrive for Business
- Collaborate using SharePoint
- Understand how to leverage Office 365 in your daily tasks

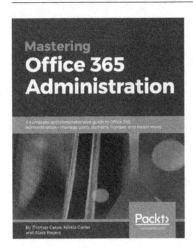

Mastering Office 365 Administration

Thomas Carpe, Nikkia Carter, and Alara Rogers

ISBN: 978-1-78728-863-8

- Understand the vast Office 365 feature set
- Understand how workloads and applications interact and integrate with each other
- Connect PowerShell to various Office 365 services and perform tasks
- Manage Skype for Business Online
- Get support and monitor Office 365 service health
- Manage and administer identities and groups efficiently

Leave a review - let other readers know what you think

Please share your thoughts on this book with others by leaving a review on the site that you bought it from. If you purchased the book from Amazon, please leave us an honest review on this book's Amazon page. This is vital so that other potential readers can see and use your unbiased opinion to make purchasing decisions, we can understand what our customers think about our products, and our authors can see your feedback on the title that they have worked with Packt to create. It will only take a few minutes of your time, but is valuable to other potential customers, our authors, and Packt. Thank you!

Index

Made in the USA
Las Vegas, NV
18 March 2024